CYBER WAR & CYBER PEACE IN THE MIDDLE EAST

CYBER WAR & CYBER PEACE IN THE MIDDLE EAST

DIGITAL CONFLICT IN THE CRADLE OF CIVILIZATION

MICHAEL SEXTON, ELIZA CAMPBELL, EDS.

All rights reserved. No part of this publication may be reproduced, distributed, or transmitted in any form or by any means, including photocopying, recording, or other electronic or mechanical methods, without the prior written permission of the publisher, except in the case of brief quotations embodied in critical reviews and certain other noncommercial Uses permitted by copyright law. For permission requests, write to the publisher.

Copyright © 2020 The Middle East Institute

The Middle East Institute
1763 N Street NW
Washington, D.C. 20036

Follow MEI:

@MiddleEastInst

/MiddleEastInstitute

Contents

FOREWORD	VII
RICHARD CLARKE	
CONDUCT OF CODE: A HISTORICAL OVERVIEW OF CYBERSPACE IN MENA	1
PAUL KURTZ AND AARON ACH	
CYBER INSURANCE AS CYBER DIPLOMACY	22
ASAF LUBIN	
INDUSTRIAL CYBERATTACKS IN THE MIDDLE EAST AND INTERNATIONAL CONSEQUENCES	37
SELENA LARSON AND SERGIO CALTAGIRONE	
INFLUENCE OPERATIONS IN THE MIDDLE EAST AND THE PROHIBITION ON INTERVENTION	56
IDO KILOVATY	
STATE-SANCTIONED HACKTIVISM: THE SYRIAN ELECTRONIC ARMY	71
EVAN KOHLMANN AND ALEX KOBRAY	
DISINFORMATION IN THE GULF	93
JAMES SHIRES	
OPERATION GLOWING SYMPHONY: THE MISSING PIECE IN THE US ONLINE COUNTER-ISIS CAMPAIGN	108
MICHAEL MARTELLE AND AUDREY ALEXANDER	
THE RISE OF DIGITAL AUTHORITARIANISM IN THE MIDDLE EAST	124
MOHAMMED SOLIMAN	
A BATTLE OF TWO PANDEMICS: CORONAVIRUS AND DIGITAL AUTHORITARIANISM IN THE ARAB WORLD	145
SAHAR KHAMIS	
TOWARD A SAFER REGIONAL CYBERSPACE	163
MICHAEL SEXTON AND ELIZA CAMPBELL	

Contributors

PAUL KURTZ
Paul Kurtz is an internationally recognized expert on cybersecurity and the co-founder and executive chairman of TruSTAR Technology. Paul began working on cybersecurity at the White House in the late 1990s. He served in senior positions relating to critical infrastructure and counterterrorism on the White House National Security and Homeland Security Councils under Presidents Clinton and Bush.

AARON ACH
Aaron Ach is an associate at Good Harbor Security Risk Management, a DC-based cyber risk consultancy. Ach graduated from Princeton in 2019, where he earned a B.A. in public and international affairs with a minor in Middle East language and culture. He will begin working with MEI's Cyber Program as a graduate fellow in November.

ASAF LUBIN
Asaf Lubin is an Associate Professor of Law at Indiana University Maurer School; Affiliate at the Berkman Klein Center for Internet and Society, Harvard University; Visiting Fellow at the Information Society Project, Yale Law School; Visiting Scholar at the Feuermann Cybersecurity Research Center, Hebrew University of Jerusalem; Fellow at the Center for Applied Cybersecurity Research, Indiana University; and Visiting Fellow at the Nebraska Governance and Technology Center.

SELENA LARSON
Selena Larson is an intelligence analyst for Dragos. As a member of the threat intelligence team, she works on reports for WorldView customers including technical, malware, and advisory group analyses. She also writes about infrastructure security on the Dragos blog and is a coauthor of Dragos' *Year in Review* reports.

SERGIO CALTAGIRONE
Sergio Caltagirone is the vice president of threat intelligence for Dragos. He spent nine years with the U.S. government and three years at Microsoft hunting the most sophisticated targeted threats in the world, applying intelligence to protect users and critical infrastructure and industrial control systems. He co-created the Diamond Model of Intrusion Analysis and serves as the technical director of the Global Emancipation Network, a non-profit NGO dedicated to ending human trafficking.

IDO KILOVATY
Ido Kilovaty is the Frederic Dorwart Endowed and Zedalis Family Fund Assistant Professor of Law, University of Tulsa, College of Law; Cybersecurity Policy Fellow, New America; Visiting Faculty Fellow, Center for Global Legal Challenges, Yale Law School; and an Affiliated Fellow, Information Society Project, Yale Law School.

ALEX KOBRAY
Alex Kobray is the senior director of physical security and counterterrorism at Flashpoint, a New York-based cyberintelligence and cyberthreat firm. Alex assists law enforcement and intelligence agencies in terrorism investigations and prosecutions and consults on physical and cyber security.

EVAN KOHLMANN
Evan Kohlmann is a founder and chief innovation officer at Flashpoint. He has consulted for the U.S. Departments of Defense and Justice, the Australian Federal Police, and Scotland Yard's Counter Terrorism Command, among others.

JAMES SHIRES
James Shires is an assistant professor at the Institute for Security and Global Affairs, University of Leiden, and a non-resident fellow with the Cyber Project at Harvard's Belfer Center for Science and International Affairs.

MICHAEL MARTELLE
Michael Martelle is the inaugural Cyber Vault Fellow at the National Security Archive. His current interests include incorporating cyber and other "emerging" fields into traditional understandings of national power and security policy.

AUDREY ALEXANDER
Audrey Alexander is a researcher and instructor at West Point's Combating Terrorism Center, where she studies terrorist exploitation of technology and investigates the nexus of gender and violent extremism.

MOHAMMED SOLIMAN
Mohammed Soliman is a non-resident scholar with MEI's Cyber Program. His work focuses on the intersection of technology, geopolitics, and business in MENA.

SAHAR KHAMIS
Dr. Sahar Khamis is an expert on Arab and Muslim media, a non-resident scholar with MEI's Cyber Program, and an associate professor of communication at the University of Maryland.

MICHAEL SEXTON
Michael Sexton is a fellow and director of MEI's Cyber Program. His work focuses on the intersection of cyber technology, international security, and governance in the Middle East.

ELIZA CAMPBELL
Eliza Campbell is the associate director of MEI's Cyber Program, research coordinator for MEI's Research Unit, and a researcher in technology and human rights at the Center for Contemporary Arab Studies at Georgetown University.

Foreword

Dear Reader,

On behalf of the Board of Governors of the Middle East Institute (MEI), it is a pleasure to provide you with this MEI Book, *Cyber War & Cyber Peace in the Middle East*, as we commence our 75th Anniversary Year.

The Middle East is the home of some of the most wired and tech-forward societies in the world. It has also been the scene of more cyber war battles than any other region. We need to better understand the dynamics of cyber activity in a region that is crucial to the global economy, one that is modernizing at a rapid pace, and one that is mired by geopolitical tensions. It is thus entirely appropriate that MEI focus on cyberspace.

MEI (www.mei.edu) is a Washington-based not-for-profit think tank, teaching institution, and cultural showcase. Our mission is to contribute to peace and prosperity by improving mutual understanding between and among Americans and people of the Middle East region.

MEI Books are a series of research publications drawing on MEI Scholars and leading non-resident experts from around the world. This volume focuses on how cyberspace affects economics, politics, social interaction, and security in the Middle East. Its publication is one of many activities of the MEI Cyber Program, which can be followed on the MEI website at https://www.mei.edu/programs/cyber.

We are grateful to the authors, to Cyber Program leaders Michael Sexton and Eliza Campbell, and to MEI's Vice President for Policy and Research, Ambassador Gerald Feierstein.

MEI welcomes members and non-members alike to its conferences, lectures, podcasts, *The Middle East Journal*, the library, and the art gallery, online and at our Washington facilities (once it becomes safe to do so again). We hope you will enjoy them all and will find this volume a valuable contribution to your understanding of the cutting-edge issues related to cyberspace in the Middle East.

Thank you, and enjoy.

Richard A. Clarke, Chair
Board of Governors
Middle East Institute

CHAPTER ONE

CONDUCT OF CODE:

A HISTORICAL OVERVIEW OF CYBERSPACE IN MENA

PAUL KURTZ AND AARON ACH

The MENA region's geopolitics have been hacked, private lives have been reprogrammed, and public opinions have been infiltrated. Activity in the cyber domain bears responsibility for the changing approaches leaders take to governing their populations and to their geostrategies over the last decade. From early experimentation with internet censorship, to crippling wiperware attacks, to disinformation[1] further polluting news and social media environments, cyberspace has presented opportunities for states to consolidate authority domestically and shift the regional balance of power. Cyberspace may be the only human-made battleground, but is hardly a borderless domain. Even this constructed realm is not exempt from domestic fractures, governance challenges, and security dilemmas, some of which have persisted in the region for generations.

Over the two-decade-long history of cyberspace in the MENA region, it has been a domain in and through which power is projected. As such, who projects power, against whom, and from what geography are all key considerations. In this chapter and throughout the book, we endeavor to shed light on how the complexities of sponsor-operator-target relationships have fostered sclerotic patterns of engagement in a domain where law often lacks implementation power or does not even exist in the first place. The cast of characters party to any cyber incident are compelled to act, react, or not act according to incentive structures that transcend cyberspace. Like other war-fighting domains, the attributability of a cyber incident to an aggressor (a matter of information completeness) and the geopolitical context in which it occurs generally govern whether and how the aggressed chooses to respond.

The Middle East Institute's Cyber Program, and the contributors to *Cyber War & Cyber Peace in the Middle East*, outline four focus areas of the region's cyber activity: (1) privacy and civil society, (2) cyber conflict, (3) information and influence operations, and (4) countering extremism online.[2] The emergence of each focus area of the region's cyber landscape has been asynchronous, making a chronological narration of the domain's evolution less productive than an overview of the groups that are most active in the region's cyberspace and their incentives for being so. In its potential to be used overtly or covertly, cyberspace affords flexibility to states in the region, non-state actors, and state actors beyond the MENA region to pursue their geopolitical, ideological, and financial agendas.

The Middle East is the region in which the first act of cyber war took place, but even that attack, commonly referred to as Stuxnet, inadvertently touched off more than just state-on-state cyber conflict. Unlike weapons of other war-fighting domains, tools of interstate cyber conflict may be repurposed by their creators or even recycled by a different actor into whose possession they fall, giving capabilities a cumulative relationship to one another.

Just as MENA nations have used capabilities domestically to control their socio-political landscapes, some of those same governments have deployed like tools against adversary states for geopolitical gain. For non-state actors native to or operating in the region, cyberspace has become an environment conducive to criminal activity, a digital arms trade, and the propagation of false information and extreme ideologies. For their part, global powers continue to treat MENA cyberspace as a proxy battleground in attempts to strategically shape norms of engagement in the domain. Native populations, some of which have only recently come online, are seen as unfortunate but distant casualties.

The ways cyberspace is being leveraged in the region testify to the flexibility it offers motivated and capable actors. Proliferating knowledge and diminishing costs to deploy both overt and covert cyber tools result in an ever-diversifying set of active parties. The domain has thus become attractive to both well-resourced groups, who may benefit from the relative difficulty of attribution and lagging laws, and less-resourced groups, who may find cyberspace allows them to punch above their weight. Cyberspace is what parties capable of acting therein want it to be, with both its creative and destructive potential tethered to its artificiality. As this collection highlights, studies of cyberspace are intersectional, as the domain agglomerates phenomena of social organization, including national security, global economies, law, civil society activities, and technological advancement, with an incomparable ease and immediacy.[3]

MENA STATE ACTORS

In the years following the United States' declaration of war with Afghanistan (2001) and its invasion of Iraq (2003), there was concern among U.S. security partners that such an alliance would make them more appealing targets for terror campaigns by proximate extremist factions. The United Arab Emirates (UAE) quickly came to appreciate that the most crippling terrorist attack would be on its critical infrastructure. To architect a homeland security strategy that emphasized critical infrastructure protection (CIP) — of seaports, airports, and nuclear and petrochemical energy projects — from a physical or cyber terrorist attack, the UAE turned outward.[4] Emirati defense and intelligence consulted current U.S. government and former national security officials, including co-author Paul Kurtz, as well as officials from the U.K., Germany, Italy, Australia, and Singapore. Abu Dhabi concluded it was imperative that the country have an organization with the capability and authority to surveil suspected terrorists. In the years between Kurtz's first defensive contracts with Abu Dhabi and the creation of the National Electronic Security Agency's (NESA) intelligence division in 2008, an irreversible linkage was fostered between defensive measures and the development of offensive capabilities that the UAE used to surveil non-terrorist persons of interest, including human rights activists, according to popular reports.[5]

While Abu Dhabi has drawn considerable attention from the international community for the genesis of its cyber capabilities, it is worth noting that its regional peers were in the process of undertaking similar efforts for some time prior to this (as were the U.S. and its intelligence partners). Initiatives to develop mass surveillance mechanisms were already underway around the same time elsewhere. A 2006 decree[6] by Qatar's telecommunications regulatory body (ictQatar) indicates the government's intent to possess surveillance capability years before that capability's development was made public in 2009.[7] Even more sophisticated tools were being developed and deployed contemporaneously in Iran. In 2005, Iranian internet service providers began using an unlicensed "Smart Filter" package,[8] a tool developed for defensive purposes by a European company, allowing the government to block content. By 2008, the Telecommunications Company of Iran had the means and capacity to conduct deep packet inspection (DPI) for every client on its network, a capability it would expand in 2010 with the help of China's ZTE Corporation to include mobile and internet communications monitoring, blocking, and user-specific web page alteration.[9]

Iran, Qatar, and the UAE were among the first to make electronic surveillance capabilities part and parcel of their national security strategies, pulling the levers of state ownership or support of telecommunications and internet service providers in a way that is common in the Gulf. More quietly, however, governments in the Maghreb were exploiting surveillance technologies for similar purposes. Tunisia, for example, purchased multiple ready-made surveillance toolkits from American and European security companies.[10] Tunisian President Zine el-Abidine Ben Ali, however, was far from the only dictator in the region to seek help from hack-for-hire outfits in an effort to quell the civil unrest on his doorstep, as detailed later in this and other chapters. Turning to non-state actors to develop and operate intrusion tools provided states a thin but real veil of deniability, a strategy also used to erode the certainty with which actions can be attributed to particular actors during interstate cyber conflict.

If in 2011 social media shed a light on the extent of civil unrest across the region, the cyber resources intelligence and law enforcement apparatuses had ready to deploy against the opposition evinced the high level of priority they had assigned to acquiring these capabilities in the years leading up to the Arab Spring. As uprisings across the region presented an opportunity for repressed peoples to raise their collective voices, many states reflexively pursued "digital authoritarianism," a trend Mohammed Soliman explores in Chapter 8, to not only silence dissidents after they organized but also to undermine movement formation in the first place. In a recent panel for a conference produced by MEI,[11] Dr. Sahar Khamis reflected on her change in attitude about the Arab Spring: Strides toward democratization have grown smaller with time since the uprisings, and it has become clear that the digital transformation has been more about how authorities exert control over their citizens than how their citizens resist that authority. (Dr. Khamis examines the role of digital authoritarianism in the regional COVID-19 pandemic response in Chapter 9.)

Surveillance platforms deployed "lawfully" in a domestic context and espionage tools deployed covertly abroad are two sides of the same coin. Acts of cyber espionage, as one of the most common modes of interstate cyber conflict, often lay the groundwork for future cyber or kinetic attacks. Espionage operations therefore entail longer lifecycles in order to obtain the desired information. One such campaign was Dark Caracal, a six-year operation discovered in 2018 as being run from within Lebanon's General Directorate of General Security (GDGS), which targeted the communications of journalists, military officers, defense contractors, financial institutions, and government officials in over 20 countries.[12] Iran, in its obsession with monitoring dissidents, is known to have conducted multiple campaigns against domestic individuals, business targets, and members of the global Iranian diaspora lasting up to 10 years.[13] Alex Kobray and Evan Kohlmann compare approaches to state-sponsored hacking activity in Chapter 5.

The more knowledge an actor can glean about a target's environment from an espionage operation the more likely an attack will be to proceed as planned when it comes time to disrupt or destroy. Government-backed espionage efforts are thus less threatening as standalone operations than they are as the first step in the larger "kill chain" of a more damaging cyberattack.[14] One of the first instances in which cyberspace was used to "prepare the battlefield" came in 2007 when the elite Unit 8200 of the Israel Defense Forces (IDF) compromised Syrian air defense radars. Through a backdoor in the system's code, Unit 8200 disabled the radar functionality and projected a "false-sky" picture as the air force executed a successful strike on a nuclear reactor at Deir ez-Zor.[15] Such sophisticated attacks are only made possible by deep knowledge of the systems in a target's environment, a lesson in delayed gratification state actors especially seem to have learned.

In a survey of state-sponsored cyber operations over the last decade, depicted in Figure 1.1 below,[16] Saudi Arabia has been subject to the greatest number of attacks. While Iran has been the victim of a similar number of operations as Saudi Arabia and Israel, it has also been the identified sponsor of more than six times as many attacks as any other MENA country, and twice the number of offensive operations sponsored by all other MENA countries combined.

As an actor that has pursued an asymmetric, offensive strategy, Iran remains a serious disruptor to its adversaries, shirking responsibility for its actions and often acting without fear of a retributive response on its soil.[17] After Symantec researchers discovered Stuxnet, a worm that targeted contractors responsible for the manufacturing, assembly, and installation of industrial control systems (ICS) at an Iranian nuclear facility between 2009 and 2010, Iran became compelled to prepare for a future of cyber conflict. It took the country only two years to develop

PUBLICLY KNOWN STATE-SPONSORED CYBER OPERATIONS IN MENA (2010-20)

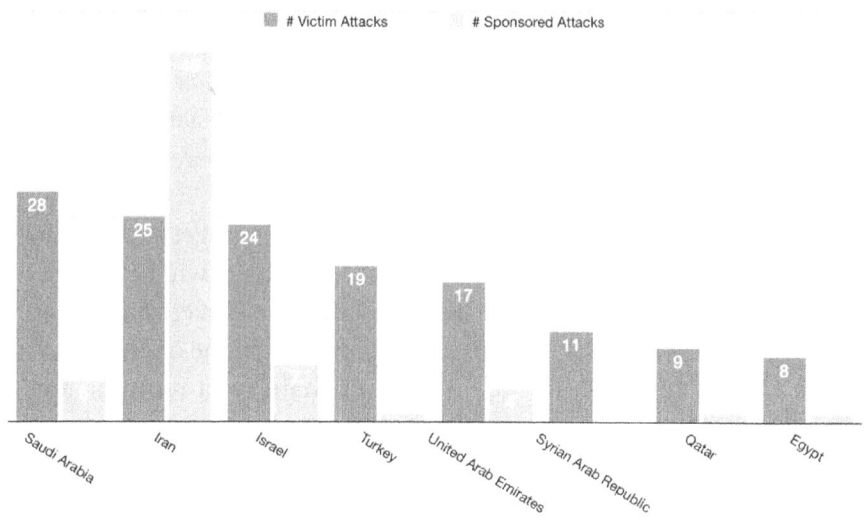

FIGURE 1.1 PLOTS THE EIGHT MENA COUNTRIES MOST FREQUENTLY VICTIMIZED BY CYBERATTACKS (DARK GRAY) AND THE FREQUENCY WITH WHICH THEY SPONSORED ATTACKS AGAINST OTHER STATES (LIGHT GRAY) FROM 2010-20. DATA: "CYBER OPERATIONS TRACKER," COUNCIL ON FOREIGN RELATIONS, 2020.

a cyberattack of its own against critical infrastructure.[18] By learning from Stuxnet, among other attacks by which Iran has been affected, the Iranian regime developed an offensive cyber playbook that capitalized on the very vulnerabilities in its adversaries of which it had first become aware as the victim.

In the last decade, Iran has proven persistent in its offensive efforts, launching successful attacks against Aramco and Saudi government agencies in 2012 and 2016, as well as attempting other operations against the operational technology environments of adversaries' critical infrastructure.[19] Examples include continued probing of the U.S. electrical grid and an attack in April 2020 against water flow and chemical treatment systems in Israel.[20] (In Chapter 2, Asaf Lubin explores the role cyber insurance can play in mitigating this risk; Sergio Caltagirone and Selena Larson expand on threats to MENA critical infrastructure in Chapter 3.) Waging offensive campaigns against symbolic institutions affiliated with enemy governments, and enlisting the country's most active underground hackers to do it, has had the added benefit of allowing the Iranian regime to portray itself at home as righteously besieged and a growing technological power.[21]

Penetration and manipulation of physical systems is expensive, knowledge-intensive, and not easily replicable. As an alternative, many MENA states have focused on advancing their agendas in the information sphere, seeking to mobilize both domestic and international support for their policies. Indeed, influence and information operations[22] (also referred to as "info-ops") have become a mainstay of political life across MENA, taking shape in what was a toxic news and social media environment well prior to their advent. The sequence of events precipitating the Gulf crisis in 2017 is a key example.

Sheikh Tamim bin Hamad al-Thani, the ruling amir of Qatar, was as surprised as news readers to be on record discussing growing tensions with the president of the U.S. (Qatar's most powerful military partner), his sympathies toward Iran, his praise for Hamas militants, and his country's warming relations with Israel.[23] The Qatar News Agency (QNA) quickly claimed that the story had been planted in an attack on its website, and the Qatari amir independently repudiated its authenticity.[24] Suspecting Abu Dhabi was behind the hack-and-info-op hybrid, Qatar allegedly retaliated by dumping the hacked personal emails of Yousef al-Otaiba, the UAE's ambassador to the U.S., and a politically connected

American with ties to the UAE.[25]

This coordinated disinformation effort is defining as both a geopolitical tripwire and as a signal for the trajectory of future hybrid operations in cyberspace. The 2017 info-op was a "checkmate" in an intensifying match between Qatar and the UAE dating back to 2013, when Doha provided support to Muslim Brotherhood affiliates that had denounced UAE leadership.[26] In the same year, Abu Dhabi signed a contract to license spyware from a top Israeli surveillance tool developer, "intended to be used exclusively for the investigation and prevention of crime and terrorism."[27] By the time of the split, Emirati intelligence had used the capability to compromise the mobile devices of 159 Qatari royal family members, including attempts on the Qatari amir's devices, as well as those of officials in other foreign governments, journalists, and Emirati dissidents.[28] Whether a fabricated QNA story used material from those surveillance efforts has not been reported, but Abu Dhabi would move to disseminate a putatively damaging narrative for Doha all the same.

The 2017 disinformation operation aimed at Qatar caused diplomatic damage rather than physical or direct economic harm. It exploited how people consume the internet more than it did the penetrability of a network, underscoring the need for further consideration of what tactics are normatively or legally permissible for states to leverage against one another in cyberspace. James Shires discusses the evolving function of disinformation in the blockade against Qatar in Chapter 6.

EXTRA-MENA STATE ACTORS

The security challenges in the region's cyberspace can be at least partially attributed to a technological outpacing of norms, specifically around what types of targets comprise a legitimate attack surface and under what circumstances attacking them is defensible. (The attack surface stands to expand rapidly with emerging technologies such as 5G and the Internet of Things.[29]) While norm-setting is also a challenge in cyberspace outside of the region, the tense geopolitical dynamics in the MENA region raise the level of complexity inherent in the relationship between physical infrastructure, proliferating knowledge, and the law. "The physical infrastructure of cyberspace maps the contours of contemporary geopolitics more than we might think," writes John Sheldon, executive director of the George C. Marshall Institute.[30]

Activity in cyberspace can thus be considered a symptom as well as a cause of geopolitical shifts and should be expected to have ramifications in the physical realm.

So it went in June 2019 when U.S. President Donald Trump ordered a cyber strike to disable a database that Iran's Islamic Revolutionary Guards Corps (IRGC) used to attack at least a half-dozen oil tankers near the Strait of Hormuz during the preceding two months.[31] In the two days before U.S. Cyber Command (USCYBERCOM) claimed responsibility for the attack against the Iranian database, a U.S. drone flying in contested airspace was downed by an Iranian surface-to-air missile. President Trump quickly approved air strikes on several Iranian missile and radar batteries, and reversed course so late that the strike group had already left the ground.[32] Claiming the air strikes would not be a "proportionate" response, he ordered USCYBERCOM to compromise the database in an operation it had been developing for weeks, if not months.[33]

Iran and the U.S. have consistently been in cyber conflict since the discovery of Stuxnet in 2010. While Iran most frequently targets adversaries in MENA, multiple attacks have been aimed at the U.S. itself, including Operation Ababil (a.k.a. Mahdi), which targeted the financial sector and a New York dam in 2012; an attack on the Sands Casino in Las Vegas that did $40 million in damage; and continued probing of its electric grid.[34] Iran does not possess the same sophistication in its offensive tooling as the U.S., Russia, or China. Iranian actors have, however, proven independently capable of sustained engagement in cyberspace below the threshold of armed conflict and should not be considered reliant on technology transfers from external partners to remain so.

While Iran is not dependent on assistance, Russia and China have willingly provided support to Tehran, among other willing recipients, in their attempts to establish spheres of influence in MENA cyberspace.[35] An ongoing example is Russia's willingness to host staging servers for Iranian cyber criminals, state-backed hackers, and proxy groups given that nearly all Iranian IP addresses are blocked in the U.S. and many European nations.[36] Amid the ongoing and global dispute between the U.S. and China over dominance in IT supply chains, for example, China and Iran agreed on united opposition to U.S. "hegemony" over the proliferation of new, strategic technologies.[37] More covertly, threat actors operating on behalf of China's Ministry of State Security breached telecommunications providers, including unnamed companies in MENA, in an espionage operation that targeted specific individuals in affected countries between 2012 and 2019.[38] These efforts are consistent with China's brazen pattern of intelligence collection and its counter-intelligence strategy across the globe, and may paradoxically be occurring in the countries that Beijing hopes to draw away from U.S. influence.

Russia has been less conspicuous yet more active than China, taking full advantage of the domain's attribution challenges and the interstate finger-pointing that follows a cyber incident. One of the most alarming cyberattacks to date, which used malware developed in a Russian state-owned research institute, sought to interfere with critical safety systems at a Petro Rabigh plant in Saudi Arabia.[39] If not for a minor execution error, this 2017 attack would have caused physical damage and likely a loss of life. Then in 2019, a prolific group of hackers operating on behalf of the Russian Federal Security Service launched an espionage campaign against MENA governments, among other targets, using Iranian tools and staging the operation from a known Iranian advanced persistent threat actor's infrastructure.[40]

Like in their intrusion operations, Russian groups often use "false flag" tactics for their influence campaigns to shape public opinion in strategic geographies. In 2015, a group declaring allegiance to ISIS claimed responsibility for a three-hour disruption to broadcasting on the French network TV5 Monde, an attack which was later linked to Russian military intelligence.[41] In more recent, pure-play information operations in Turkey, the Kremlin has sought to foment suspicion of NATO and Western allies; minimize opposition to Russian activity in the Middle East and Eurasia; and interfere in elections to assist candidates that would make Ankara a more pliant partner to Moscow.[42]

As an active and early agent in MENA cyberspace, the United States also plays a dynamic role. Cyberattacks purportedly architected by U.S. military and intelligence organizations have been consequential both in terms of their immediate effects as well as the proliferation of capabilities that has ensued among their targets. (In cyberspace, victimization can also be highly educational, as demonstrated by Iran.) Since the late Obama administration and throughout the Trump administration, the U.S. has taken a more active approach to engaging its adversaries, a shift noticeable in policy proposals and institutional adjustments.[43] Washington's approach more recently has been to "defend forward," particularly against Iran, but perhaps quietly against the other global cyber powers described in this section as well.

The U.S. has also been active against non-state actors in the region, specifically when it comes to extremist threats. Beginning in 2016 and continuing through the present, the U.S. campaign known as Operation Glowing Symphony has seriously disrupted ISIS's internal communications and problematized the content dissemination techniques upon which the organization relied heavily for recruitment and public-facing legitimization efforts. Developed by Joint Task Force Ares, the operation sought to deny access to and destroy the few key nodes through which almost the entire ISIS network was brought online, favoring a systematic and top-down disruption to ISIS operations over a discrete, conventional military campaign.[44] Michael Martelle and Audrey Alexander more fully discuss government intervention from a U.S. foreign policy perspective in Chapter 7.

The value of deep reconnaissance to Operation Glowing Symphony was that it enabled a rapid and systematic execution of a subsequent cyberattack. Iran has gained notoriety among its regional adversaries and the U.S. for its sophisticated reconnaissance efforts, prompting anxiety about Tehran's interest in conducting more damaging cyberattacks than it has proved capable of carrying out thus far. In part due to such anxieties about Iran, U.S. policies have recently given far more latitude to military commands and intelligence agencies to respond to cyberattacks with kinetic force and retaliatory cyberattacks, respectively.[45] These shifts in U.S. posture may create new potential for the interplay between kinetic and cyber force deployment, as in the June 2019 skirmish with Iran, despite Washington's general regard for cyber operations below the threshold of armed conflict.[46] Whether a more proactive U.S. approach to the region's cyberspace will function to deter adversaries and limit spillover into the physical realm, as intended, or whether it will instead accelerate escalation in the most tenuous of moments, remains to be seen.

NON-STATE ACTORS

In MENA and elsewhere, the increased activity of non-state actors in cyberspace is a by-product of the domain's maturation and the spread of technical know-how. At a more formative point for the domain, few people or groups were well-resourced enough to develop offensive capabilities, and those that did have expertise were often recruited by their governments. The gulf between what it costs to develop versus buy a capability, however, plays a paramount role in the possession of sophisticated capabilities by less-resourced groups. In 2009, for example, Iraqi insurgents downloaded an off-the-shelf package from a dark-web marketplace that allowed them to intercept U.S. Predator drone video feeds.[47] For the low price of $25.95, the Iraqi militia got better counterintelligence than it ever would have been able to cultivate with its own resources.

Some states have also encouraged the emergence of capable non-state actors, realizing both the financial and diplomatic benefits of having non-state actors operate on their behalf. In exchange for the financial resources, technology transfers and training, and other incentives states may offer, non-state actors insulate their state backers from culpability when those governments feel compelled to go on offense. Iran has a demonstrated track record of financial and human resource investment in its cyber proxies, such as Cyber Hezbollah, the Syrian Electronic Army (SEA), Hamas, and the Yemen Cyber Army.[48] In 2015, for example, an attack known as "Volatile Cedar" primarily targeted contractors for the IDF and was suspected to have been carried out by Hezbollah.[49] Iran's known tactical support for Hezbollah's disinformation operations[50] and active involvement in its cyber recruitment efforts suggest that Iran may seek to provide expertise, products, and processes to its other proxies. If that is the case, future operations from these groups may draw on the Iranian playbook, which includes credential harvesting, powerful password-spraying, distributed denial of service attacks, and domain name system hijacking. In its pursuit of an outsized geopolitical strategy, cyber proxies afford Tehran a greater level of deniability in a preferred domain of engagement — and at far lower cost than Iran's historic strategy of conventional proxy warfare.

While Iran is the most active sponsor of non-state offensive actors in the region, it is hardly alone. Until late 2019, for example, the UAE had a close partnership with DarkMatter, an intelligence firm staffed in part by Western technical experts to which the Emirati government contracted much of its surveillance, cyber defense, and intrusion efforts.[51] Unlike Iran's proxies, which receive training and other assistance from the IRGC, DarkMatter sold tools and provisioned services to the UAE. (In this light, DarkMatter was more akin to a private security firm that also engaged offensively.) Although its relationship to Emirati intelligence was not shrouded in mystery, DarkMatter nonetheless provided the UAE a modicum of deniability, and could recruit talent to catalyze the development of cyber capabilities the UAE would later bring under state control.[52]

MENA states with less mature cyber operations than the UAE have made a similar judgement. Rather than invest the time and resources necessary to build in-house capabilities, the existing marketplace for cyber tools and offensive services has provided the opportunity for regimes to more cheaply and quickly deploy capabilities against their targets. This was a phenomenon that became especially widespread during the Arab Spring, a time of crisis during which regimes depended on the services of sophisticated hacking groups and the repurposing of capabilities already developed by legitimate IT security companies.[53] At the time, such organizations were largely based in Europe and claimed to be legally exporting their technologies.

Documents leaked from the Egyptian State Security Headquarters reveal that U.K.-based Gamma International Group, a parent for its better-known German subsidiary FinFisher, delivered a proposal to Egyptian intelligence for its remote intrusion malware product, dubbed "FinSpy."[54] Research by the University of Toronto's Citizen Lab confirmed that the specialized Technological Research Department (TRD) of Egypt's intelligence service was deploying FinSpy against domestic targets, and that the TRD had also acquired a full remote control tool for mobile devices from the Italy-based Hacking Team.[55] Gamma International is also suspected of having sold FinSpy to Bahraini authorities, where it was subsequently used to monitor activists' Skype calls and other communications during its 2011 uprising.[56] The Bahraini government purchased similar tools from Trovicor, a Germany-based joint venture between Siemens and Nokia. Transcripts of phone calls and text messages obtained using Trovicor's intrusive surveillance technology were read aloud to activists, journalists, and other opponents of the Bahraini government as they were tortured.[57]

The Arab Spring confirmed that there was and remains a burgeoning market for products that enable purported "lawful interception" of all kinds of electronic activity. The indiscriminate sale of technical knowledge sent a profound signal to authoritarian regimes both in and beyond the region: The possibility of tightening digital control domestically, and even of dislocating a state's enemies abroad, was no longer a function of know-how but of price. In the years since, capabilities supplied by organizations outside of the region have continued to proliferate, and companies native to the region have sprung up in Egypt, the UAE, and especially in Israel.[58] Israeli firms lead the private cyberintelligence market both with high-profile names, like NSO Group and Black Cube, and lesser-known ones, like Intellexa and Verint.[59] Similar firms have increasingly provided the means for smaller, less-resourced governments around the world to harness the power of emerging technologies they once perceived as threatening. (Michael Sexton and Eliza Campbell explore the role of these and other non-state actors more fully in the Conclusion.) As stated plainly in a 2019 Department of Homeland Security report, "Proliferation of capabilities by way of transaction is the new normal."[60] The long-term implications of this state of affairs, however, remain an open question.

Despite their relative novelty, information operations and influence campaigns have become highly commodified as well. Private groups offering influence-as-a-service[61] are key drivers of new methods for both content generation and content dissemination, the combination of which has upped the sophistication of info-ops considerably in recent years. Even by global comparison, info-ops dominate MENA social and news media. In Oxford's 2019 ranking of countries with the greatest incidence of what it labels "computational propaganda,"[62] Egypt, Iran, Saudi Arabia, Syria, and the UAE all make the top 12.[63] In instances where they are not the architects of information operations, non-state actors (including private industry, internet forums, and even social media influencers) are often relied upon to elevate and amplify disinformation.[64]

Influence-as-a-service is often delivered by mercenary organizations operating under the benign but shadowy labels of public relations (PR) firms, social media analytics providers, and political consultancies. The Archimedes Group, a self-described PR firm in Israel, openly marketed its services with the slogan, "winning campaigns worldwide," and was later linked to a campaign that took place during Tunisia's 2019 elections.[65] The firm's techniques capitalized on a toxic information environment; it spun up websites and social media pages for a watchdog organization that appeared to be focused on fact-checking and stopping the spread of disinformation in Tunisia.[66] In reality, it was a network of fake Facebook profiles and accounts spreading disinformation itself.

For some non-state actors, information operations and influence campaigns are cheap, convenient, and potentially effective at inciting division and sowing confusion. For extremists aiming to exert territorial control and striving for legitimacy and influence across the region, information operations are existential (if ISIS's attempts at a digital caliphate are anything to go by). The weaponization of social media platforms by extremists is not a type of use that has emerged organically, but one that should be considered the tactical adoption of platforms "ideally suited to the strategic and organizational approach" extremists take.[67] The violence committed by a group like ISIS or its affiliates features unspeakable atrocities that would be far less meaningful if not for their constant digital reproduction. As hybrids between human and technological resources, extremists' networks are dynamic phenomena that must be "constantly built and maintained."[68]

The applications and platforms that extremists use to recruit and disseminate fear campaigns are as integral to jihad as the ideologues who commit violence under its flag. The constant propagation of specifically designed and decentralized content is imperative for extremist organizations to "achieve operational penetration," or an illusion of it, in geographies beyond their control.[69] The 2010 bombing of the Boston Marathon, for example, was carried out by two men who had been inspired by al-Qaeda in the Arabian Peninsula's English language digital magazine.[70] If decentralization of violent acts is one technique, high message volume (i.e., redundancy) is a reinforcing one that is key to an extremist group's validation of its ideological system. Consistently demonstrating and electronically disseminating acts of violence is a way of shoring up a sense of the group's legitimacy among a global audience (including both opponents and proponents of that ideology). At peak output, ISIS accounts sent as many as 90,000 tweets per day.[71]

While extremists' dependence on social media makes their operations vulnerable to disruptive efforts like Operation Glowing Symphony, their content remains a scourge on the platforms they do use. Major social media companies have consequently come under scrutiny for nefarious usage of their platforms, highlighting how their fundamental accessibility remains a principal benefit and drawback. On the one hand, the opportunities online platforms provide for expression of individual thought and access to information are especially critical in a region where both are often restricted. On the other, such platforms are easily abused and a challenge to moderate. Confronting the spread of violent messaging by extremists, and that of disinformation more broadly, will require platforms to preserve low enough barriers to entry that they may be used both legitimately and widely. Ido Kilovaty addresses these and adjacent issues from a legalistic perspective in Chapter 4.

What may once have been overt, largely state-driven propaganda machines are now covert operations executed by a range of actors with varied incentives. As emerging technologies, such as deepfakes, artificial intelligence, and the Internet of Things become increasingly available, non-state actors both in and beyond MENA are well positioned to exercise ever-greater influence in already fraught social and news media environments.[72]

Cyberspace in a MENA context serves as a domain both in and through which operational and psychological forces are deployed, as the rest of the book will lay forth. It shapes geopolitical realities, reflects states' and non-state actors' risk appetites, and provides more flexibility than ever for a growing number of capable parties. So what are the next iterations of these tools? Who will develop them? And how do we move toward a safer cyberspace in the MENA region? As rivals seek to develop or acquire increasingly sophisticated capabilities, often motivated by having themselves been compromised, the cyber domain stands to become more unruly the longer its dangers are not mitigated by norms, regulated markets, secure architecture, and law.

ENDNOTES

1. Disinformation, originating from the Russian word *dezinformatsiya*, is the deliberate spread of false information intended to mislead, incite, or harm a targeted audience. Adapted from William Gangware and Christina Nemr, "Weapons of Mass Distraction: Foreign State-Sponsored Disinformation in the Digital Age," U.S. Department of State, March 18, 2019, https://www.state.gov/wp-content/uploads/2019/05/Weapons-of-Mass-Distraction-Foreign-State-Sponsored-Disinformation-in-the-Digital-Age.pdf.

2. "Cyber Program," Middle East Institute, est. 2019, https://www.mei.edu/programs/cyber.

3. Trey Herr, "Governing Proliferation in Cybersecurity," *Global Summitry*, no. 1 (April 2017), https://ssrn.com/abstract=2958978.

4. Christopher Bing and Joel Schectman, "White House veterans helped Gulf monarchy build secret surveillance unit," *Reuters*, December 10, 2019, https://www.reuters.com/article/us-usa-raven-whitehouse-specialreport/special-report-white-house-veterans-helped-gulf-monarchy-build-secret-surveillance-unit-idUSKBN1YE1OB.

5. See Ibid.; and Christopher Bing and Joel Schectman, "Inside the UAE's secret hacking team of American mercenaries," *Reuters*, January 30, 2019, https://www.reuters.com/article/us-usa-spying-raven-specialreport/special-report-inside-the-uaes-secret-hacking-team-of-u-s-mercenaries-idUSKCN1PO19O.

6. مرسوم بقانون رقم (34) لسنة 2006 بإصدار قانون الاتصالات، وزارة المواصلات والاتصالات، دولة قطر، 06 تشرين الثاني 2006; Decree Law No. (34) of 2006 on the Promulgation of the Telecommunications Law, Ministry of Transport and Communications, State of Qatar, 2006, https://www.motc.gov.qa/en/documents/document/decree-law-no-34-2006-promulgation-telecommunications-law.

7. Qatar, OpenNet Initiative, August 6, 2009, https://opennet.net/research/profiles/qatar.

8. "Tightening the Net Part 2: The Soft War and Cyber Tactics in Iran," Article 19, 56, 2017, https://www.article19.org/resources/tightening-the-net-part-2-the-soft-war-and-cyber-tactics-in-iran/.

9. Ibid.

10. The Tunisian government purchased: DPI infrastructure from Blue Coat Systems (U.S.), NetApp (U.S.), and Utimaco Gmbh (Germany); VoIP and data interception capability, in addition to an intelligence feed platform, from Trovicor (Germany), a subsidiary of Nokia-Siemens Systems; targeted web traffic analysis and user profile construction technologies from Sundby ETI (Denmark), a subsidiary of BAE Systems; and satellite monitoring, web traffic analysis, and data retention from ATIS Uher (Germany). See "State of Surveillance Tunisia," Privacy International, March 14, 2019, https://privacyinternational.org/state-privacy/1012/state-surveillance-tunisia.

11. Sahar Khamis in Mahsa Alimardani, Avi Ascher-Schapiro, Eliza Campbell, Sahar Khamis, and Spandana Singh, "Panel II: Privacy and Surveillance, Freedom and Censorship: The Social Contract in the Digital Age," Middle East Institute, June 9, 2020, https://www.mei.edu/events/cyber-domain-middle-east-implications-business-security-and-society.

12. "Dark Caracal: Cyber espionage at a global scale," Lookout, Inc. and the Electronic Frontier Foundation (EFF), 2018, https://www.lookout.com/info/ds-dark-caracal-ty.

13. "Significant Cyber Incidents," CSIS, 2020, https://www.csis.org/programs/technology-policy-program/significant-cyber-incidents.

14. Rohan M. Amin, Michael J. Cloppert, Eric M. Hutchins, "Intelligence-Driven Computer Network Defense Informed by Analysis of Adversary Campaigns and Intrusion Kill Chains," Lockheed Martin Corporation, 2009, https://www.lockheedmartin.com/content/dam/lockheed-martin/rms/documents/cyber/LM-White-Paper-Intel-Driven-Defense.pdf.

15. Oliver Holmes, "Israel confirms it carried out 2007 airstrike," *The Guardian*, March 21, 2018, https://www.theguardian.com/world/2018/mar/21/israel-admits-it-carried-out-2007-airstrike-on-syrian-nuclear-reactor.

16. An earlier version of this data appeared in Kristina Kausch, "Cheap Havoc: How Cyber-Geopolitics Will Destabilize the Middle East," GMFUS, 2017, https://www.gmfus.org/publications/cheap-havoc-how-cyber-geopolitics-will-destabilize-middle-east. Data from: "Cyber Operations Tracker," Council on Foreign Relations (CFR), 2020, https://www.cfr.org/cyber-operations/.

17. Scott Stewart, "How Iran's Cyber Game Plan Reflects Its Asymmetrical War Strategy," Stratfor, December 18, 2018, https://worldview.

stratfor.com/article/how-irans-cyber-game-plan-reflects-its-asymmetrical-war-strategy; and Jon Gambrell, "Oil tanker attacks echo Persian Gulf's 1980 'Tanker War,'" *The Associated Press*, June 14, 2019, https://apnews.com/article/ceb6e7a86bf14a9a8d8ecf81c9dcc7ef.

18. Eric Chien, Nicolas Flliere, Liam O Murchu, "W32.Stuxnet Dossier," Symantec Security Response, November 2010, https://www.wired.com/images_blogs/threatlevel/2010/11/w32_stuxnet_dossier.pdf; and Kim Zetter, "An Unprecedented Look at Stuxnet, the World's First Digital Weapon," *Wired*, November 3, 2014, https://www.wired.com/2014/11/countdown-to-zero-day-stuxnet/.

19. Robert Falcone, "Shamoon 2: Return of the Disttrack Wiper," Palo Alto Networks, November 30, 2016, https://unit42.paloaltonetworks.com/unit42-shamoon-2-return-disttrack-wiper/.

20. For U.S. electrical grid probing, see Andy Greenberg, "Iranian Hackers Have Been 'Password-Spraying' the US Grid," *Wired*, January 9, 2020, https://www.wired.com/story/iran-apt33-us-electric-grid/; for Israeli water supply attack, see Ellen Nakashima and Joby Warrick, "Foreign intelligence officials say attempted cyberattack on Israeli water utilities linked to Iran," *The Washington Post*, May 8, 2020, https://www.washingtonpost.com/national-security/intelligence-officials-say-attempted-cyberattack-on-israeli-water-utilities-linked-to-iran/2020/05/08/f9ab0d78-9157-11ea-9e23-6914ee410a5f_story.html.

21. Insikt Group, "The History of Ashiyane: Iran's First Security Forum," Recorded Future, January 16, 2019, https://www.recordedfuture.com/ashiyane-forum-history/; and Sanil Chohan, Levi Gundert, and Greg Lesnewich, "Iran's Hacker Hierarchy Exposed," Recorded Future, May 9, 2018, https://www.recordedfuture.com/iran-hacker-hierarchy/; and Michael Sulmeyer, "Cyberspace: A Growing Domain for Iranian Disruption" in Melissa G. Dalton and Kathleen H. Hicks, eds., *Deterring Iran After the Nuclear Deal* (Lanham: Rowman & Littlefield, March 2017), chap. 4, https://www.belfercenter.org/sites/default/files/files/publication/Deterring%20Iran%20after%20the%20Nuclear%20Deal%202.pdf.

22. Information and influence campaigns include the collection of tactical information about an adversary and the dissemination of false information to manipulate foreign publics' opinions in pursuit of a competitive advantage over an opponent. Adapted from: "Information Operations," Rand Corporation, 2020, https://www.rand.org/topics/information-operations.html.

23. Sheera Frenkel and David Kirkpatrick, "Hacking in Qatar Highlights a Shift Toward Espionage-for-Hire," *The New York Times*, June 8, 2017, https://www.nytimes.com/2017/06/08/world/middleeast/qatar-cyberattack-espionage-for-hire.html.

24. Tom Finn and Karin Strohecker, "Qatar says media report reveals UAE role in hack that sparked crisis," *Reuters*, July 17, 2017, https://www.reuters.com/article/us-gulf-qatar-emirates/qatar-says-media-report-reveals-uae-role-in-hack-that-sparked-crisis-idUSKBN1A20P1.

25. Julie Bykowicz, "U.S. Judge Dismisses Qatar from Elliott Broidy Hacking Lawsuit," *The Wall Street Journal*, August 8, 2018, https://www.wsj.com/articles/u-s-judge-dismisses-qatar-from-elliott-broidy-hacking-lawsuit-1533768624.

26. Azam Ahmed and David Kirkpatrick, "Hacking a Prince, an Emir and a Journalist to Impress a Client," *The New York Times*, August 31, 2018, https://www.nytimes.com/2018/08/31/world/middleeast/hacking-united-arab-emirates-nso-group.html; Eric Trager, "The Muslim Brotherhood Is the Root of the Qatar Crisis," *The Atlantic*, July 2, 2017, https://www.theatlantic.com/international/archive/2017/07/muslim-brotherhood-qatar/532380/.

27. Ron Deibert, Bill Marczak, Sarah McKune, Bahr Abdul Razzak, and John Scott-Railton, "Hide and Seek: Tracking NSO Group's Pegasus Spyware to Operations in 45 Countries," Citizen Lab, 2018, https://citizenlab.ca/2018/09/hide-and-seek-tracking-nso-groups-pegasus-spyware-to-operations-in-45-countries/; "Amnesty International Staff targeted with malicious spyware," Amnesty International, August 1, 2018, https://www.amnesty.org/en/latest/news/2018/08/staff-targeted-with-malicious-spyware/.

28. >>الإمارات تجسّست على أمير قطر وأمير سعودي<< وصحافي... كيف تمكّنت من تنفيذ خطّتها؟<<، رصيف٢٢، ٣١ الثامن ٢٠١٨. "How the UAE spied on the Emir of Qatar, a Saudi prince and a journalist," *Raseef22*, August 31, 2018.

29. 5G refers to the fifth generation of standards for cellular or otherwise wireless communications; Internet of Things is a global infrastructure that integrates objects of the physical

world (physical things) or the information world (virtual world) into information and communication technology networks. Adapted from: "ITU-T Y.4000/Y.2060 - Overview of the Internet of Things," International Telecommunications Union, June 2012, https://www.itu.int/rec/T-REC-Y.2060-201206-I.

30. John Sheldon, "Geopolitics and Cyber Power: Why Geography Still Matters," *American Foreign Policy Interests* 36, no. 5 (2014): pp. 286-293, https://doi.org/10.1080/10803920.2014.969174.

31. Ellen Nakashima, "Trump approves cyber-strikes against Iranian computer database used to plan attacks on oil tankers," *The Washington Post*, June 22, 2019, https://www.washingtonpost.com/world/national-security/with-trumps-approval-pentagon-launched-cyber-strikes-against-iran/2019/06/22/250d3740-950d-11e9-b570-6416efdc0803_story.html.

32. Michael Crowley, Maggie Haberman, Eric Schmitt, and Michael Shear, "Strikes on Iran Approved by Trump, Then Abruptly Pulled Back," *The New York Times*, June 20, 2019, https://www.nytimes.com/2019/06/20/world/middleeast/iran-us-drone.html.

33. Nakashima, "Trump approves cyber-strikes."

34. For Operation Ababil, see "Seven Iranians Working for Islamic Revolutionary Guard Corps-Affiliated Entities Charged for Conducting Coordinated Campaign of Cyber Attacks Against U.S. Financial Sector," U.S. Department of Justice, March 24, 2016, https://www.justice.gov/opa/pr/seven-iranians-working-islamic-revolutionary-guard-corps-affiliated-entities-charged; for attack on Sands Casino, see Alyza Sebenius, Kartikay Mehrotra, and William Turton, "Iran's Cyber Attack on Billionaire Adelson Provides Lesson on Strategy," *Bloomberg*, January 5, 2020, https://www.bloomberg.com/news/articles/2020-01-05/iranian-attack-on-adelson-provides-lesson-on-cyber-strategy; for U.S. grid, see Greenberg, "'Password-Spraying' the US Grid"; and "Rising Cyber Escalation Between US, Iran, and Russia: ICS Threats and Response," Dragos, Inc., June 25, 2019, https://www.dragos.com/blog/industry-news/rising-cyber-escalation-between-us-iran-and-russia-ics-threats-and-response/.

35. "Iran: Military Power: Ensuring Regime Survival and Securing Regional Dominance," U.S. Defense Intelligence Agency, August 2019, https://www.iranwatch.org/sites/default/files/iran_military_power_v13b_lr.pdf.

36. Colin Anderson and Karim Sadjadpour, "Iran's Cyber Threat: Espionage, Sabotage, and Revenge," Carnegie Endowment for International Peace (CEIP), January 4, 2018, https://carnegieendowment.org/2018/01/04/iran-s-cyber-threat-espionage-sabotage-and-revenge-pub-75134; Brian Merchant, "Is This the Leader of the Syrian Electronic Army?" *VICE News*, August 28, 2013, https://www.vice.com/en_us/article/4xxjp9/is-this-19-year-old-the-leader-of-the-syrian-electronic-army. "Rising Cyber Escalation," Dragos, Inc.

37. Zak Doffman, "Cyber Warfare Threat Rises as Iran and China Agree 'United Front' Against U.S.," *Forbes*, July 6, 2019, https://www.forbes.com/sites/zakdoffman/2019/07/06/iranian-cyber-threat-heightened-by-chinas-support-for-its-cyber-war-on-u-s/.

38. Assaf Dahan, Mor Levi, and Amit Serper, "Operation Soft Cell: A Worldwide Campaign Against Telecommunications Providers," Cybereason, June 25, 2019, https://www.cybereason.com/blog/operation-soft-cell-a-worldwide-campaign-against-telecommunications-providers.

39. "TRITON Attribution: Russian Government-Owned Lab Most Likely Built Custom Intrusion Tools for TRITON Attackers," FireEye, October 23, 2018, https://www.fireeye.com/blog/threat-research/2018/10/triton-attribution-russian-government-owned-lab-most-likely-built-tools.html.

40. "Russian-Linked Turla Group Compromised Iran's Infrastructure for False Flag Operations," Binary Defense, October 22, 2019, https://www.binarydefense.com/threat_watch/russian-linked-turla-group-compromised-irans-infrastructure-for-false-flag-operations/.

41. "Compromise of TV5 Monde," Council on Foreign Relations (CFR), 2020, https://www.cfr.org/cyber-operations/compromise-tv5-monde#:~:text=In%20May%202015%2C%20threat%20actors,the%20network's%20social%20media%20accounts.

42. Katherine Costello, "Russia's Use of Media and Information Operations in Turkey: Implications for the United States," RAND Corporation, 2018, https://www.rand.org/pubs/perspectives/PE278.html.

43. Sen. Angus King and Rep. Mike Gallagher, chrs., United States Cyberspace Solarium Commission, March 2020, https://

drive.google.com/file/d/1ryMCIL_dZ30QyjFqFkkf10MxIXJGT4yv/view.

44. Dina Temple-Raston, "How the U.S. Hacked ISIS," *NPR*, September 26, 2019, https://www.npr.org/2019/09/26/763545811/how-the-u-s-hacked-isis.

45. The 2019 John S. McCain National Defense Authorization Act (NDAA) for the Fiscal Year 2019, for example, calls for the use of "all instruments of national power, including the use of offensive cyber capabilities, to deter if possible, and respond to when necessary, all cyber attacks or other malicious cyber activities of foreign powers that target United States interests," in United States Congress, House Committee on Armed Services, John S. McCain National Defense Authorization Act For Fiscal Year 2019: Report of the Committee on Armed Services, Pub. L. 115–232, div. A, title XVI, §1636, Aug. 13, 2018, 132 Stat. 2126, House of Representatives on H.R. 5515, Washington: *U.S. Government Publishing Office*, 2018; "The CIA's new powers ... open the way for the agency to launch offensive cyber operations with the aim of producing disruption," in Zack Dorfman, Jenna McLughlin, Sean D. Naylor, and Kim Zetter, "Exclusive: Secret Trump order gives CIA more powers to launch cyberattacks," *Yahoo! News*, July 15, 2020, https://news.yahoo.com/secret-trump-order-gives-cia-more-powers-to-launch-cyberattacks-090015219.html.

46. "Summary: Department of Defense Cyber Strategy 2018," U.S. Department of Defense, September 2018 ctd. in: Richard Clarke and Robert Knake, *The Fifth Domain: Protecting Our Country, Our Company, and Ourselves in the Age of Cyber Threats* (New York: Penguin Random House Press, 2019).

47. August Cole, Yochi Dreazen, Siobhan Gorman, "Insurgents Hack U.S. Drones," *The Wall Street Journal*, December 17, 2009, https://www.wsj.com/articles/SB126102247889095011.

48. "How Cyber-Geopolitics Will Destabilize the Middle East," German Marshall Fund of the United States.

49. Ben Schaefer, "The Cyber Party of God: How Hezbollah Could Transform Cyberterrorism," *Georgetown Security Studies Review*, March 11, 2018, https://georgetownsecuritystudiesreview.org/2018/03/11/the-cyber-party-of-god-how-hezbollah-could-transform-cyberterrorism/.

50. Mike Wagenheim, "Hezbollah hones expertise in training cyber-warfare agents," *The Jerusalem Post*, August 16, 2020, https://www.jpost.com/middle-east/hezbollah-hones-expertise-in-training-cyber-warfare-agents-638800.

51. "Commodification of Cyber Capabilities: A Grand Cyber Arms Bazaar," Analytic Exchange program, U.S. Department of Homeland Security (DHS) and Office of the Director of National Intelligence (ODNI), November 2019, https://nsiteam.com/social/wp-content/uploads/2019/11/191119-AEP_Commodification-of-Cyber-Capabilities-Paper.pdf.

52. Ibid.; and David Reid, "UAE announces Middle East defense giant in the wake of Aramco attacks," *CNBC News*, November 5, 2019, https://www.cnbc.com/2019/11/05/uae-announces-middle-east-defense-giant-in-the-wake-of-aramco-attacks.html.

53. See Vernon Silver, "EU Legislators Ask for Inquiry into Spy Gear Abuses in Bahrain," *Bloomberg*, August 24, 2011, https://www.bloomberg.com/news/articles/2011-08-24/eu-legislators-ask-for-inquiry-into-spy-gear-abuses-in-bahrain; Nour Malas, Pal Sonne, and Jennifer Valentino-DeVries, "U.S Firm Acknowledges Syria Uses Its Gear to Block Web," *The Wall Street Journal*, October 2, 2011; and "The President's Men? Inside the Technical Research Department, the secret player in Egypt's intelligence infrastructure," Privacy International, February 2016, https://privacyinternational.org/report/666/presidents-men-inside-technical-research-department-secret-player-egypts-intelligence.

54. "Egypt, FinFisher Intrusion Tools and Ethics," F-Secure Labs, March 8, 2011, https://archive.f-secure.com/weblog/archives/00002114.html.

55. Bill Marczak, Sarah McKune, Irene Poetranto, John-Scott Railton, and Adam Senft, "Pay No Attention to the Server Behind the Proxy," Citizen Lab, October 15, 2015, https://tspace.library.utoronto.ca/handle/1807/97784.

56. Parker Higgins, "Elusive FinFisher Spyware Identified and Analyzed," Electronic Frontier Foundation (EFF), July 25, 2012, https://www.eff.org/deeplinks/2012/07/elusive-finfisher-spyware-identified-and-analyzed.

57. "The President's Men?" Privacy International, 16.

58. For companies in Egypt, see "The President's Men?" Privacy International; for companies in the UAE, see Nancy Hopkins and Matthew Taylor, "Private firms selling mass surveillance systems around world, documents show,"

The Guardian, November 18, 2013, https://www.theguardian.com/world/2013/nov/18/private-firms-mass-surveillance-technologies; for companies in Israel, see "Hide and Seek," Citizen Lab; and "NSO Group / Q Cyber Technologies: Over One Hundred New Abuse Cases," Citizen Lab, October 29, 2019, https://citizenlab.ca/2019/10/nso-q-cyber-technologies-100-new-abuse-cases/; and "Commodification of Cyber Capabilities," Analytic Exchange Program.

59. "Commodification of Cyber Capabilities," Analytic exchange Program.

60. Ibid.

61. Influence-as-a-service draws on the popularized nomenclature of cloud computing, in which "-as-a-service" refers to a type of solution that is centrally managed, hosted, designed, or executed by a third party.

62. Computational propaganda is the application of algorithms and automation to amplify or repress political content, disinformation, hate speech and junk news. Adapted from: The Computational Propaganda Project, Oxford Internet Institute, 2020, https://comprop.oii.ox.ac.uk.

63. Samantha Bradshaw and Philip Howard, "The Global Disinformation Order: 2019 Global Inventory of Organised Social Media Manipulation," Oxford University: Project on Computational Propaganda (Oxford, UK, 2019), https://comprop.oii.ox.ac.uk/research/cybertroops2019/.

64. Ibid.

65. "Inauthentic Israeli Facebook Assets Target the World," DFRLab (on Medium), Atlantic Council, May 17, 2019, https://medium.com/dfrlab/inauthentic-israeli-facebook-assets-target-the-world-281ad7254264; and "Sorting fact from fiction in Tunisia's presidential election," DFRLab (on Medium), Atlantic Council, October 11, 2019, https://medium.com/dfrlab/sorting-fact-from-fiction-in-tunisias-presidential-election-862bcc05bdaf.

66. Vanessa Szakal, "Tunisia target by Israeli disinformation campaign," Nawaat, June 7, 2019, https://nawaat.org/2019/06/07/la-tunisie-ciblee-par-une-campagne-de-desinformation-israelienne/.

67. Levi J. West, "#jihad: Understanding Social Media as a Weapon," *Security Challenges* 12, no. 2 (2016), 9-26, https://www.jstor.org/stable/26465604. Retrieved from Jstor July 8, 2019.

68. Teodor Mitew and Ahmed Shehabat, "Black-boxing the Black Flag: Anonymous Sharing Platforms and ISIS Content Distribution Tactics," *Perspectives on Terrorism* 12, no. 1 (February 2018), 81-99, https://www.jstor.org/stable/26343748. Retrieved from Jstor July 7, 2020.

69. Charlie Winter, "Making Sense of Jihadi Stratcom: The Case of the Islamic State," *Perspectives on Terrorism* 13, no 1 (2019), 53-61, https://www.jstor.org/stable/26590508. Retrieved from Jstor July 8, 2019.

70. Antonia Ward, "ISIS's Use of Social Media Still Poses a Threat to Stability in the Middle East and Africa," RAND Corporation, December 11, 2018, https://www.rand.org/blog/2018/12/isiss-use-of-social-media-still-poses-a-threat-to-stability.html.

71. West, "#jihad"; Shehabat and Mitew, "Black-boxing the Black Flag."

72. Deepfakes are technologically synthesized media that rely on computer graphics, computer vision, and machine learning. Meant to seem real, they undermine visual and aural authenticity to enable the production of disinformation by bad actors. Adapted from: Nicholas Diakopoulos and Deborah Johnson, "Anticipating and Addressing the Ethical Implications of Deepfakes in the Context of Elections," New Media & Society, November 1, 2019, https://dx.doi.org/10.2139/ssrn.3474183.

CHAPTER TWO

CYBER INSURANCE AS CYBER DIPLOMACY

ASAF LUBIN[*]

INTRODUCTION

The delicate art of managing foreign affairs is one of the oldest in human history. This long-established practice has recently experienced a renaissance with the introduction of "cyber diplomacy" as an exciting new frontier for traditional diplomatic work. Under this novel banner a pincer movement is gradually taking form: While ambassadors and foreign relations experts are being called to engage further with "the geopolitics of cyberspace," computer scientists and cybersecurity specialists are invited, perhaps for the first time, to meaningfully contribute to discussions at "the heart of foreign policy."[1] Cyber diplomacy is thus better understood as an umbrella term, encompassing a whole array of diplomatic activities that center around the control and management of our interconnected digital environments and resources. As summarized by the former coordinator for cyber issues at the U.S.

Department of State, Christopher Painter:

> *Among other things, effective cyber diplomacy involves: (1) building strategic partnerships with other countries around the world and engaging the many, many multilateral forums that are shaping cyber policy; (2) using diplomacy and diplomatic tools to directly respond to cyber threats; and (3) working with other agencies to facilitate law enforcement and technical cooperation and provide capacity building so other countries can better work with us.*[2]

Estonia offers a great example of leadership in cyber diplomacy. As the victim of one of the first strategically significant cyberattacks in history, it has emerged as a pioneer and revolutionary in the promotion of global cyber norms.[3] In July 2019 it hosted the "first-ever 'summer school' training on cyber diplomacy," inviting dozens of NATO and EU diplomats to take part.[4] In October 2019, it was the first country to establish within its Ministry of Foreign Affairs a whole department devoted to cyber diplomacy, focused predominantly on enhancing international cooperation around "compliance with cyber norms, trust-building measures, and existing international law."[5]

One way of explaining the efforts of nation states like Estonia in the field of cyber diplomacy is through the lens of constructivism theory in international relations studies. Constructivist thinkers place a premium on non-material intersubjective factors such as ideas and identities.[6] A fundamental theme in constructivist thought is the notion of "norm diffusion,"[7] according to which states act with the belief that by securing such ideational alliances they could simultaneously strengthen their own soft power while resolving the coordination problems that are so prevalent in world politics. Reaching consensus around a certain set of normative rules-of-the-road "reduc[es] transaction costs" by developing a shared "language and grammar" for conceptualizing and understanding global social and political challenges.[8]

A cyber diplomat can thus be seen as an importer/exporter of norms. On their agenda is the trade in a growing list of cyber normative commodities. In the morning a bilateral meeting on internet freedom in Myanmar, in the afternoon negotiations at the U.N. Open-Ended

Working Group (OEWG) discussing principles for responsible state behavior in cyberspace, and over dinner a conversation with the legal advisors of a few corporate tech giants about encryption and backdoors. These, of course, are all hot topics, ripped straight from the headlines.

But dare interrupt the cyber diplomat's busy schedule with questions about insurance underwriting, premiums and deductibles, brokers and risk polls and most will run for the hills, horrified by the idea that they might be required to master such jargon. The reality, however, is that cyber insurance is proving to be an important tool for cyber risk prevention and mitigation on the local, regional, national, and international levels. If cyber diplomacy is truly concerned with enhancing cyber deterrence[9] and promoting norms that ensure global cyber stability and cyber peace,[10] it must broaden its perspective to include international insurance norms for modeling and indemnifying the perils of cyberspace.

In this chapter I therefore argue that norms surrounding cyber insurance should be added to the diplomatic portfolio of nation states. To illustrate this point, I discuss a recent initiative of the Israel National Cyber Directorate to transform Israel into a beta site for cyber insurance regulation. The goal of this trial is to experiment with various prescriptive and regulatory solutions for some of the most fundamental problems that plague the still-emerging cyber insurance market. By collaborating with a number of reinsurers and foreign governments, Israel hopes to successfully chart the way forward for other commercial insurers and insurance regulators around the world. In so doing, it is demonstrating how cyber diplomacy might be augmented and expanded to encompass certain norms, best practices, and governance mechanisms that have so far been deemed wholly domestic, jurisdiction-specific, and purely technical.

The chapter proceeds in the following order. Section I briefly explores the current state of the cyber insurance market and its existing global limitations. Section II moves to discuss the new initiative to turn Israel into a cyber insurance beta site, its scope and rationale. The chapter concludes by extrapolating from the Israeli case study to propose a broader research agenda for international norms around cyber insurance.

SECTION I: THE CYBER INSURANCE MARKET

Cyber insurance, as the name suggests, is an economic device through which the risk from various types of cyber perils is transferred from the policyholder to a third party, traditionally a commercial entity, in exchange for a fee — the insurance premium. As with all lines of insurance, cyber coverage is differentiated between first- and third-party harms. Coverage for first-party harms may include, for example, loss of revenue from network business interruptions, data restoration costs, and post-incident forensic investigations. Coverage for third-party harms will center around liabilities for breach of personal information, transmission of malicious code, or statutory fines and penalties triggered by violations of data protection regimes.[11]

The global cyber insurance market is booming. In 2018 it had a market size of roughly $4.8 billion worldwide, and according to some researchers it is likely to grow to more than $28 billion by 2026.[12] The U.S. currently controls the lion's share of this market. As of 2017 it accounted for approximately 90 percent of all gross written premiums worldwide.[13] Recently, the COVID-19 pandemic has intensified the demand for cyber insurance globally. A recent study which surveyed more than 3,000 cybersecurity experts from Japan, Australia, Germany, the U.K., and Singapore found that "91% of enterprises reported an increase in cyberattacks with more employees working from home amidst the coronavirus outbreak."[14] Even more troubling was that 80 percent of those surveyed noted "an increase in the level of sophistication in such threats."[15] With the expansion of remote work strategies by businesses and the continued straining of their network IT resources, malicious cyber actors are finding new opportunities to exploit vulnerabilities introduced by a rapidly changing COVID-19 digital environment.[16] In the wake of this reality "[i]nsurance brokers and industry attorneys say they're seeing a spike in both cyber insurance claims and more general inquiries about how such policies can offset some of the liabilities they're confronting."[17]

Nonetheless, the race of insurers toward cyber insurance might be nothing more than a gold rush. The European Insurance and Occupational Pensions Authority concluded in a recent report that insurers were "broadening coverage, terms, and conditions" in an attempt to sell more policies, all due to "increasing competition and a limited understanding of the risks."[18] Warren Buffet was even more disparaging, suggesting recently that if anyone said they knew what they were doing when writing cyber policies, they were "kidding themselves!"[19]

Three particular challenges stand out. First, the market is plagued with informational gaps and asymmetries. Insurance companies lack sufficient expertise around mitigation of cyber risks and perils, expertise that is held by a handful of intelligence agencies and cybersecurity firms. Prospective policyholders too lack information. Many are blind to their own cybersecurity needs and lack awareness as to the value of cyber insurance as a tool in the cybersecurity toolbox. Two factors might widen informational gaps. First, the dominance of a few insurance companies and their reluctance to share much of their emerging claims datasets entrench the reality of a concentrated market with a few major players. Moreover, the refusal of victims of cyberattacks to publicly disclose necessary security data out of reputational concerns makes it even harder for insurers to mature their understanding of the risks and perils. The result is an insurance market that is lacking reliable actuarial data to effectively compute pricing or model exposures.[20]

Second, cybersecurity underwriting is more susceptible to aggregated risks. Think of insurance for natural disasters. A particular geographical region might be prone to hurricanes, earthquakes, or flooding. An insurer could thus diversify its portfolio by offering coverage across geographical lines in areas that are less likely to suffer an insurable event.[21] Cyberattacks, however, are blind to geographical borders. The interconnectivity that is part and parcel of our digital economy makes mega cyber-catastrophes a real possibility, as we have already witnessed in the WannaCry and NotPetya cyberattacks.[22] Moreover, monopolies in the tech landscape have forced us to rely on only a few operating systems, online platforms, services, devices, and cloud providers. As a result, we are all subject to the same common vulnerabilities. Exploiting one of us is exploiting all of us.[23]

A third hurdle to cyber insurance maturity concerns lack of uniformity around scope of coverage across the industry. Contemporary policies suffer from an array of definitional ambiguities.[24] Both under domestic and international law, no clear classifications have yet been codified as to what constitutes an "act of war" or "terrorism" in cyberspace, nor have we developed clear evidentiary rules for attributing cyberattacks to state or non-state actors.[25] As a result, uncertainty plagues the cyber insurance market and raises skepticism on the part of both existing and future policyholders.

The combination of information asymmetries, aggregation risks, and lack of uniform language results in an underperforming market. Such underperformance could lead to negative consequences. Instead of substituting governmental regulation through commercial monitoring and enhancement of safety enforcement,[26] insurers could increase cyber instability through moral hazards.[27]

SECTION II: ISRAEL AS A BETA SITE FOR CYBER INSURANCE REGULATION

Israel has a small but growing cyber insurance market. While the market "has grown six fold over the past five years and continues to grow at a similar rate,"[28] it currently does not come close to reaching its full potential.[29] In 2019 the Israel National Cyber Directorate conducted a survey among 4,242 Israeli companies. The survey found that while 80 percent of companies identify cyber risk as a top corporate priority, only 13 percent had acquired cyber insurance, and among those only 18 percent had coverage of 5 million Israeli shekels (roughly $1.5 million) or above.[30] Most of those surveyed reported a lack of awareness and a lack of economic worthwhileness as the two primary reasons they were hesitant to acquire such a policy.[31]

The Israeli insurance industry is also a highly concentrated market dominated by a few composite insurance groups, each relying heavily on foreign reinsurers.[32] This trend is even more visible in the cyber insurance context, where only a handful of actors provide standalone cyber insurance products across the country. Moreover, in Israel the Capital Market, Insurance, and Savings Authority, within the Ministry of Finance, possess expanded authorities to regulate and monitor the local insurance industry.

More broadly, Israel is a cybersecurity powerhouse. As of the end of 2019 the Israel's cyber industry was second only to the U.S., taking 22 percent of "the overall venture-backed cyber investment worldwide."[33] Investment in cybersecurity firms in Israel reached a record high of $1.6 billion with 540 active cybersecurity startups operating across the country.[34]

Israel is thus well positioned to develop and test cyber insurance regulations. Its relatively small, concentrated, and emerging cyber insurance market is met with statutorily powerful insurance and cybersecurity regulators, as well as a bustling broader cybersecurity ecosystem.[35] At the end of 2019, the Israel National Cyber Directorate, together with the Federmann Cyber Security Center at the Hebrew University of Jerusalem, co-convened a policy workshop to discuss the progression of the Israeli cyber insurance market. The event, which was supported by both the Carnegie Endowment for International Peace and the William and Flora Hewlett Foundation, was centered around an innovative idea by the Israeli government, exploring "how Israel could responsibly develop a beta site for testing the solutions identified by the workshop participants"[36] for enhancement of its cyber insurance market. The event saw participation from foreign government regulators, reinsurers, insurers, Israeli government officials, academics, and cyber research centers.

One of the most important takeaways from the event was the conclusion that cyber insurance regulation requires an inter-state multi-stakeholder collaboration. As was further summarized by Ariel E. Levite of the Carnegie Endowment, who moderated the event:

> *In fact, it seems crystal clear that the evolution of a more mature cyber risk management market (including an insurance one) would benefit greatly from collaborative efforts by a group of states as well as from leading players in the (re) insurance world who will take the lead to develop a multinational/multi-stakeholder platform. Some other private sector entities, such as leading credit rating agencies and companies with risk modelling expertise, could be valuable partners in such an undertaking and appear to be willing partners to engage in such an undertaking. Similar logic applies to collaboration with and between academic research institutes as well as policy-oriented think tanks. It is precisely because the issue we are dealing with cuts across several academic disciplines (inter alia business and finance, computer science and engineering, law, public policy, security studies) that some exchanges are important in order to help develop workable models for enhancing cyber resiliency and risk management.*[37]

Following the event, the Israel National Cyber Directorate took the lead in developing its proposed beta site regulatory plans. The program is still being developed but we can already learn from some of Israel's achievements to date in the areas of cyber modeling and cyber risk mitigation, to get a sense of what the program might include in the future. In this regard it might be useful to highlight a few existing initiatives of the Israel National Cyber Directorate:

- To increase information sharing between the private sector and the government the Israeli Cyber Emergency Response Team (CERT) created a social platform known as CyberNET. This program now has more than 2,000 members, including analysts, chief information security officers, and information security researchers. Each member has an individual profile and is able to both share and receive information in public and anonymous forms. The system alerts about various cyber incidents and reported security events on the national and international level. It also operates internal chat and discussion groups to facilitate conversation. Finally, the program allows participants to share information directly with the CERT or with members in their sector, and even upload malicious software to be further analyzed.[38] The growth of the cyber insurance industry, and its appropriate regulation, will depend on accurate and detailed information exchange between insurers and government and programs like CyberNET may present a prototype for what such information sharing might look like.

- The Israel National Cyber Directorate has devoted significant resources to the development of a number of projects aimed at "improving Israel's capacity to detect and prevent cyber incidents, enhance coordination and intelligence, increase readiness and risk management, and facilitate data sharing and distribution processes across institutions."[39] Three of these projects in particular are worth mentioning. *High Castle* "is a platform for governmental and private stakeholders to improve detection, investigation, and blocking capabilities."[40] *Crystal Ball*, meanwhile, "combines various threat intelligence collection tools, adds the findings from *High Castle* and creates a unified threat projection to improve situation analysis capabilities for intelligence services and civilian stakeholders."[41] Finally, *Showcase* "evaluates risk exposure and the degree of preparedness in critical infrastructure."[42] The more the Israeli regulators are capable of assessing industry-specific risks and levels of exposure, the more they will be able to articulate effective mitigation strategies of the kind that the insurance industry will wish to rely on in promulgating its own cyber insurance-related programming.

- In recent months, the Directorate has developed models for assessing national cyber catastrophes. The models try to evaluate the length of business interruptions, the depth of such disturbances on the markets, and the unique vulnerabilities of particular sectors. In this context, a particular focus of the models was the level of under-insurance and insurance coverage exclusions, across industries, and how the lack of an insurance solution might trigger cascading effects across the economy.[43] Another area for national risk modeling of relevance to the cyber insurance industry is the risk posed by cyber terrorism. In this context, the Directorate recently joined the International Forum for Terrorism (Re)Insurance Pools (IFTRIP) and has been directly involved in dialogue on developing uniform language for cyber insurance coverage for cyber terrorism risks and beyond.[44]

It is still unclear whether and how this program will roll out or how successful it will be in the long run. But the very idea alone is already worth highlighting. Treating cyber insurance as an area of commercial practice that goes beyond its pure technical and jurisdiction-specific dimensions, and examining it as a broader phenomenon with potential global effects, is both innovative and promising. Understanding that the issues that plague the Israeli cyber insurance industry are not unique to Israel, but rather reflect universal concerns that can only be tackled by cross-border collaboration and capacity building, is an important step in the stabilization of this emerging market. In this regard, it might be worth noting that the U.S. Cybersecurity and Infrastructure Security Agency recently highlighted Israel as an example of a success story to be emulated, for its government's efforts to collaborate with its emerging cyber insurance market.[45]

CONCLUSION: A RESEARCH AGENDA FOR INTERNATIONAL NORMS AROUND INSURANCE REGULATION

On December 5, 2018 the U.N. General Assembly adopted Resolution 73/27, which established the OEWG, involving all interested U.N. member states, "to further develop the rules, norms and principles of responsible behaviour of States"[46] in cyberspace. Among those rules, norms, and principles, the General Assembly included the following list:

- The development and application of measures "to increase stability and security in the use of ICTs [information and communications technology] and to prevent ICT practices that are acknowledged to be harmful or that may pose threats to international peace and security."[47]

- The cooperation, assistance and exchange of information around use of ICTs for terrorist and criminal purposes.[48]

- Protection of critical infrastructure from ICT threats by taking appropriate measures and the creation of a "global culture of cybersecurity and the protection of critical information infrastructures."[49]

- Protecting the "integrity of the supply chain so that end users can have confidence in the security of ICT products."[50]

- Encouragement of "responsible reporting of ICT vulnerabilities" and the sharing of "[a]ssociated information on available remedies for such vulnerabilities to limit and possibly eliminate potential threats to ICTs and ICT-dependent infrastructure."[51]

- Encouragement of "the private sector and civil society to play an appropriate role to improve security of and in the use of ICTs, including supply chain security for ICT products and services."[52]

Each of the six general rules, norms, and principles listed above has immediate and obvious interactions with and effects on cyber insurance development. Cyber insurers can be a force for good in enhancing best practices around the reporting of vulnerabilities and improvement of security. Cyber insurers can also indirectly play a negative role as incentivizers of cyber instability, enhancing the likelihood of unmitigated cybercrime and uninsurable cyber events, like state-sponsored cyberattacks and acts of cyber terrorism. Cyber insurance can be a promoter of an enhanced culture of cyber standardization or a demoter of proper and efficient security budgeting and the adoption of best practices in cyber hygiene.

In their article "Constructing Norms for Global Cybersecurity," Martha Finnemore and Duncan Hollis highlight that one of the most obvious challenges in developing international cyber norms and governance regimes is a failure to properly identify "whom does the cybernorm govern," "what does the norm say," and "where does it say it," as well as "what promotion and socialization tools should be deployed to make the norm effective."[53] Cyber diplomats have focused much of their attention in norm design and promulgation on a narrow set of responsibilities owed by states, and to a lesser extent responsibilities owed by major ICT companies.

In an effort to expand the multi-stakeholder understanding of the risks cyber threats pose to society, we must begin to draw additional actors into the fold. Involving commercial reinsurers and insurers, brokers, underwriters, cyber risk insurance pool directors, corporate chief cyber risk officers, and insurance law and policy scholars and think tanks in a larger conversation about the future of international cybersecurity would be a pivotal first step toward a more democratic and inclusive dialogue. Such a dialogue would offer more nuanced solutions to practical challenges, and would ensure better norm design by the very actors that will ultimately be tasked with ensuring the norms' proper implementation.

Endnotes

*Asaf Lubin is an Associate Professor of Law at Indiana University Maurer School; Affiliate at the Berkman Klein Center for Internet and Society, Harvard University; Visiting Fellow at the Information Society Project, Yale Law School; Visiting Scholar at the Feuermann Cybersecurity Research Center, Hebrew University of Jerusalem; Fellow at the Center for Applied Cybersecurity Research, Indiana University; and Visiting Fellow at the Nebraska Governance and Technology Center. This work was supported by funding from the Federmann Cyber Security Center in conjunction with the Israel National Cyber Directorate. I wish to thank Itai Benartzi for comments provided on previous versions of this chapter.

1. See Shaun Riordan, *Cyber-diplomacy: Why Diplomats Need to Get Into Cyberspace*, 22 PUB. DIPL. MAG. 9, 10 (2019); *See also* André Barrinha & Thomas Renard, Cyber-diplomacy: the making of an international society in the digital age, 3 GLOBAL AFF. 353, 355-56 (2017) (defining cyber diplomacy as "diplomacy in the cyber domain or, in other words, the use of diplomatic resources and the performance of diplomatic functions to secure national interest with regards to cyberspace." Elsewhere they note that cyber diplomacy "is a relatively new concept," and that the "absence of literature results from the novelty of cyber-diplomacy, whose origins we situate at the turn of the first decade of the twenty-first century"). *See also* Khristo Ayad & Abed Shirzai, *Cyber-diplomacy in Qatar: A Virtue of Necessity?*, 22 PUB. DIPL. MAG. 28, 28 (2019) (Noting that the delineation of the term cyber diplomacy is "not without debate," arguing further that the term is better understood as distinguishable from digital diplomacy, an older term which centers on the "use of digital means in exercising diplomacy." Instead Ayad and Shirazi define cyber diplomacy the employment of diplomacy "to respond to challenges in cyberspace.").

2. *U.S. Cyber Diplomacy in an Era of Growing Threat: Hearing Before the H. Comm. On Foreign Relations*, 105th Cong. 5 (2018) (statement of Christopher Painter, Commissioner for the Global Commission for the Stability of Cyberspace).

3. *See generally* Daniel E. White, *Estonian Leadership in the Cyber Realm*, 22 PUB. DIPL. MAG. 31-32 (2019).

4. *See* Shannon Vavra, *Estonia debuts first-ever cyber diplomacy training*, CYBERSCOOP (Jul. 29, 2019), https://www.cyberscoop.com/cyber-diplomacy-estonia-summer-school/.

5. *See* Fredrico Plantera, *Estonia takes on a major role in cyber diplomacy with a new department for international cooperation*, E-ESTONIA (Oct. 2019), https://e-estonia.com/estonia-cyber-diplomacy-international-cooperation/.

6. Martha Finnemore & Kathryn Sikkink, *Taking Stock: The Constructivist Research Program in International Relations and Comparative Politics*, 4 ANN. REV. POL. SCI. 391, 392-393 (2001) ("constructivism is an approach to social analysis that asserts the following: (a) human interaction is shaped primarily by ideational factors, not simply material ones; (b) the most important ideational factors are widely shared or "intersubjective" beliefs, which are not reducible to individuals; and (c) these shared beliefs construct the interests and identities of purposive actors.").

7. *See* Carla Winston, *Norm structure, diffusion, and evolution: A conceptual approach*, 24(3) EUR. J. INT'L RELATIONS 638, 642 (2018) (discussing the dual nature of norms — being "both stable and flexible" — Winston highlights the process of norm diffusion: "in which states will variously interact with norms as they are (stable) or change them, either purposefully or accidentally (flexible). This duality presents a problem for norms researchers studying the diffusion and evolution of norms throughout the international system, as it complicates the relationship between actor (norm adopter), process (diffusion mechanism), and object (the norm itself).").

8. Andrew P. Cortell & James W. Davis, Jr., *Understanding the Domestic Impact of International Norms: A Research Agenda*, 2(1) INT'L STUD. REV. 65, 65-66 (2000).

9. *See e.g.* Martin Libicki, *Cyber Deterrence and Cyber War* 7 (2009) (noting that "[i]f deterrence is anything that dissuades an attack, it is usually said to have two components: deterrence by denial (the ability to frustrate the attacks) and deterrence by punishment (the threat of retaliation)."). *But cf.* Max Smeets and Stefan Soesanto, *Cyber Deterrence Is Dead. Long Live Cyber Deterrence!*, Council

on Foreign Relations (Feb. 18, 2020), https://www.cfr.org/blog/cyber-deterrence-dead-long-live-cyber-deterrence ("Born in the 1990s, the thinking on cyber deterrence was nurtured by the U.S. Department of Defense in numerous war-gaming exercises. Hitting puberty in the aftermath of the distributed denial-of-service campaign against Estonia in 2007, cyber deterrence matured after Stuxnet and received peak attention from policymakers and academics from 2013 to 2016 during the golden age of 'cyberwar' scholarship. From 2016 onward, the interest in cyber deterrence started to fade to the extent that it is now intentionally neglected.").

10. *See e.g.* Group of Governmental Experts on Developments in the Field of Information and Telecommunications in the Context of International Security, UN Doc. A/70/174, 7 ¶ 13 (Jul. 22, 2015) (as part of its list of "recommendations for the consideration by States for voluntary, non-binding norms, rules or principles of responsible behaviour of States aimed at promoting an open, secure, stable, accessible and peaceful ICT environment," the UNGGE included the following recommendation: "Consistent with the purposes of the United Nations, including to maintain international peace and security, States should cooperate in developing and applying measures to increase stability and security in the use of ICTs and to prevent ICT practices that are acknowledged to be harmful or that may pose threats to international peace and security.").

11. For a general overview see *Understanding Cyber Insurance: A Structured Dialogue With Insurance*, European Insurance and Occupational Pensions Authority (2018); *Enhancing the Role of Insurance in Cyber Risk Management*, OECD (2017); Christopher C. French, *Insuring Against Cyber Risk: The Evolution of an Industry*, 122(3) PENN. ST. L. REV. 607 (2018); Jay P. Kesan and Carol M. Hayes, *Strengthening Cybersecurity with Cyberinsurance Markets and Better Risk Assessment*, 102 MINN. L. REV. 191 (2017); Shauhin A. Talesh, *Data Breach, Privacy, and Cyber Insurance: How Insurance Companies Act as "Compliance Managers" for Businesses*, 43(2) L. & SOC. INQ. 417 (2018).

12. *Cyber Insurance Market Outlook – 2026*, Allied Market Research (Mar. 2020), https://www.alliedmarketresearch.com/cyber-insurance-market.

13. *Cyber Insurance: A Key Element of the Corporate Risk Management Strategy*, Deloitte 4 (2017), https://www2.deloitte.com/content/dam/Deloitte/cy/Documents/risk/CY_Risk_CyberInsurance_Noexp.PDF.

14. Eileen Yu, *COVID-19 fuels cyber attacks, exposes gaps in business recovery*, ZDNET (Jul. 21, 2020), https://www.zdnet.com/article/covid-19-fuels-cyber-attacks-exposes-gaps-in-disaster-recovery/.

15. *Id.*

16. *See e.g.* Dep't Homeland Sec., *Covid-19 Exploited by Malicious Cyber Actors*, Alert (AA20-009A) (Apr. 8, 2020), https://us-cert.cisa.gov/ncas/alerts/aa20-099a.

17. Allisson Grande, *Cyber Insurance Demand Heats Up As COVID-19 Hacks Rise*, LAW360 (May 14, 2020), https://www.law360.com/articles/1258119/cyber-insurance-demand-heats-up-as-covid-19-hacks-rise (quoting a law firm partner who represents cyber insurance policy holders who noted that: "Cyber was already a hot area where we were seeing a lot of claims before the pandemic hit. … Now with the massive abrupt change of so many working from home, that's just thrown gas on the fire.").

18. *Understanding Cyber Insurance – A Structured Dialogue with Insurance Companies*, European Insurance And Occupational Pensions Authority, 23 (2018), https://www.eiopa.europa.eu/sites/default/files/publications/reports/eiopa_understanding_cyber_insurance.pdf [hereinafter: EIOPA 2018 Report].

19. Katherine Chiglinsky and Sonali Basak, *Buffett Cautious on Cyber Insurance Because No One Knows Risks*, Bloomberg (May 5, 2018), https://www.bloomberg.com/news/articles/2018-05-05/buffett-cautious-on-cyber-insurance-because-no-one-knows-risks.

20. *See e.g.* Michael Faure and Bernold Nieuwesteeg, *The Law and Economics of Cyber Risk Pooling*, 14(3) NYU J. L. & BUS. 923, 932 (2018) ("A general problem which often emerges in insuring against relatively new risks is that insurance companies may lack sufficient information to correctly calculate so-called "actuarially fair premiums," which is, as previously mentioned, a particular problem for cyber risks… [E]mpirical observations show that the market has not yet fully developed, precisely because of the lack of past data…"); EIOPA 2018 Report, supra note

18, at 15 ("Lack of data is a primary obstacle to a detailed understanding of fundamental aspects of cyber risk. It is challenging to build adequate models to assure accuracy in the risk management if the availability of data is limited. That might not only reinforce the fact that there is a need for a deeper understanding of cyber risks, but also foment the insufficient level of risk information in the market."); Cybersecurity and Infra. Sec. Agency, *Assessment of the Cyber Insurance Market*, Department of Homeland Security (Jul., 2019), https://www.cisa.gov/sites/default/files/publications/19_1115_cisa_OCE-Cyber-Insurance-Market-Assessment.pdf [hereinafter: CISA 2019 Report] ("Cyber insurance is a new and specialized market with significant risks and difficulties for underwriting due to challenges presented by a lack of data, methodological limitations, and a lack of information sharing. These core challenges make it difficult for insurance companies to underwrite the risk at the right price. To do so, insurance companies would need underwriting guidelines, a risk management process, and robust and reliable pricing models that are continuously validated, especially given the dynamic nature of cyber risk.").

21. For further reading see Michael L. Smith and Stephen A. Kane, *The Law of Large Numbers and the Strength of Insurance*, in INSURANCE, RISK MANAGEMENT, AND PUBLIC POLICY 1 (Gustavson and Herrington eds., 1994).

22. *See e.g. Cyber Insurance and Systemic Market Risk*, EastWest Inst. 14, 38 (Jun., 2017), https://www.eastwest.ngo/sites/default/files/ideas-files/cyber-insurance-and-systemic-market-risk.pdf ("Contagion, which is the propagation of adverse effects within and across sectors, happens when the digital interconnection of critical systems and the underlying technical, functional, economic and financial dependencies are of sufficient depth to allow the incident to breach the cyber realm and affect the broader economy and society. ... [The insurance industry] has the potential to be significantly damaged from such systemic cyber risk — an event with large contagion factors that hits the entire insurance market at once.").

23. *Id.*, at 13 ("The risk from a "common vulnerability" comes from the presence of a component or vulnerability that is widespread throughout systems (e.g., a bug in the OpenSSL library in the case of Heartbleed, vulnerabilities that were exploited in the WannaCry and NotPetya cyberattacks, or a common Linux vulnerability.").

24. *See e.g.* Koyejo-Isaac Idowu, *The Insurance Data Security Model Law: Strengthening Cybersecurity Insurer-Policyholder Relationships and Protecting Consumers*, 24(1) ROGER WILLIAMS UNIVERSITY L. REV. 115, 128 (2019) ("Insurers' sweeping risk-averse approach and lack of uniform language spells trouble for companies who often do not realize that a 'cyber' breach is not covered under its cyber policy or its traditional insurance policy until it is too late.").

25. For further reading see Adam B. Shniderman, *Prove It! Judging the Hostile-or-Warlike-Action Exclusion in Cyber-Insurance Policies*, 129 YALE L. J. FORUM 64 (15 Oct., 2019).

26. *See* Omri Ben-Shahar and Kyle D. Logue, *How Insurance Substitutes for Regulation*, 36(1) REGULATION 36, 44 (2013) (discussing how "insurers perform many of the same regulatory functions that government regulators and courts perform" by "mandating specific investments in risk reduction, to offering premium discounts for favorable claims experience, to selling cost-containment expertise to policyholders, and even to the design of safety technologies and codes.").

27. By moral hazard I refer to the economics doctrine which confirms the idea that "a party who is insured against risk has a suboptimal incentive to reduce it." (*Id.*, at 36). For an example of a moral hazard in the context of cyber insurance consider Danny Palmer, *Ransomware: Cyber-insurance payouts are adding to the problem, warn security experts*, ZDNET (17 Sept., 2019), https://www.zdnet.com/article/ransomware-cyber-insurance-payouts-are-adding-to-the-problem-warn-security-experts/.

28. Tal Pavel, *Cyber Insurance Market in Israel – What is the Official Policy?*, in 2020 INTERNATIONAL CONFERENCE ON CYBER SITUATIONAL AWARENESS, DATA ANALYTICS AND ASSESSMENT, reprinted in IEEE Xplore DOI 10.1109/CyberSA49311.2020.9139722, 5 (Jul. 14, 2019), https://ieeexplore.ieee.org/document/9139722.

29. *Id.*

30. *Cybersecurity in the Israeli Civilian Sector: Concluding Empirical Findings Report*, ISRAELI NAT'L CYBER DIR., 32 (in Hebrew)

(May, 2019).

31. *Id.*, at 34.

32. *Id.*, at 34.

33. *2019 in the Cyber Industry: A Year and Decade Overview*, ISRAELI NAT'L CYBER DIR. (Jan. 27, 2020), https://www.gov.il/he/departments/news/2019innumbers; Shoshanna Solomon, *Cybersecurity investment in Israel surges 47% to over $1b in 2018*, TIMES OF ISRAEL (Jan. 28, 2019), https://www.timesofisrael.com/cybersecurity-investment-in-israel-surges-47-to-over-1b-in-2018-report/#gs.fjxg2f.

34. *Id.*

35. For more on this latter point consider Dr. Nee-Joo Teh, *Cybersecurity in Israel* (2018), https://admin.ktn-uk.co.uk/app/uploads/2019/03/216_KTN_CyberSecurity_Israel_v4.pdf (discussing the cybersecurity and innovation landscape and ecosystem in Israel with a focus on its drivers and sources of policy, regulation and funding).

36. *See Compass Initiative: Policy Workshop for the Cyber Insurance Market Progression*, HEBREW FEDERMANN CYBER SECURITY CENTER, CYBER LAW PROGRAM(Dec. 3-4, 2019), https://csrcl.huji.ac.il/event/Compass-Initiative.

37. Ariel E. Levite, *Select Takeaways from the Jerusalem Cyber Insurance Workshop (the Compass Initiative)*, December 3-4, 2019, CARNEGIE ENDOWMENT FOR INTERNATIONAL PEACE (Jan. 27, 2020) (copy kept by the author).

38. For further reading see *CyberNET – A professional network for information exchange on cyber attacks*, ISRAELI NAT'L CYBER DIR. (in Hebrew) (Aug. 16, 2020), https://www.gov.il/he/departments/general/joincybernet.

39. Jasper Frei, *Israel's National Cybersecurity and Cyberdefense Posture Policy and Organizations*, Cyber Defense Project, Center for security Studies, ETH ZURICH, 11 (Sep., 2020), https://css.ethz.ch/content/dam/ethz/special-interest/gess/cis/center-for-securities-studies/pdfs/Cyber-Reports-2020-09-Israel.pdf.

40. *Id.*

41. *Id.*

42. *Id.*

43. Information is based on email exchanges with Itai Benartzi, Director of Policy Advancement at ISRAELI NAT'L CYBER DIR. (Sep. 8, 2020).

44. For an example of work products from the IFTRIP in this area consider *Cyber War and Terrorism: Towards a Common Language to Promote Insurability*, IFTRIP (Jul., 2020), https://www.genevaassociation.org/sites/default/files/research-topics-document-type/pdf_public/cyber_war_terrorism_commonlanguage_final.pdf.

45. See CISA 2019 Report, supra note 20, at 22.

46. GA Res. 73/27, para. 5, U.N. Doc. A RES/73/27 (Dec. 11, 2018). This recent effort is supplemental to an ongoing process at the U.N. level to develop cyber rules, norms, and principles, led by a Group of Governmental Experts (GGE). For further reading on both processes and their interrelation see Alex Grigsby, *The United Nations Doubles Its Workload on Cyber Norms, and Not Everyone Is Pleased*, COUNCIL ON FOREIGN RELATIONS (Nov. 15, 2018), https://www.cfr.org/blog/united-nations-doubles-its-workload-cyber-norms-and-not-everyone-pleased.

47. *Id.*, para. 1.1.

48. *Id.*, para. 1.4.

49. *Id.*, para. 1.7.

50. *Id.*, para. 1.9.

51. *Id.*, para. 1.11.

52. *Id.*, para. 1.13.

53. Finnemore, Martha and Duncan Hollis, *Constructing Norms for Global Cybersecurity*, 110 AM. J. INT'L. L. 425, 428, 465-472 (2016).

CHAPTER THREE

INDUSTRIAL CYBERATTACKS IN THE MIDDLE EAST AND INTERNATIONAL CONSEQUENCES

SELENA LARSON AND SERGIO CALTAGIRONE

In August 2017, one of the systems preventing an oil and gas refinery from exploding failed. The world's most dangerous malware had just infected the Petro Rabigh facility in Saudi Arabia. It caused the safety systems within the industrial control system (ICS) to shut down, and plant operations came to a standstill.[1] Designed to target the equipment protecting the lives of refinery employees, the malware known as TRISIS represented an escalation of attacks on ICSs. While the plant and its staff were unharmed, the attack could have resulted in fatal consequences never seen before. On this occasion, malware had gone beyond shutting down equipment and plant operations — it could now end lives.

"The capability of the attack was unprecedented," said Julian Gutmanis, who responded to the incident in Saudi Arabia and is now a principal industrial incident responder at Dragos. "It had a global impact regarding safe operations of critical infrastructure."

As extraordinary as the Petro Rabigh attack may seem, the story does not begin or end there. The TRISIS attack was only one event on an active timeline of malicious cyber activity targeting industrial companies in the Middle East. The region remains a hotbed for adversaries seeking to disrupt or destroy infrastructure critical for the safety, health, and comfort of its inhabitants. It has the highest likelihood of a catastrophic cyberattack of any region in the world, and deadly malware targeting safety systems has not appeared anywhere else. In order to understand the value and interest that industrial entities provide attackers, it is useful to first understand what an ICS is.

ICS IN THE MIDDLE EAST

The term ICS is relatively new, but control systems date back to ancient times, as in the case of the ancient Egyptian water clock, which is often cited as the first example of an ICS.[2] ICS is an umbrella term for software and hardware that control and automate industrial processes and data collection to support critical infrastructure. It is separate from the "enterprise," in which business functions like human resources, sales, legal, and others operate. There are many control systems, like building automation and ventilation systems, but the "I" in ICS is important. ICSs are used in industries including oil and gas, electricity generation, and critical manufacturing. It is easy to understand these environments as "things that get hot, things under pressure, things that spin fast, and things that go boom." Equipment in ICS environments may include switchgears and circuit breakers that control the flow of power, robotic manufacturing arms that help produce goods in a factory, and safety equipment that prevents explosions.

In the Middle East, almost all cyberattacks targeting ICS entities focus on the energy industry, and attackers targeting the oil and gas vertical specifically are most active in this region. Based on the visibility our company, Dragos, has in the Middle East, ICS-targeting adversaries are most active in Saudi Arabia, and multiple disruptive cyber events have occurred there. Oil and gas is the largest and most important industrial vertical in the region. Primarily state-owned, it drives economies, politics, and military activities around the globe. The industry provides a high-value target for state-associated adversaries, largely because a disruptive attack can further political, economic, and national security goals, and potentially cause global chaos.

According to the U.S. Energy Information Administration, the

Middle East accounts for almost 30 percent of global oil production, with Saudi Arabia providing 12 percent of the world's total[3] (only the U.S. produces more oil, at 19 percent). However, usage in the region is considerably lower: The Middle East is responsible for less than 15 percent of global oil consumption. According to the Organization of the Petroleum Exporting Countries (OPEC), Saudi Arabia is the world's largest oil exporter.[4] A disruptive attack on the region's oil production would impact economies, transportation, and businesses around the world that rely on Middle Eastern oil or the supply chain supporting it.

In August 2012, state-owned oil and gas company Saudi Aramco was targeted with malware called Shamoon. The attack destroyed 35,000 computers and disrupted communications, logistics tracking, and payment systems. Although the attack did not affect production, the disruption of business-critical systems jeopardized the entire energy supply chain.[5] According to *The Financial Times*, Saudi Aramco's vice-president for corporate planning, Abdullah al-Saadan, told local media months after the Shamoon event that "the main target in this attack was to stop the flow of oil and gas to local and international markets."[6]

An attacker aiming to disrupt the flow of oil and gas via cyberattack may target any point across the three major stages of oil and gas operations: upstream, midstream, or downstream. Upstream ICSs and process control network operations refer to exploration, drilling wells, and production infrastructure. Midstream operations provide the link between upstream and downstream, and include field gathering systems, processing plants, pipelines, maritime and rail transportation, and storage. Downstream operations include refining raw materials and distribution to customers.[7] From exploration and production to customer distribution, operational technology (OT) environments are in close proximity to information technology (IT) networks for logistics, fleet management, sales operations and fulfillment, inventory, and custody transfer functions. The intertwined nature of the relationship between IT and OT networks enables adversaries to leverage interconnections for initial access and lateral movement techniques. Currently, most malicious activity is found in the downstream oil and gas segment, and adversaries will likely target refining operations to achieve disruptive effects. Several adversaries have demonstrated the intent or capability to target downstream environments in refining, including XENOTIME, the cyber threat actor responsible for TRISIS.

Cyberattacks specifically targeting ICSs for disruptive or destructive purposes require different skills, capabilities, techniques, and tools to attacks targeting IT environments. Additionally, the way companies detect, respond to, and prevent attacks from each will vary depending on environment, risk analysis, and business decisions.

IMPACTS OF CYBERATTACKS

To understand and differentiate the potential targeting of and impacts on enterprise and operations environments, it is useful to examine the principles of cybersecurity adopted by security practitioners in each space. Most professionals in the information security industry are aware of the acronym CIA, which stands for confidentiality, integrity, and availability. This foundational model governs security policies and procedures that address data privacy, trustworthiness, and system maintenance (respectively), all of which can be compromised in the event of a cyberattack. The cybersecurity fundamentals within ICSs are unique and the CIA model does not directly apply to the cyber-physical elements of an industrial system.

To better illustrate the potential impacts of a cyberattack on industrial systems, Dragos created the VICES model, which describes the cybersecurity properties within ICS: view, input and output, control, engineering, and safety within an ICS environment.

- View refers to the ability to monitor or read system state.

- Input and output relates to the equipment used to communicate within the OT and data flowing between systems, and the physical relationship.

- Control refers to the ability to modify a system state with either a hard loss, in which a device is unable to respond to input, or a soft loss, in which a device continues to respond to inputs based on pre-programmed logic but prevents an operator from intervening.

- Engineering refers to the physical controls and specifications implemented that are not linked to digital assets, like a nuclear centrifuge spinning within certain parameters until it breaks.

- Safety is the most important. Asset owners and operators within ICSs care about safe and reliable power, the safety of workers and the environment, chemical safety processes, and food safety — all of which could be impacted by targeted cyberattacks or operational disruptions.

If a cyberattack affects any or all of these properties, then industrial operations will be compromised and possibly rendered unstable or unsafe.

In the TRISIS event in August 2017, the XENOTIME activity group demonstrated its ability to disrupt operations by leveraging specialized malware targeting equipment directly within the ICS environment using a vulnerability in the Triconex safety controller, an important piece of industrial equipment that protects the safety of workers and the environment at the organization. It impacted safety and control mechanisms at the target facility.

TRISIS malware is a good representation of the capabilities required to interact with complex control systems. There are many digital and physical safety controls in place, and tampering with an ICS device may either damage a system or have no impact at all. To achieve a desired effect within an ICS, an adversary needs to understand the equipment and software within the environment. This requires significant reconnaissance operations both externally and internally. In the case of TRISIS, attackers remained in the refinery's network for months before executing the attack, becoming familiar with the ICS network, and targeted devices to create malware specifically targeting safety systems. XENOTIME attempted a TRISIS attack in June 2017 targeting the same safety equipment, and engineers at the facility failed to detect the malicious activity. The adversary remained in the network, improved attack capabilities, and launched a second attack months later.

Although the TRISIS attack demonstrated the adversary's deep understanding of the target facility and its sophisticated capabilities, it is possible to repurpose this attack to use on other equipment. "Injecting unauthorized code and/or logic into safety controllers is likely to be a key step to achieve maximum damage in attacks going forward," said Gutmanis.

The petrochemical plant recruited Gutmanis and his team of three others to assist with the investigation into an unexpected shutdown caused by the safety controllers. He immediately suspected a cyber incident, possibly related to an insider breach, but did not know with certainty. Two teams of investigators dug into the network and plant operations — including endpoint collection and network artifacts like infrastructure logs and configurations — and ultimately identified suspicious communications to the plant systems, and the creation of TRISIS executable code in close proximity to the outage.

"TRISIS was built to communicate with Triconex safety controllers using the Tristation protocol and exploit a vulnerability in the specific model of the controllers present within the plant," Gutmanis said. "The toolkit itself would need to be modified with additional protocols and exploits for other vendor infrastructure. TRISIS would, however, work for other Triconex environments running the same version of controller."

THE EVOLUTION OF ICS THREATS

Almost a decade before TRISIS, one of the most sophisticated attacks on ICSs wormed its way through Iran. First identified in 2010, Stuxnet became a touchstone for all the ICS attacks that followed due to its sophistication and highly targeted nature. The worm, first deployed in 2008, targeted Iranian-owned programmable logic controllers responsible for controlling centrifuges used in uranium enrichment.[8] Attackers used a USB drive to load the malware onto the target machine, which then propagated the malware throughout the network. The worm destroyed about a fifth of Iran's nuclear centrifuges, according to *The New York Times*, and is believed to have hobbled the country's nuclear weapons program.[9] Unprecedented at the time, this cyberattack was the first to cause physical damage to computerized systems. While specifically targeted at Iran's nuclear program, the worm had global consequences. It infected hundreds of thousands of computers worldwide by automatically spreading to vulnerable machines. Since it was specifically targeted toward special equipment operating uranium enrichment processes, any infected machines outside of this specific group did not suffer any consequences.

In the years that followed, adversaries became more adept at targeting ICS entities, and developing new malware and attack capabilities.

Just days after the 2012 Shamoon attack rocked Saudi Aramco, adversaries infected liquified natural gas company RasGas in Qatar with the same malware.[10] In 2016, a new strain of Shamoon appeared, targeting at least 15 Saudi government agencies, organizations, and joint ventures associated with Saudi Aramco.[11] December 2018 saw yet another new version of Shamoon targeting companies with links to oil and gas operations in Saudi Arabia.[12]

Wipers, a type of malware designed to destroy data, remain a prominent threat to ICS companies in the Middle East. In 2019 and 2020, multiple new destructive malware strains targeted energy companies in the region. KILLGRAVE, a wiper malware identified by Dragos, targeted oil and gas contractors and shipping companies in the Middle East. ZeroCleare infected oil and gas and other energy firms in the region[13] and Dustman impacted oil and gas and electric entities in Saudi Arabia.[14] Although such malware is targeted at enterprise resources, it has the capability to potentially disrupt operations due to interdependencies between IT and OT networks, including Windows operating systems.

A cousin of wiper malware, ransomware infiltrates victim environments, locks files across the system, and demands a ransom to unlock them. It is a threat to ICS entities both in the Middle East and around the world. Various strains have affected critical infrastructure entities globally, and although most ransomware is focused on the enterprise, it can have disruptive impacts on operations. Ransomware can directly impact the OT environment if it is able to bridge the gap between IT and OT systems due to improper security hygiene.[15] It can also have indirect effects on operations by impacting business-critical resources used for management, tracking, and distribution, or causing loss of visibility into enterprise resource management tools.

Ransomware operators are evolving techniques that enable them to specifically target industrial processes. In 2020, Dragos discovered a new type of ransomware called Ekans with the ability to kill specific ICS processes that manage or control operations.[16] Further research found that adversaries had included the same type of behaviors in ransomware samples used in 2019. Ekans actors may have targeted the Bahrain state oil company, Bapco, though this is unconfirmed. The adoption of ICS-specific process targeting in ransomware suggests that adversaries are becoming more familiar with industrial processes, and are capable of building ICS-specific functions into ransomware to potentially achieve disruptive operational effects. Historically, publicly known disruptive ransomware events at industrial entities all featured IT-focused ransomware that spread into control system environments through enterprise mechanisms and lacked ICS functionality.

Ransomware attackers tend to be financially motivated cybercriminals aiming to cause enterprise disruption. Another type of adversary known as hacktivists illegally access networks and information to obtain and publish data that they claim is of importance to the general public. According to a 2019 report from IBM, public hacktivism has dropped by 95 percent since 2015, possibly due to fewer attacks by the disorganized Anonymous hacking collective and an increase in legal action taken against hacktivist operations.[17] However, such adversaries remain a threat. In late 2019, well-known hacker Phineas Fisher reportedly released a manifesto saying it would pay for hacked or leaked data from a variety of industries — including oil and gas companies — with operations in the Middle East. Phineas Fisher claimed it would give up to $100,000 to people who provided documents and sensitive information or other material of "public interest." In an interview with *Vice News*, the hacker said, "hacktivism has only been used to a fraction of its potential."[18]

Generally, hacktivists use fairly unsophisticated means to infiltrate companies and expose sensitive data. More advanced adversaries targeting industrial entities in the Middle East largely conduct reconnaissance activities, long-term compromises, and destructive attacks to support their sponsor's mission objectives. These groups' activities generally align with the interests of specific countries, including Iran, Russia, Israel, and the U.S.

ICS THREAT LANDSCAPE

Dragos currently tracks six activity groups targeting ICSs in the Middle East: XENOTIME, RASPITE, HEXANE, CHRYSENE, MAGNALLIUM, and PARISITE. Of these, only XENOTIME has successfully developed and deployed ICS-specific malware, in the form of TRISIS. However, the other groups demonstrate the ability to infiltrate and potentially disrupt IT operations. MAGNALLIUM and CHRYSENE both likely are developing, or already have, the capability to bridge the gap between enterprise and ICS resources to achieve potentially disruptive consequences. These two adversaries are linked to wiper malware activity in the region. Activity groups use different methods, behaviors, and capabilities to compromise a target and achieve their objectives. For instance, PARISITE is the initial access group that helps facilitate MAGNALLIUM activity. PARISITE also uses known vulnerabilities in enterprise services, like virtual private networks, to infiltrate a target, and can establish a foothold for MAGNALLIUM to conduct reconnaissance, obtain company data, and potentially gain access to the operations environment.

Dragos does not attribute activity groups to individuals or states. However, various third parties have linked behaviors associated with the groups Dragos tracks to state-associated activities. In 2018, the U.S. National Counterintelligence and Security Center released a report on espionage activities globally.[19] The agency attributed OilRig, a group largely focusing on Saudi Arabia, and APT33, which targets energy sector companies in the Middle East and elsewhere, to Iran. OilRig overlaps with CHRYSENE activity, and APT33 is associated with MAGNALLIUM.

Iranian cyber adversaries have targeted companies and government entities across the Middle East for years. Iranian state-associated adversaries are the biggest threat to OT organizations in the region, especially those maintaining friendly relationships with Western countries. Such groups regularly conduct reconnaissance and initial access operations against critical infrastructure, aerospace, government authorities, and financial organizations in countries across the region, including Saudi Arabia, Kuwait, Bahrain, Qatar, Turkey, and the United Arab Emirates (UAE).

Iran's ICS-related targeting extends across North America, Europe, and parts of Asia and Africa, and it was believed to be responsible for the 2012 Shamoon attack.[20] Subsequent attacks employed various strains of the virus used by threat actors aligned with Iranian strategic interests. The newer versions of wiper malware previously discussed also appeared to be linked to Iranian interests. Operation Cleaver, revealed in 2014, was a years-long campaign by Iranian attackers to infiltrate and steal data from multiple critical infrastructure firms, including some in the Middle East.[21] In 2019, attackers likely linked to Iran infiltrated Bahrain's Electricity and Water Authority, among other government entities, with the reported goal of testing the attackers' ability to disrupt the entire country.[22] Dragos regularly identifies ongoing activity from groups associated by others with Iran targeting industrial entities, particularly in the Middle East.

Iran's cyber operations complement their kinetic capabilities. The country is involved in ongoing, violent, and decades-long conflicts with its neighbors including Saudi Arabia, Bahrain, and the UAE. The U.S. and Israel are also allied against Iran, with all three countries developing and deploying sophisticated cyber capabilities as well as traditional kinetic weaponry against military targets. In addition, Iran is involved in numerous proxy conflicts against Saudi Arabia in neighboring wars, supporting belligerents such as President Bashar al-Assad in the ongoing Syrian civil war and the Houthi rebels in Yemen, where Saudi Arabia supports the internationally recognized government of President Abed Rabbo Mansour Hadi.

Not always on the cyber offensive, Iran is also a regular victim of cyber adversaries that seek to disrupt or destroy computerized systems controlling industrial processes. Though neither country claimed responsibility, Stuxnet is widely attributed to a joint operation between the U.S. and Israeli intelligence services.[23] Throughout 2012, multiple cyberattacks targeting Iran impacted critical infrastructure providers. This included an unattributed malware attack on the country's oil industry, specifically the control systems of Kharg Island export terminal.[24] Espionage malware named Flame, discovered in 2012, is attributed to the U.S. and Israel, and is reportedly aimed at disrupting Iran's nuclear efforts.[25] Additionally, the Mahdi trojan discovered the same year targeted critical infrastructure, engineering companies, and government agencies in the country.[26]

The identity of the entity responsible for TRISIS remains a mystery. No government intelligence organization or third-party security firm definitively identified the likely state-sponsored actor behind the attack, as they have done with previous hacking events. The U.S. named North Korea as being responsible for the Sony hack in 2014,[27] and the U.K.'s national security agency blamed Russian intelligence services for multiple attacks on global sporting entities, governments, transportation systems, and business operations.[28] Some elements within the malware point to its development possibly originating at the Russian government-owned technology research institution called the Central Scientific Research Institute of Chemistry and Mechanics. However, it is also possible that attackers simply compromised the Russian institute's infrastructure to confuse analysts when the attack came to light. The adversaries' ultimate goal in this event is unclear.

"It could have been a testing ground for other more sensitive sites — a lot of nuclear facilities leverage Triconex safety controllers," Gutmanis said. "Or potentially an attempt to destabilize Saudi [Arabia's] petrochemical and oil refining reputation, which could result in positive oil price movements for other countries."

Russia is the world's third-largest oil producer, and its wealth chiefly comes from its vast energy resources. Disrupting oil and gas operations in the Middle East via cyberattack could support its own financial interests. The country is in many ways beholden to the intergovernmental cartel known as OPEC. This group of oil-producing nations exists to manipulate oil prices, and can impact the value of Russian oil flowing through global markets by increasing or decreasing its own production and distribution. In early 2020, in response to lower demand due to the coronavirus pandemic, OPEC, which includes Saudi Arabia, agreed to cut production by 1.5 million barrels a day if Russia agreed to lower production as well. Russia, which is not an OPEC member, refused and in response, Saudi Arabia cut prices of its crude oil output and increased its production in an already oversupplied market.[29] The price war lasted for approximately one month, after which Russia agreed to cut its production, along with others, to prevent a market collapse.[30]

Russia's entanglement with the Middle East does not just involve oil — the country is also deeply involved with Middle Eastern conflicts and frequently intervenes in military activities in the region, as in the case of its support for al-Assad in the war in Syria. Like Iran, Russia uses cyberattacks on entities across the globe to support its political, military, and economic interests. Russia's cyber capabilities include sophisticated ICS malware that can cause widespread disruption. The 2016 CRASHOVERRIDE cyberattack on a transmission substation in Ukraine knocked out electricity in part of Kiev for an hour. The group behind the attack is known as ELECTRUM or Sandworm, and its activities are associated with Russian state interests.[31]

POTENTIALLY DEADLY CONSEQUENCES

Regardless of which entity was responsible for TRISIS, a deadly cyberattack could cause widespread disruptions in the precarious geopolitical landscape and open a new chapter in the power competition in the Middle East. With the region already a hotbed of kinetic war, a cyberattack on critical infrastructure would likely fuel more military activity and put lives at risk due to its disruptive effects.

Industrial processes are vital to everyday life. Energy resources comprise large parts of Middle East economies, and citizens rely on safe and reliable water and power supply to survive. In this region especially, the supply of potable water is intrinsically linked to electric power generation. Gulf countries devote considerable electric and natural gas resources to desalination efforts that turn seawater into water people can drink, cook with, and bathe in safely.[32] In effect, a prolonged disruption to the power system could impact the availability and safety of water resources.

Kinetic conflict and refugee crises in the region already put infrastructure at risk, causing people to suffer both mentally and physically. In 2017, a *New Yorker* investigation into power outages across the region — including in Lebanon, Iraq, Egypt, and the Gaza Strip — described tens of millions of people suffering regular power outages that disrupted electricity, running water and sewage services, health care, and daily activities. People froze in winter and suffered through sweltering heat in the summer, forcing them to change their behavior and adapt to frequent blackouts.[33]

The causes of these outages range from government inefficacy leading to fundamental infrastructure weaknesses to political and economic disenfranchisement. While critical infrastructure is vital in sustaining safe and healthy communities, it is also inherently political, and can experience negative consequences from government neglect, military violence, and financial collapse. Cyberattacks add a further threat to already delicate infrastructure in a region that relies disproportionately on electricity due to its climate, especially in the Gulf.

Prolonged power outages — which cyberattacks have yet to cause — can quickly turn into humanitarian crises. In Venezuela, widespread power outages in March 2019, likely due to poor infrastructure maintenance, caused dozens of deaths, forced people to strictly ration water and food, and disrupted public transportation.[34] The Red Cross sent volunteers to help distribute humanitarian aid during the crisis.[35]

The environmental consequences of disruptive attacks on critical infrastructure can be disastrous. One notorious incident occurred in Queensland, Australia in 2000, when a former engineer for a local wastewater management entity executed an attack releasing over 250,000 gallons of sewage into a river and surrounding area.[36] Destructive attacks on infrastructure responsible for providing energy could also damage the planet. Throughout the world, oil spills caused by malfunctions, military action, or other activities cause significant environmental impacts on marine life and the health of ocean ecosystems.[37] In 2019, four oil tankers off the coast of the UAE experienced sabotage attacks, giving rise to significant concerns over the health of local ecosystems. Although such attacks caused by cyber means have not been observed in the region, the consequences of disruptions to vital energy infrastructure would have detrimental impacts on ecological communities and industries like fishing, tourism, and shipping.

It is not unusual for states to signal their intent and operational capability to target and disrupt foreign critical infrastructure.[38] The efficacy and believability of these signals in state interaction illustrates the reality that many states could deploy ICS-disrupting capabilities very quickly, hobbling other countries, and causing humanitarian and environmental crises. Nobody is bluffing and nobody believes they are.

GLOBAL CYBERWEAPON PROLIFERATION

It is becoming easier for state-backed adversaries to develop and execute industrial cyberattacks. This is caused by the increasing proliferation and commoditization of hacking tools, increasing understanding of industrial vulnerabilities, and knowledge of industrial processes and human resources. Governments are also investing money and personnel into developing and acquiring such tools. Private cybersecurity and surveillance companies now sell sophisticated hacking tools, zero-day vulnerabilities, and data interception technologies to governments and companies around the world to enhance their cyberweapon capabilities.[38]

The desire and capability to develop cyberweapons to disrupt critical infrastructure is not just in the hands of technologically advanced states. Threat proliferation combined with the relatively low cost of development compared to traditional weaponry means that almost any state can develop and deploy these capabilities with intent.

In an interview with Michael Morell, the former acting director of the U.S. Central Intelligence Agency, Chris Krebs, the Department of Homeland Security's director of the Cybersecurity and Infrastructure Security Agency, described the development of cyberweapons as a "commodity game."[40] Krebs said, "We focus a lot on the big four of China, Russia, North Korea, and Iran. But every country is developing tools. If they're not, they're not trying."

States are deploying these weapons now. TRISIS disrupted oil and gas operations in Saudi Arabia and CRASHOVERRIDE disrupted Ukrainian electric power. The world has yet to see consequences for adversaries executing cyber actions on the scale one would receive for kinetic attacks on foreign soil. For instance, no entity faced any consequences following the CRASHOVERRIDE malware attack that caused widespread temporary blackouts throughout Kiev. Despite government intelligence agencies attributing the attack to Russia,[41] no governing authority acted against the country specifically for the attack through retaliatory cyber/kinetic activities or sanctions.

In 2018 the International Committee of the Red Cross (ICRC) convened the first international experts' committee to discuss the humanitarian effects of cyber warfare, documented in the report, *The Potential Human Cost of Cyber Operations*.[42] It concluded, "In the view of the ICRC, many of the operations described in the report would be contrary to International Humanitarian Law (IHL) if carried out during armed conflict. However, there is insufficient consensus today as to the interpretation of IHL in cyber space to provide clear legal protection for the civilian population."

As the ICRC concluded, there were no clear standards or guidelines on the applications of cyberwarfare against civilian populations in or out of warfare. This leaves a gap for abuse and potentially the loss of innocent human lives, resulting in a humanitarian crisis with little in the way of international legal repercussions.

THE NEED FOR CIVILIAN PROTECTIONS

Despite cyber warfare capabilities existing and being deployed for over a decade, cyber warfare norms and civilian protections are nonexistent. This is an unacceptable situation for the most mature, deliberative international community in human history. At a minimum, countries should prohibit cyberattacks impacting or harming civilians, which would include any disruption to critical infrastructure. Building on the work of civil society organizations, governments, and technology firms, Microsoft in 2017 released a whitepaper suggesting 10 rules that a digital Geneva Convention should contain. The first rule is, "Refrain from attacking systems whose destruction would adversely impact the safety and security of private citizens (i.e., critical infrastructures, such as hospitals, electric companies)."[43]

Until norms are established and enforced, cyberspace will effectively be a lawless landscape internationally, with adversaries targeting any entity that furthers their economic and national interests, regardless of the humanitarian cost. Espionage, disruptive malware, and destructive attacks can ultimately endanger societal structures and individual welfare. The ultimate and early costs of international inaction will land squarely on the shoulders of civilians, given the current cyber threat environment.

Prior to the TRISIS event in Saudi Arabia, most decision makers in the region did not think that the attack space extended to the OT environment, according to Naser Aldossary, a former ICS security analyst at Saudi Aramco and current principal industrial incident responder at Dragos. "The OT environment was always considered to be a black box built by original equipment manufacturers (OEMs) and operated by the ICS companies," Aldossary said. "The OEMs included themselves in the change management process to ensure any changes are approved by them; doing otherwise would violate the support contracts." OEMs effectively assumed responsibility for ICS security practices and believed that disruptive cyberattacks would not move beyond the enterprise.

The TRISIS attack proved to be groundbreaking, and government entities responded by implementing new cybersecurity rules to address the threat posed by XENOTIME. In 2018, the National Cybersecurity Authority in Saudi Arabia issued a new Essential Cybersecurity Controls document outlining security requirements for critical infrastructure organizations operating in the country. It included a rule specifically requiring companies to isolate safety instrumented systems, a direct response to the TRISIS attack. Other countries where oil and gas is a state-owned industry also have government cybersecurity standards, including Qatar, Bahrain, and the UAE.

Globally, government authorities and infrastructure regulators should do more to encourage asset owners and operators to adopt security practices that align with defending against the current threat landscape. General best-practice enterprise cybersecurity guidelines are not comprehensive enough to address cyber threats to oil and gas OT environments and the supply chain supporting this industry. However, community-created standards exist to fill the gap. For instance, the nonprofit International Society for Automation has developed standards for securing ICS environments that many companies rely on but are not mandated to adopt.[44] The organization also provides training and certification opportunities for engineers and operators to learn how to secure critical systems. Governments should leverage the work already done by third-party organizations and develop regulations specifically for industrial operations and critical infrastructure.

The global community must consider the following position and the humanitarian imperative confronting us, as described by Dragos' vice-president of intelligence, Sergio Caltagirone:

> *Any illicit access into civilian industrial control systems, like electric power, unacceptably places innocent human lives at risk. Decision makers and policymakers worldwide must establish a red line disallowing all forces from operating within civilian industrial networks to ensure civilian safety.*[45]

Attacks against industrial entities in the Middle East are expected to increase as adversaries become better equipped to disrupt operations and the components supporting them. To combat the growing threat landscape, greater support and security must be provided to companies with industrial operations to safeguard the services and safety of the communities they support, and the surrounding environment.

Endnotes

1. Blake Sobczak, "The inside story of the world's most dangerous malware," *E&E News*, March 7, 2019, https://www.eenews.net/stories/1060123327.
2. "A Walk Through Time – Early Clocks," NIST, June 25, 2019, https://www.nist.gov/pml/time-and-frequency-division/popular-links/walk-through-time/walk-through-time-early-clocks
3. "What countries are the top producers and consumers of oil?" Frequently Asked Questions, U.S. Energy Information Administration, April 1, 2020, https://www.eia.gov/tools/faqs/faq.php?id=709&t=6.
4. "Saudi Arabia facts and figures," Organization of the Petroleum Exporting Countries, accessed September 14, 2020, https://www.opec.org/opec_web/en/about_us/169.htm.
5. Jose Pagliery, "The inside story behind the biggest hack in history," *CNN Business*, August 5, 2015, https://money.cnn.com/2015/08/05/technology/aramco-hack/.
6. Camilla Hall and Javier Blas, "Aramco cyber attack targeted production," *The Financial Times*, December 10, 2012, https://www.ft.com/content/5f313ab6-42da-11e2-a4e4-00144feabdc0.
7. "Dragos Oil and Gas Threat Perspective Summary," Dragos, Inc, August 1, 2019, https://dragos.com/resource/dragos-oil-and-gas-threat-perspective-summary/.
8. Kim Zetter, "An Unprecedented Look at Stuxnet, the World's First Digital Weapon," *Wired*, November 3, 2014, https://www.wired.com/2014/11/countdown-to-zero-day-stuxnet/.
9. William J. Board, John Markoff, and David E. Sanger, "Israeli Test on Worm Called Crucial in Iran Nuclear Delay," *The New York Times*, January 15, 2011, https://www.nytimes.com/2011/01/16/world/middleeast/16stuxnet.html?pagewanted=all.
10. Kim Zetter, "Qatari Gas Company Hit With Virus in Wave of Attacks on Energy Companies," *Wired*, August 30, 2012, https://www.wired.com/2012/08/hack-attack-strikes-rasgas/.
11. Jim Finkle, Tom Finn, and Jeremy Wagstaff, "Shamoon virus returns in Saudi computer attacks after four-year hiatus," *Reuters*, December 1, 2016, https://www.reuters.com/article/us-cyber-saudi-shamoon-targets/shamoon-virus-returns-in-saudi-computer-attacks-after-four-year-hiatus-idUSKBN13Q4AX.
12. Threat Hunter Team: Symantec, "Shamoon: Destructive Threat Re-emerges with New Sting in its Tail," *Broadcom*, December 14, 2018, https://symantec-blogs.broadcom.com/blogs/threat-intelligence/shamoon-destructive-threat-re-emerges-new-sting-its-tail.
13. Limor Kessem and X-force Iris, "New Destructive Wiper ZeroCleare Targets Energy Sector in the Middle East," Security Intelligence. December 4, 2019, https://securityintelligence.com/posts/new-destructive-wiper-zerocleare-targets-energy-sector-in-the-middle-east/.
14. Sean Lyngaas, "Saudi cyber authority uncovers new data-wiping malware, and experts suspect Iran is behind it," *Cyberscoop*, January 8, 2020, https://www.cyberscoop.com/saudi-arabia-iran-cyberattack-soleimani/.
15. Security hygiene refers to best practices for securing networks, data, and endpoints. In this case, IT and OT networks should be separate domains from each other and employ a single, secure point of entry, often called a jumpbox, to move from IT into OT. This is a form of "segmentation," which can prevent IT ransomware from affecting ICS networks, if multi-factor authentication is also deployed.
16. "EKANS Ransomware and ICS Operations," Dragos, Inc, February 2, 2020, https://dragos.com/blog/industry-news/ekans-ransomware-and-ics-operations/.
17. Camille Singleton, "The Decline of Hacktivism: Attacks Drop 95 Percent Since 2015," Security Intelligence, May 16, 2019, https://securityintelligence.com/posts/the-decline-of-hacktivism-attacks-drop-95-percent-since-2015/
18. Lorenzo Franceschi-Bicchierai, "Phineas Fisher Offers $100,000 Bounty for Hacks Against Banks and Oil Companies," *Vice*, November 17, 2019, https://www.vice.com/en_us/article/vb5agy/phineas-fisher-offers-dollar100000-bounty-for-hacks-against-banks-and-oil-companies.
19. "Foreign Economic Espionage in Cyberspace," National Counterintelligence and Security Center, June 24, 2018, https://www.dni.gov/files/NCSC/documents/news/20180724-economic-espionage-pub.pdf.
20. Tom Shanker and David E. Sanger, "U.S. Suspects Iran Was Behind a Wave of Cyber-

attacks," *The New York Times*, October 13, 2012, https://www.nytimes.com/2012/10/14/world/middleeast/us-suspects-iranians-were-behind-a-wave-of-cyberattacks.html.

21. "Operation Cleaver," Cylance, 2018, https://www.cylance.com/content/dam/cylance/pdfs/reports/Cylance_Operation_Cleaver_Report.pdf.

22. Bradley Hope, Warren P. Strobel, and Dustin Volz, "High-Level Cyber Intrusions Hit Bahrain Amid Tensions with Iran," *The Wall Street Journal*, August 7, 2019, https://www.wsj.com/articles/high-level-cyber-intrusions-hit-bahrain-amid-tensions-with-iran-11565202488?mod=hp_lead_pos3.

23. Ellen Nakashima and Joby Warrick, "Stuxnet was work of U.S. and Israeli experts, officials say," *The Washington Post*, June 2, 2012, https://www.washingtonpost.com/world/national-security/stuxnet-was-work-of-us-and-israeli-experts-officials-say/2012/06/01/gJQAlnEy6U_story.html.

24. Reuters Staff, "Suspected cyber attacks hit Iran oil industry," *Reuters*, April 23, 2012, https://www.reuters.com/article/us-iran-oil-cyber-idUSBRE83M0YX20120423.

25. Ellen Nakashima, Greg Miller, and Julie Tate, "U.S., Israel developed Flame computer virus to slow Iranian nuclear efforts, officials say," *The Washington Post*, June 19, 2012, https://www.washingtonpost.com/world/national-security/us-israel-developed-computer-virus-to-slow-iranian-nuclear-efforts-officials-say/2012/06/19/gJQA6xBPoV_story.html.

26. Kim Zetter, "Mahdi, the Messiah, Found Infecting Systems in Iran, Israel," *Wired*, July 17, 2012, https://www.wired.com/2012/07/mahdi/

27. Ellen Nakashima, "U.S. attributes cyberattack on Sony to North Korea," *The Washington Post*, December 19, 2014, https://www.washingtonpost.com/world/national-security/us-attributes-sony-attack-to-north-korea/2014/12/19/fc3aec60-8790-11e4-a702-fa31ff4ae98e_story.html.

28. "Reckless campaign of cyber attacks by Russian military intelligence service exposed," National Cyber Security Center, October 3, 2018, https://www.ncsc.gov.uk/news/reckless-campaign-cyber-attacks-russian-military-intelligence-service-exposed.

29. Brian Sullivan, "Putin just sparked an oil price war with Saudi Arabia – and the US energy companies may be the victims," *CNBC*, March 8, 2020, https://www.cnbc.com/2020/03/08/putin-sparks-an-oil-price-war-and-us-companies-may-be-the-victims.html.

30. Javier Blas, Salma El Wardany, and Grant Smith, "Saudi Arabia and Russia end their oil-price war with output cut agreement," World Oil, April 9, 2020, https://www.worldoil.com/news/2020/4/9/saudi-arabia-and-russia-end-their-oil-price-war-with-output-cut-agreement.

31. "CRASHOVERRIDE: Analyzing the Malware that Attacks Power Grids," Dragos, Inc., June 12, 2017, https://dragos.com/resource/crashoverride-analyzing-the-malware-that-attacks-power-grids/.

32. Ian James, "The Middle East, countries spend heavily to transform seawater into drinking water," The Republic|azcentral, November 29, 2019, https://www.azcentral.com/story/news/local/arizona-environment/2019/11/29/middle-east-oman-water-desalination-reliance-costs/2123698001/.

33. Robin Wright, "The Lights Are Going Out In The Middle East," *The New Yorker*, May 21, 2017, https://www.newyorker.com/news/news-desk/the-lights-are-going-out-in-the-middle-east.

34. Gabe Gutierrez and Annie Ross Ramos, "Venezuela's hospitals see rising death toll from blackouts," *NBC News*, April 1, 2019, https://www.nbcnews.com/news/latino/venezuela-s-hospitals-see-rising-death-toll-lack-power-blackouts-n989776.

35. Isayen Herrera and Anatoly Kurmanaev, "In Polarized Venezuela, Red Cross Grapples with Aid Distribution," *The New York Times*, April 17, 2019, https://www.nytimes.com/2019/04/17/world/americas/red-cross-venezuela-aid.html.

36. Tony Smith, "Hacker jailed for revenge sewage attacks," *The Register*, October 31, 2001, https://www.theregister.co.uk/2001/10/31/hacker_jailed_for_revenge_sewage/.

37. Jennifer Bell, "Marine ecosystems endangered by tanker sabotage in the Gulf," *Arab News*, May 28, 2019, https://www.arabnews.com/node/1502996/middle-east

38. Ivan Nechepurenko, "Kremlin Warns of Cyber-war After Report of U.S. Hacking into Russian Power Grid," *The New York Times*, June 17, 2019, https://www.nytimes.com/2019/06/17/world/europe/russia-us-cyberwar-grid.html.

39. Patrick Howell O'Neill, "Champagne, shotguns, and surveillance at spyware's grand bazaar," *MIT Technology Review*, November 25, 2019, https://www.technologyreview.com/2019/11/25/131837/champagne-shotguns-and-surveillance-at-spywares-grand-bazaar/.

40. "Transcript: Chris Krebs talks with Michael Morell on "Intelligence Matters," *CBS News*, June 26, 2019, https://www.cbsnews.com/news/transcript-chris-krebs-talks-with-michael-morell-on-intelligence-matters/.

41. "Press release: UK condemns Russia's GRU over Georgia cyber-attacks," Foreign & Commonwealth Office, National Cyber Security Center, The Rt Hon Dominic Raab MP, February 20, 2020, https://www.gov.uk/government/news/uk-condemns-russias-gru-over-georgia-cyber-attacks.

42. Ritchie B. Tongo, "The potential human cost of cyber operations," International Committee of the Red Cross, May 29, 2019, https://www.icrc.org/en/document/potential-human-cost-cyber-operations.

43. "A Digital Geneva Convention to protect cyberspace," Digital Geneva Convention Policy Paper, Microsoft, last modified 2020, https://www.microsoft.com/en-us/cybersecurity/content-hub/a-digital-geneva-convention-to-protect-cyberspace.

44. "Cybersecurity," ISA Cybersecurity Brochure. International Society of Automation, accessed September 14, 2020, https://www.isa.org/technical-topics/cybersecurity/.

45. Sergio Caltagirone, "Escalating Cyber Tensions Risk Human Life," Dragos, Inc, June 28, 2019, https://dragos.com/blog/industry-news/escalating-cyber-tensions-risk-human-life/.

CHAPTER FOUR

INFLUENCE OPERATIONS IN THE MIDDLE EAST AND THE PROHIBITION ON INTERVENTION

Ido Kilovaty[*]

Introduction

Influence operations in the Middle East have proliferated in recent years. While to some, the emergence of social media platforms has heralded more democratization, transparency, and accountability, the reality is that these platforms are double-edged swords. Authoritarian regimes have leveraged the internet and social media platforms to pursue their goals, which in turn has enabled them to engage in influence, disinformation, interference, disruption, and propaganda operations across the world.

In 2018, Facebook, Instagram, and Twitter reported that they had removed thousands of Iranian accounts that were engaged in trolling and influence operations.[1] Iranian influence activity online has been aimed at audiences in the U.S., the U.K., Latin America, and the Middle East.[2] As with other influence operations, the Iranian efforts were focused on promoting the interests of the Iranian regime by spreading news sources that are in line with its narrative.[3] In Iran's case, this narrative has often been anti-America, anti-Israel, anti-Saudi Arabia, and pro-Palestine.[4]

However, Iran is not alone in its efforts to influence foreign governments and their citizens. Other Middle Eastern nations have their own political narratives, which they promote through influence operations in cyberspace. Saudi Arabia, together with Iran, was identified by Oxford researchers Mona Elwash and Philip Howard as using "computational propaganda for foreign influence operations."[5] Saudi Arabia was similarly involved in planting fake news to destabilize political debate in other countries.[6] As a result, Facebook announced that it removed inauthentic accounts linked to an operation in Saudi Arabia.[7] Among other nations involved in a separate influence operation, Facebook cites Egypt and the United Arab Emirates (UAE).[8]

One such example would be the influence operation allegedly carried out by the UAE through social media, where it compromised Qatari news and social media in order to post fabricated controversial and scandalous comments attributed to the Qatari amir.[9] In response to many of these influence operations, both Twitter and Facebook have been suspending accounts engaged in state-backed information operations.[10]

These influence operations proliferate for many reasons, though the availability, ease, and effectiveness of using social media to sway public opinion may be among the most likely explanations.

The increasing sophistication of these operations helps actualize the doctrine of "reflexive control." Reflexive control, a doctrine developed by the Soviet Union that has found renewed utility in the age of borderless internet and ubiquitous social media networks, is defined as the "process of imitating the enemy's reasoning or imitating the enemy's possible behavior and cause[ing] him to make a decision unfavorable to himself." Reflexive control explains the widespread resort to influence operations across the world. This contribution will begin with an overview of reflexive control before delving into international law, and in particular the prohibition on intervention.

How, then, does international law respond to tools used in the reflexive control context? Primarily, international law offers a prohibition on intervention, which is one of the bedrock principles of the international legal system. While this prohibition may apply to many abusive uses of cyberspace, it is also inadequate in how it applies to influence operations, and may therefore offer a glimpse as to the reasons why these operations have proliferated in the Middle East and elsewhere.

At first blush, international law's prohibition on intervention may serve as a framework through which those states abusing influence operations would be held accountable. However, therein lies the rub. The prohibition on non-intervention is not well-equipped to address the abusive use of cyberspace for influence, disinformation, and propaganda. This contribution seeks to elaborate on the shortcomings of the prohibition on non-intervention in the era of influence and disinformation.

REFLEXIVE CONTROL AND INFLUENCE OPERATIONS

The increasing use of influence and disinformation lead one to observe that information has become weaponized in the era of social media and global internet. As Tim Stevens put it, "Cyber warfare of the future may be less about hacking electrical power grids and more about hacking minds by shaping the environment in which political debate takes place."[11] The literature on the weaponization of information focuses primarily on the injection of disinformation, and the proliferation of fake news on social media and other platforms. Iran, Saudi Arabia, and Israel are among the Middle Eastern nations that have expanded their use of cyber operations with a view to swaying public opinion and advancing their narrative. The growing adoption of these operations in the Middle East is grounded in the reflexive control theory.[12]

Reflexive control is the study by one state of an adversarial power to identify and then exploit its weaknesses so as to encourage it to reach a decision that benefits the controlling state. The idea is to study the moral, psychological, and personal factors of the target so that they can be mimicked or manipulated to shape the enemy's perceptions and disconnect them from reality. This requires adversaries to "analyse their own ideas, and to model their adversary's behaviour in accordance."[13] According to this theory, the side with the "highest degree of reflex (the side best able to imitate the other side's thoughts or predict its behavior) will have the best chances of winning."[14] Two of the four elements constituting reflexive control are "providing false information" and "affecting the adversary's decision-making process" through the "publication of deliberately distorted doctrines."[15] As such, reflexive control may be achieved by creating an informational reality of a certain kind (propaganda, manipulation, disinformation), such that one's opponent will *voluntarily* (or seemingly voluntarily) make a decision favoring the state that created this reality.[16]

The decision made by the controlled actor stems directly from the information, or disinformation, communicated to them by the controlling adversary.[17] Reflexive control theory is gradually becoming a part of a broader phenomenon enabled by the digital era, which allows adversaries to disseminate information that may lead to a strategically desirable outcome. In the pre-cyber era, this was usually achievable only during times of war, when interactions between adversaries were a daily occurrence and geographical proximity allowed the activities associated with reflexive control to take place.

Cyberspace empowers reflexive control because it allows the dissemination of information at scale, doing so across political borders, at low cost, and more or less instantaneously. States like Russia, China, Iran, and the U.S. are especially well positioned to take advantage of these new circumstances.[18]

Reflexive control theory, developed by the Soviet Union in the 1960s[19] and discussed in literature dating back 30 years,[20] most recently appeared in headlines in connection to the war in Ukraine.[21] In that context, reflexive control was not purely informational on Russia's behalf; for example, it was reported that Russia concealed its forces (colloquially referred to as "little green men"),[22] publicly denied the real reasons that the Kremlin engaged in war with Ukraine, and shaped the narrative in a way that benefited the Kremlin, primarily by using social media and other online platforms.[23] These actions allowed the Russian government to "create whatever story" it wanted "for whatever audience it want[ed]."[24]

The Middle Eastern nations involved in influence operations are leveraging reflexive control for their own benefit. Dissemination of narratives and fake news is leading to certain reactions both in the target government and its population. The use of influence operations is unlikely to disappear in the near future, which begs the question of law. How does international law address a phenomenon grounded in reflexive control? Does international law deem "influence" as improper in certain circumstances? The next section addresses the prohibition on intervention and influence operations.

THE PROHIBITION ON INTERVENTION AND INFLUENCE OPERATIONS

One of the most fundamental yet obscure aspects of international law is the prohibition on intervention.[25] This prohibition derives its rationale from the principles of territorial sovereignty,[26] sovereign equality,[27] and political independence,[28] and prohibits states from coercively interfering in the domestic or foreign affairs of other states.

The Permanent Court of International Justice, which was the predecessor to the International Court of Justice (ICJ), stated in its 1927 ruling: "The first and foremost restriction imposed by international law upon a State ... [is that] it may not exercise its power in any form in the territory of another State."[29] The same framing of the prohibition appears in many other judicial decisions and legal instruments.[30]

In the context of influence operations, however, the prohibition on intervention comes up short, and a closer look at its constitutive elements can shed more light on why that is. The modern conception of the prohibition on intervention is understood to contain two constitutive elements that transform an act of mere interference,[31] which is not illegal under international law, into an act of intervention, which is unlawful.[32] Both elements are required in order to hold a state accountable for a violation of non-intervention. The elements provide that an act of interference is unlawful when (1) the act is directed at the *domaine réservé* of a state,[33] and; (2) the act is of coercive nature.[34]

Are states in MENA engaging in influence operations violating international law by doing so? Or, in other words, are influence operations that target the *domaine réservé* of the target state in a coercive manner unlawful?

DOMAINE RÉSERVÉ

To be wrongful, an act of interference must target a specific subset of protected state prerogatives. These prerogatives constitute the activities that are so deeply entrenched in the state's sovereignty and political independence that no external interference with them is permissible. While the notion seems straightforward, it is often unclear what falls into this area of activity.[35]

The ICJ in its *Nicaragua* decision has provided some guidance on what falls within the *domaine réservé*. In that case, the court concluded that the financial support and training provided by the U.S. to an opposition armed group within Nicaragua was a "clear breach of the principle of non-intervention."[36] The court explained:

> *A prohibited intervention must accordingly be one bearing on matters in which each State is permitted, by the principle of State sovereignty, to decide freely. One of these is the choice of a political, economic, social and cultural system, and the formulation of foreign policy. Intervention is wrongful when it uses methods of coercion in regard to such choices, which must remain free ones.*[37]

Michael Schmitt, while exploring grey zones in international law, attempted to draw the line between matters under the sole discretion of the state and those that are not.[38] Schmitt provides that "elections fall within the *domaine réservé*" while "commercial activities typically do not."[39] Intuitively, if a state engaged in an act of interference "intended to afford business advantages to its national companies" it would not run afoul of the principle of non-intervention.

While these two extremes are uncontroversial, Schmitt acknowledges that there may be a grey zone in the context of online communications.[40] States typically regulate online communications to a certain degree, yet this is not within the sole discretion of the regulating state.

Would interfering with online communications constitute an act against the *domaine réservé*? The answer, to many, is in the negative. In practical terms, an interference through social media is unlikely to reach the state prerogatives protected by international law.

This categorical determination does not solve the *should* question: *Should* it be unlawful for states to interfere with online communication or political discourse on social media platforms? International law has not been able to address this timely question, particularly given the growing role of private speech platforms, namely social media, which have become the new public squares. Is the notion of *domaine réservé* still relevant in a world where social media platforms have transformed online communications and political campaigning?

The world in which social media has taken such a central role in public discourse is creating a unique challenge. On the one hand, the emergence of these platforms has led to the democratization of speech. Users from all over the world can communicate with each other in an open and transparent manner. On the other hand, states have found these platforms to be appealing for their own goals. Promotion of biased narratives, fake news, disinformation, propaganda, and influence operations are but a few examples of state activity on social media.

There is a historical reason why international law does not extend to influence operations carried out on private platforms. However, the current reality suggests that international law ought to adapt itself to the pressing challenges presented by influence operations on social media and other platforms.

COERCION

Coercion is a *sine qua non* in the context of intervention. The ICJ in *Nicaragua* exemplified the importance and centrality of coercion to the prohibition on intervention, where it held that "intervention is wrongful when it uses methods of coercion"[41] and that coercion is "the very essence"[42] of intervention.

While the ICJ did not use the term *coercion* in its *Corfu Channel* case, it rejected the argument that there is a "right of intervention" recognized by international law, by noting that it views "the alleged right of intervention as the manifestation of a policy of force, such as has, in the past, given rise to the most serious abuses."[43]

In addition, the 1970 United Nations Declaration on Friendly Relations provides that: "No state may use or encourage the use of economic, political or any other type of measures to coerce another State in order to obtain from it the subordination of the exercise of its sovereign rights and to secure from it advantages of any kind."[44]

The prohibition on intervention and its coercion requirement carry over to the cyberspace context as well. The *Tallinn Manual 2.0 on the International Law Applicable to Cyber Operations* provides that "States may not intervene, including by cyber means, in the internal or external affairs of another State"[45] and subsequently clarifies that to be wrongful under international law, such intervention "must be coercive in nature."[46]

According to this widely accepted view, there can be no unlawful intervention without coercion. Any act of interference falling below the threshold of coercion is not unlawful under international law. But what does coercion actually mean? The relevant instruments on non-intervention do not provide a clear answer, which may signify that non-intervention suffers from a serious gap.[47] After all, if there is no intervention without coercion, and there is no robust theory on what coercion is, then the legitimacy of the principle dissipates.

Oppenheim, however, provides some useful guidance on coercion, by asserting that to qualify as prohibited intervention, "interference must be *forcible or dictatorial, or otherwise coercive; in effect depriving the State intervened against of control over the matter in question*."[48] In other words, an act of coercion exists when the victim state is forced to do something by an external state actor, or when it is faced with an ultimatum — do X (or refrain from doing X), or else.[49] Schmitt, similarly, defines an act of coercion as an action "intended to cause the State to do something, such as take a decision that it would otherwise not take, or not to engage in an activity in which it would otherwise engage."[50]

Coercion, therefore, is an action that deprives the state of its sovereign will. It is an action that seeks "to force a policy change in the target state."[51] A state loses its independence when its sovereignty is forcefully usurped by an external state actor. But sovereign will and independence may still be undermined even if something other than the *domaine réservé* is targeted, or when interference is not designed to be coercive. Consider for example a foreign state government that is engaged in microtargeting users on social media with disinformation, with the purpose of leading to a certain outcome in the victim state. This is another shortcoming of the prohibition on intervention, whereby it is unable to apply to the current challenges posed by the unique architecture of influence operations.

REFLEXIVE CONTROL, INTERVENTION, AND THE MIDDLE EAST

The growing appeal of reflexive control techniques in influence operations in the Middle East should be of concern to the region and the international community. International law and the prohibition on intervention are unable to fully address the dangers arising from the use of influence operations. In the MENA context, influence operations present an increased risk of escalation in an already fragile and deeply divided region. Due to the ambiguity of international law at this time, more nations in the region may find influence operations an appealing political and military tool, which would further exacerbate existing conflicts and lead to the emergence of new ones.

While currently the prohibition on intervention is unable to fully grasp the problematic and disruptive nature of influence operations, this essay offers a few reflections on how best to approach them from a law and policy perspective.

INTERVENTION AND CUSTOMARY INTERNATIONAL LAW

The prohibition on intervention appears unable to address influence operations. This begs the question of whether its elements — d*omaine réservé* and coercion — require a revision that can account for the unique characteristics of today's influence operations. This can be achieved through either emerging customary international law or a new treaty.

Customary international law is the development of international law through widespread state practice accompanied by the sense of legal obligation: *opinio juris*. In fact, the roots of the prohibition on intervention are in customary international law, whereby states have engaged in a norm of non-intervention over the decades as a matter of law. But any reliance on customary international law as a solution to the lawlessness of influence operations is likely doomed to fail. This is primarily because the lack of transparency, involvement of private actors such as social media platforms, and state interest in maintaining obscurity may stifle the progression of customary international law on the issue.

Dan Efrony and Yuval Shany identify three separate strategies adopted by states that may hinder such development: *optionality*, *parallel tracks*, and *gradation in law enforcement*,[52] all of which suggest that there is a serious transparency issue with respect to cyberspace and new technologies of interference. The emergence of new standards and elements of the prohibition on intervention may be hindered by the transparency challenge identified by Efrony and Shany.

The building blocks of a new norm of customary international law include information about the occurrence of an act of interference, the method used, direct and indirect consequences, and the response (or lack thereof) of the victim state. But in the technological context, it is difficult to access such evidence due to the secrecy that states maintain by default in that space. Middle Eastern nations involved in influence operations are particularly non-transparent in their efforts, exacerbating the challenge. The optionality and parallel tracks strategies identified by Efrony and Shany are emblematic of this evidentiary challenge.

The covert nature of interference operations has become the norm since states have come to believe that publicity or transparency "might expose their vulnerabilities, adversely affect their offensive or defensive capabilities, and weaken their power of deterrence."[53] Brian Egan acknowledged this difficulty in a speech given at the University of California, Berkeley, in which he highlighted the need for "increased transparency ... to clarify how the international law on non-intervention applies to States' activities in cyberspace."[54] Schmitt, reacting to Egan, seems to support the need for more transparency on the part of states operating in cyberspace.[55] Secrecy, however, remains the norm. How, then, will the prohibition on intervention be revised?

Until more public information and evidence become available, identifying a new customary international legal standard for cyber intervention may prove difficult to impossible. Schmitt believes that this will likely increase the role and weight of *opinio juris* serving as an "interpretive function, rather than a law-creating one" in the absence of public state practice.[56] This is a persuasive outlook, since prohibition on intervention already exists, and all that is required is a consistent and uniform consensus in the international community that states now follow new standards with respect to the prohibition on intervention as a matter of law.

In addition, states still have some incentive to be transparent, because those states whose practices with respect to new technologies of influence are transparent may benefit from the ability to control and steer the development of customary international law in a desirable direction, or at the very least, convince states to reveal information about their shadowy practices with respect to new technologies and cyberspace.[57]

A NEW STANDARD: UNDUE INFLUENCE? MANIPULATION? DISINFORMATION?

The ambiguities surrounding the prohibition on intervention call for a new standard. Assuming that we can overcome the difficulties presented in this section, what should this standard be?

Previously, I have argued that we are entering an era of disruption.[58] Coercion is still an important threshold for the wrongfulness of intervention, but disruption is becoming far too commonplace to be ignored by the current interpretation of non-intervention.[59] An act of interference that significantly disrupts a political process in another state therefore should constitute an act of unlawful intervention.[60] The severity and magnitude thresholds of such disruption may need to be determined before disruption is to become an alternative standard to coercion, but McDougal and Feliciano's consequentiality approach may serve as a starting point.

Severe manipulation, influence, and disinformation may also constitute alternative standards to coercion. Emerging technologies allow states to engage in interference that is not coercive by nature, but that manipulates and unduly influences political, economic, and social processes to a degree that deprives the victim state of its sovereign will and freedom of choice.

Manipulation and influence are not new phenomena, but recent technological advancements, the availability of data, and the global nature of the internet give them a far more menacing form than ever before.[61] As Roberto Gonzales put it: "[s]ince we are never totally free of outside influence, what gives us (part) authorship over our own actions is that we regard our own reasons for acting as authoritative. Manipulation thwarts that."[62] Manipulation and influence can undermine sovereign will directly, but also indirectly where they reach a critical mass of the population, which may then force the state to make a decision that it otherwise would not.

The same threshold question comes up with respect to manipulation and influence as well. At what point does manipulation become illegitimate? How severe should an influence operation be to cross the unlawfulness threshold?

Manipulation allows the interfering state to influence the subconscious of the victim state or misinform its citizens to a degree that they demand policy change from their own government. Is this really any different to coercion? I argue that the outcome would be no different, and that the difference is in the means: Coercion is forceful, manipulation is subtle, but wrongfulness should attached to both.

CONCLUSION

The increasing reliance of Middle Eastern nations on reflexive control techniques in their influence operations illustrates the inability of international law to deter and hold accountable those that abuse our information and technology ecosystems. The prohibition on intervention is among international law's most fundamental norms, yet the sophistication and uniqueness of today's influence operations do not seem to fall within the existing scope of the prohibition. The development of the norm through customary international law — and in particular the addition of manipulation, undue influence, and disinformation — may serve the purpose of modifying the prohibition to encompass the nature of influence operations.

ENDNOTES

* Frederic Dorwart Endowed and Zedalis Family Fund Assistant Professor of Law, University of Tulsa, College of Law; Cybersecurity Policy Fellow, New America; Visiting Faculty Fellow, Center for Global Legal Challenges, Yale Law School; Affiliated Fellow, Information Society Project, Yale Law School.

1. "Iranian Offensive Cyber Attack Capabilities (Jan. 13, 2020) https://fas.org/sgp/crs/mideast/IF11406.pdf
2. FireEye, Suspected Iranian Influence Operation Leverages Network of Inauthentic News Sites & Social Media Targeting Audiences in U.S., U.K., Latin America, Middle East (Aug. 21, 2018), https://www.fireeye.com/blog/threat-research/2018/08/suspected-iranian-influence-operation.html
3. *Id.*; Sheera Frenkel and Nicholas Fandos, Facebook Identifies New Influence Operations Spanning Globe, NY TIMES (Aug. 21, 2018), https://www.nytimes.com/2018/08/21/technology/facebook-political-influence-midterms.html
4. Mona Elwash, Philip Howard, Vidya Narayanan, *Iranian Digital Influence in the Arab World*, Comprop Data Memo (2019).
5. Samantha Bradshaw, Philip Howard, The Global Disinformation Order 2019 Global Inventory of Organised Social Media Manipulation, https://comprop.oii.ox.ac.uk/wp-content/uploads/sites/93/2019/09/CyberTroop-Report19.pdf
6. Nathaniel Glacier, Removing Coordinated Inauthentic Behavior in UAE, Egypt and Saudi Arabia, Facebook (Aug. 1, 2019), https://about.fb.com/news/2019/08/cib-uae-egypt-saudi-arabia/
7. *Id.*
8. *Id.*
9. Marc Jones, Alexei Abrahams, *A Plague of Twitter Bots is Roiling the Middle East*, The Washington Post (Jun. 5, 2018), https://www.washingtonpost.com/news/monkey-cage/wp/2018/06/05/fighting-the-weaponization-of-social-media-in-the-middle-east/
10. *See* Twitter, *New Disclosures To Our Archive Of State-Backed Information Operations* (Dec. 20, 2019), https://blog.twitter.com/en_us/topics/company/2019/new-disclosures-to-our-archive-of-state-backed-information-operations.html; Nathaniel Glacier, *Removing Coordinated Inauthentic Behavior in UAE, Egypt and Saudi Arabia* (Aug. 1, 2019), https://about.fb.com/news/2019/08/cib-uae-egypt-saudi-arabia/.
11. Ben Quinn, "Revealed: the MoD's secret cyberwarfare programme," *The Guardian*, March 16, 2014, http://www.theguardian.com/uk-news/2014/mar/16/mod-secret-cyberwarfare-programme.
12. *See* Annie Kowalewski, *Disinformation and Reflexive Control: The New Cold War*, GEO. SEC. STUD. REV. F. (Feb. 1, 2017), http://georgetownsecuritystudiesreview.org/2017/02/01/disinformation-and-reflexive-control-the-new-cold-war
13. ML Jaitner, H Kantola, *Applying Principles of Reflexive Control and Cyber Operations*, 15 Journal of Information Warfare 27, 29 (2016).
14. *Id.* at 242
15. M.D. Ionov, *On Reflexive Control Of The Enemy In Combat*, Military Thought, 46-7 (1995).
16. *Id.* at 237.
17. *Id.* at 241.
18. *See* Reuben Johnson, *Experts: DNC Hack Shows Inadequate Security Against Russian Cyber Attacks*, WASH. FREE BEACON (July 27, 2016), http://freebeacon.com/national-security/experts-dnc-hack-shows-u-s-no-defense-russian-cyber-attacks/
19. Robert Rasmussen, *Cutting Through the Fog: Reflexive Control and Russian Stratcom in Ukraine*, CTR. INT'L MAR. SEC. (Nov. 26, 2015), http://cimsec.org/cutting-fog-reflexive-control-russian-stratcom-ukraine/20156.
20. Thomas, *supra* note 11, at 238.
21. Maria Snegovaya, 'Reflexive Control': Putin's Hybrid Warfare in Ukraine is Straight out of the Soviet Playbook, BUS. INSIDER (Sep. 22, 2015), http://www.businessinsider.com/reflexive-control-putins-hybrid-zxwarfare-in-ukraine-is-straight-out-of-the-soviet-playbook-2015-9.
22. *See* U.S. Army Special Ops. Command, *"Little Green Men": A Primer on Modern Russian Unconventional Warfare, Ukraine 2013–2014*, at 31 (2015), http://www.jhuapl.edu/ourwork/nsa/papers/ARIS_LittleGreenMen.pdf ("Groups of unidentified armed men began appearing throughout the region, often in coordination with local pro-Russian militias. Both the Ukrainian government and most

Western intelligence sources claimed that the 'little green men' were Russian operatives.").

23. Id.
24. Rasmussen, *supra* note 66, Id.
25. *See also* Nicaragua v. United States, 1986 I.C.J. at 106-07, ¶ 202 ("the Court considers that it is part and parcel of customary international law").
26. Michael Schmitt, Sean Watts, *Beyond State-Centrism: International Law and Non-State Actors in Cyberspace*, 21 J. Conf. & Sec. L. 595, 600 (2016) ("The prohibition of intervention by a state into the internal or external affairs of other states derives directly from the principle of sovereignty.")
27. e.g. Article 2(1) of the U.N. Charter ("The Organization is based on the principle of the sovereign equality of all its Members.") and Article 2(7) ("Nothing contained in the present Charter shall authorize the United Nations to intervene in matters which are essentially within the domestic jurisdiction of any state or shall require the Members to submit such matters to settlement under the present Charter; but this principle shall not prejudice the application of enforcement measures under Chapter VII.")
28. Jennings, S. R., & Watts, S. A., Oppenheim's International Law. Intervention, 1, 430-449.
29. S.S. Lotus (Fr. v. Turk.), 1927 P.C.I.J. (ser. A) No. 10, at 18 (Sept. 7).
30. Corfu Channel Case (U.K. v. Alb.), Judgment, 1949 I.C.J. Rep. 4, 35 (Apr. 9); Military and Paramilitary Activities in and Against Nicaragua (Nicar. v. U.S.), Judgment, 1986 I.C.J. Rep. 14, ¶¶ 202, 205, 251 (June 27); Armed Activities on the Territory of the Congo (Dem. Rep. Congo v. Uganda), Judgment, 2005 I.C.J. Rep. 168, ¶¶ 16165 (Dec. 19); G.A. Res. 2625 (XXV), Declaration on Principles of International Law Concerning Friendly Relations and Co-operation among States in Accordance with the Charter of the United Nations, ¶ 3, (Oct. 24, 1970)
31. By "interference" I mean "activities that disturb the territorial State's ability to perform the functions as it wishes." Though, interference by itself is currently not illegal under international law, unless it is coercive and targets the *domaine réservé*. See Michael Schmitt, *"Virtual" Disenfranchisement: Cyber Election Meddling in the Grey Zones of International Law*, 19 Chi. J. Int'l. L. 30, 45 (2018).

32. Jennings, S. R., & Watts, S. A., Oppenheim's International Law, Intervention, 1, 432 (1992) ("the interference must be forcible or dictatorial, or otherwise coercive, in effect depriving the state intervened against of control over the matter in question. Interference pure and simple is not intervention").
33. Ohlin, *Did Russian Cyber Interference in the 2016 Election Violate International Law?* 95 Tex. L. Rev. 1579, 1587 (2017) (a state's *domaine réservé* refers to "its exclusive power to regulate its internal affairs without outside interference").
34. Military and Paramilitary Activities in and Against Nicaragua (Nicar. v. U.S.), Merits, 1986 ICJ Rep. 14, para. 205 (June 27) ("Intervention is wrongful when it uses methods of coercion in regard to such choices, which must remain free ones. The element of coercion, [...] defines, and indeed forms the very essence of, prohibited intervention").
35. Ohlin, *supra* note 30, p. 1588; Michael Schmitt, *"Virtual" Disenfranchisement: Cyber Election Meddling in the Grey Zones of International Law*, 19 Chi. J. Int'l. L. 30, 45 (2018) ("The inherently governmental function concept lacks granularity, although some cases are clear. On the one hand, purely commercial activities, even if engaged in by State-owned enterprises, do not qualify, for they obviously are not within the exclusive purview of a State. On the other hand, law enforcement and defense of the State from external attack are inherently governmental in character. ... Between these extremes lies a great deal of uncertainty.")
36. Nicar. V. U.S., 1986 I.C.J. ¶ 242.
37. Nicar. V. U.S., 1986 I.C.J. ¶ 205.
38. Michael N. Schmitt, *Grey Zones in the International Law of Cyberspace*, 42 Yale J. Int'l L. 1, 7 (2017)
39. Schmitt, Grey Zones, 7.
40. Schmitt, Grey Zones, 7.
41. Military and Paramilitary Activities in and Against Nicaragua (Nicar. v. U.S.), Merits, 1986 ICJ Rep. 14, para. 205 (June 27).
42. Id.
43. Corfu Channel (United Kingdom v. Albania) (Merits) ICJ Rep. 9, at 35 (1949).
44. U.N. Doc. A/RES/2625 (XXV).
45. *Tallinn Manual 2.0 on the International Law Applicable to Cyber Operations*, 312, Rule 66

(Michael N. Schmitt ed., 2017) [hereinafter Tallinn Manual 2.0].

46. Id.

47. Ohlin 1581 ("there is little in international law that outlines a complete theory of coercion")

48. Jennings, S. R., & Watts, S. A., Oppenheim's International Law. Intervention, 1, 430-449.

49. Ido Kilovaty, *The Elephant in the Room: Coercion*, 113 AM. J. INT'L. L. UNBOUND 87, 89 (2019).

50. Schmitt, *Disenfranchisement*, 51.

51. Maziar Jamnejad and Michael Wood, *The Principle of Non-Intervention*, 22 LEIDEN JOURNAL OF INTERNATIONAL LAW 345, 348 (2009).

52. Dan Efrony & Yuval Shany, *A Rule Book on the Shelf? Tallinn Manual 2.0 on Cyberoperations and Subsequent State Practice*, 112 AM. J. INT'L. L. 583, 648-52 (2018).

53. Dan Efrony, Yuval Shany, supra note.

54. Brian Egan, *Legal Adviser, U.S. Dep't of State, Address at University of California-Berkeley School of Law: International Law and Stability in Cyberspace*, JUST SECURITY (Nov. 10, 2016).

55. Michael Schmitt, US Transparency Regarding International Law in Cyberspace, JUST SECURITY (Nov. 15, 2016).

56. Schmitt, Grey Zones 20 ("it will likely be left to States to address grey zones through State practice and expressions of opinio juris. However, because most State practice in cyberspace is classified, the bulk of the heavy lifting will likely have to be accomplished by opinio juris").

57. Ido Kilovaty, *The Elephant in the Room: Coercion*, 113 AM. J. INT'L. L. UNBOUND 87, 90 (2019).

58. Ido Kilovaty, *Doxfare: Politically Motivated Leaks and the Future of the Norm on Non-Intervention in the Era of Weaponized Information*, 9 HARV. NAT'L. SEC. J. 146, 169 (2018).

59. See e.g. William Mattessich, *Digital Destruction: Applying the Principle of Non-Intervention to Distributed Denial of Service Attacks Manifesting No Physical Damage*, 54 COLUM. J. TRANSNAT'L L. 873 (2016) (applying the norm on non-intervention to distributed denial of service attacks).

60. Ido Kilovaty, *Doxfare: Politically Motivated Leaks and the Future of the Norm on Non-Intervention in the Era of Weaponized Information*, 9 Harv. Nat'l. Sec. J. 146, 169 (2018).

61. See Ido Kilovaty, *Legally Cognizable Manipulation*, 34 BERK. TECH. L. J. 457, 472-6 (2019).

62. Helen Nissenbaum et al., *Online Manipulation: Hidden Influences in a Digital World* 16 (Jan. 8, 2019) (unpublished manuscript) https://papers.ssrn.com/sol3/papers.cfm?abstract_id=3306006 [https://perma.cc/4KJU-DABA].

CHAPTER FIVE

STATE-SANCTIONED HACKTIVISM:

THE SYRIAN ELECTRONIC ARMY

EVAN KOHLMANN AND ALEX KOBRAY

Although state-sponsored hacking and electronic warfare are hardly new developments for either the world at large or the Middle East in particular, they have evolved greatly over the past decade. In 2020 we live in an online universe dominated by advanced persistent threat (APT) actors, who operate behind the scenes in stealth mode to quietly obtain unauthorized access to sensitive systems and exfiltrate useful information over long periods. These actors eschew publicity or notoriety, their methodology is professional and sophisticated, and their targets are carefully chosen. Attacks by APT actors closely resemble traditional espionage or sabotage operations, and the level of technical prowess involved in some sense reflects the democratization of the skills required to carry out advanced digital subterfuge.

However, this obviously has not always been the case. As recently as five years ago, the global cyber threat landscape was remarkably different, and still immersed in the twilight of the great hacktivist era. From the Occupy Wall Street movement in the U.S. to the Arab Spring uprisings, the early 2010s witnessed a surge in populism, nationalism, and anti-corporate revolutionary ideologies. On the internet, this manifested itself as a steady flow of lurid website defacements and occasional data leaks by eccentric "Anonymous" hacktivists whose tactics were relatively basic, but whose loud personas and claims of responsibility attracted an outsized degree of public attention.

Western Anonymous-style actors were mimicked by others from around the world and across the political spectrum, including those affiliated with international terrorist organizations and rogue foreign regimes. A wave of amateurish populist hacker groups appeared on the internet, some referring to themselves as electronic armies. They included entities that appeared to be tacit fronts for state-sponsored (or at least state-sanctioned) electronic warfare, such as Parastoo, the Iranian Cyber Army, the Izzadeen al-Qassam Cyber Fighters, and the Syrian Electronic Army (SEA). These hacktivist entities, backed by rogue regimes, operated with the barest veneer of deniability — publicly acknowledging their solidarity with those regimes but dancing around the more delicate question of whether they were explicit state actors — as broadcasting their national identity was an essential aspect of gaining value from their operations.

THE EMERGENCE OF THE SEA

Ironically, given its approach, the SEA was essentially a reactionary response to the Arab Spring in 2011 and the sudden siege that encircled the regime of President Bashar al-Assad and its supporters on the ground, in the media, and online. U.S. and European journalists were largely reporting favorably on the nascent uprisings against decades of autocratic rule, and major social media platforms in the West welcomed their new beneficent role of serving as a virtual megaphone for young Arab Spring activists seeking the downfall of anti-democratic regimes around the Middle East. Not everyone was possessed of such positive views on these popular protests, however, among them supporters and associates of the Assad regime in Syria. According to the SEA's own narrative, "The SEA was created in 2011 when the Arab and Western media started their bias in favor of terrorist groups that have killed civilians, the Syrian Arab Army, and [that] have destroyed private and public property. The Arab and Western media formed a cover for the continuation of these groups and their actions through the blackout on terrorism in Syria and sabotaged the Syrian Arab Army."[1] The SEA upheld from the start the tenets of Syrian nationalism (rarely touching on any theological or jihadi themes) under the slogan "Nation, Honor, Loyalty."[2]

According to the SEA's official history, the group began not specifically as a hacker collective, but rather as a pro-Assad social media campaign aimed at "reporting pages that were accomplices in shedding the blood of Syrians" and "spreading awareness of the truth on media and international politics pages."[3] The essential notion behind the founding of the SEA was "let's fight them using their own weapon."[4] The SEA began abusing its access to mainstream American social media — Facebook, Twitter, YouTube, Instagram, Google Plus, and Pinterest — in order to broadcast pro-Assad news clips, images, and video "reporting the truth of events in Syria ... relating correct information."[5]

However, "making the world listen to the voice of truth" proved a significant challenge, due to "all the highly reputable channels and agencies still speaking the story from one side and completely silencing the other. ... Here came the idea of 'attacking' certain Facebook pages that target the sought audience."[6] SEA members and supporters began flooding official Facebook pages for foreign leaders like Barack Obama, Nicolas Sarkozy, and Dmitri Medvedev with comments "expressing their anger at foreign interference in Syria" and offering "gratitude" to Russia and other Syrian allies for their continuing solidarity.[7] By the summer of 2011, the initial social media campaign had evolved into a more focused operation aimed at trolling Assad's enemies among Syrian dissidents, other Arab states, Western media, human rights organizations, and the U.S. government. The group's methodology likewise evolved from promoting propaganda to actively sabotaging competing online voices.

THE SOCIAL MEDIA WAR

This hostile behavior quickly came to the attention of others, including officials at Facebook who, according to the SEA, "... didn't like our activities, so they closed our pages with no previous warnings. Simply, an anonymous 'Privacy and Security' official notified us ... that 'a decision has been made which clearly stated that this page and the pages similar to it shall be closed' and it described that what happened in Barak [sic]

Obama's official Facebook page as 'offensive to the Facebook policy because the criticism was very acrimonious.'"[8] The SEA began to declare open war on Facebook, accusing the company of "unfair practices" and "following its double standards, classifying pages as acceptable and unacceptable without relying on fair standards."[9]

Over a period of months, Facebook administrators allegedly shut down more than 22 separate attempts by the SEA to create new Facebook accounts for itself in spite of the ban: "After closing the first page, a new page was opened almost immediately, and the number of the participants in the page exceeded ten thousand after only a few hours. The new page got closed too, and a new page was opened once again."[10] As the SEA's activities began to receive more media attention, it received a similar chilly reception from Twitter and other major social media companies, which were quick to suspend official SEA accounts on their platforms as well. By April 2013, the SEA claimed that Twitter had already removed at least 11 iterations of its official account created on the popular online service.[11] According to the SEA, "the frequent closure of the Syrian Electronic Army accounts on Twitter ... made us in a state of war with the Security team of Twitter."[12] The group continued to regularly post taunts, threats, and "new challenge[s] to the management of Twitter [sic] website: So you will keep suspending our accounts?"[13]

In June 2011, the SEA furiously lashed out at Facebook and insisted that its supporters should stop providing the company "with any important personal information or any phone numbers or any image of personal identity, or any personal data, because that data is subject to analysis for use in its aggression against our dear country, Syria."[14] By August, the SEA conceded that it had become "absurd for us to create backup pages [on Facebook] because Facebook detects our movement so quickly. They deleted many of our groups and personal accounts and many, many backup and non-backup pages — and even secret groups that did not even carry the name of the army or any link with it." Nonetheless, the SEA insisted that "we are still coming up with many methods and we have many gaps in the Facebook system through which we can squeeze."[15]

Perhaps it is no surprise therefore that Western social media companies — and particularly Facebook and Twitter — became the focus of many of the SEA's attacks over the next four years. Simply describing these attacks as "hacking" is arguably misleading, as there was generally very little actual technical work involved. There do not appear to have been any novel software or hardware exploits involved. This was not the work of sophisticated elites who had outsmarted the highly capable engineers at Facebook or Twitter. It amounted to more of a constant trial-and-error game of scam artistry involving easily guessed passwords and email spear-phishing. The SEA was using the anonymity of the internet to dupe corporate social media managers and those with administrative access to influential accounts into clicking on suspicious links and mistakenly handing over their credentials, which could then be (briefly) hijacked for propaganda purposes.

Given that many of these account hijackings lasted for a few hours at most, and that these were public accounts with little sensitive information attached to them, the damage was mostly reputational. However, several of the attacks demonstrated the potential for real secondary damage as a result of these operations. In April 2013, SEA members sent a fake email to a group of Associated Press (AP) journalists posing as a fellow AP journalist in San Diego with an apparent link to a *Washington Post* blog article. When clicked, the link actually brought visitors to "a bogus site requesting you to log on."[16] Within an hour of the phishing email lure being sent, the SEA was able to gain access to the credentials for the official AP Twitter feed and posted a message reading, "Breaking: Two Explosions in the White House and Barack Obama is injured."[17] In the three minutes it took for major media outlets to discount the report as fake, there was a brief panic and the U.S. stock market dropped approximately 150 points, temporarily wiping out $136 billion in equity value.[18]

Similarly, in June 2014, the SEA acknowledged targeting an Israel Defense Forces (IDF) spokesman in a phishing scheme "and [being] able to access the personal email account of the spokesperson and other accounts belong[sic] to him."[19] Shortly thereafter, the SEA seized control of the IDF's official Twitter account and posted a bogus message warning of a "possible nuclear leak in the region after 2 rockets hit Dimona nuclear facility" in Israel's Negev region.[20] The message was quickly deleted, but not before it had already been retweeted dozens of times. Three hours later, the real IDF Twitter administrator was forced to post a new message that "apologize[d] for the incorrect tweets[.] Our twitter account was compromised. We will combat terror on all fronts including the cyber dimension."[21]

Even when the hijackings and defacements were immediately recognized as obvious acts of trolling, the reputational damage from such relatively low-skill attacks could still be quite significant given the high-profile nature of the targets. In early 2014, the SEA targeted a variety of social media properties owned by Microsoft Corporation, including those for its Skype Voice over Internet Protocol (VoIP) service and Microsoft Office, posting threats and trolling on corporate Facebook and Twitter accounts as well as company blogs.[22] One such blog post from Skype was altered to be titled, "Hacked by Syrian Electronic Army.. Stop Spying!"[23]

Given White House support for Syrian rebels fighting the Assad regime, U.S. President Barack Obama was also an attractive propaganda target for the SEA. Apparently unable to find a direct route into the White House or Obama campaign social media accounts, in October 2013, SEA members reportedly took a more sophisticated backdoor by targeting a vulnerable URL shortener service operated by his old campaign website, BarackObama.com. Shortened links that had already been posted on Obama's Twitter account were manipulated and "redirected to a video showing the truth about Syria."[24] In order to do this, the SEA apparently targeted one of the website's administrators in yet another email spear-phishing attack. "As you might expect all the necessary information was in their emails," an alleged SEA spokesperson told the website Mashable.com. "They didn't even enabled [sic] two-step verification."[25] Questions about White House cybersecurity procedures in the wake of the episode were eventually posed to White House Press Secretary Jay Carney, who refused to offer any comment.[26]

THE PRINT MEDIA WAR

Amid early optimism at the possibilities of the Arab Spring — followed by violent crackdowns by the Assad regime (among others in the region) — traditional journalists were no more sympathetic or receptive to the propaganda line of Assad and his supporters than the social media giants had been. The SEA later complained: "Unfortunately, we discovered that what we used to call as 'independent and professional' media agencies and channels turned out to be biased and turned to have certain political agendas. ... The news that western media publicizes and the stories that news agencies adopt ... are closer to action/sci-fi movies than to reality."[27]

Consequently, a sweeping majority of public SEA attacks have targeted international media organizations that have dared to offend the Assad regime with unfriendly headlines. Taken in abstract, the lengthy list of major news services that have been successfully sabotaged by the SEA is impressive: AP, Reuters, *The Washington Post*, *The New York Times*, Agence France Press, CNN, Al-Jazeera, Al-Arabiya, Channel 4 UK, *The Telegraph*, *The Guardian*, *The Financial Times*, *The International Business Times*, *The Sunday Times*, *The Sun*, *Le Monde*, the U.K. *Mirror*, ITV News, Sky News, Vice News, the Daily Dot, CBS News, NPR, the BBC, and more. Indeed, there are few hacker collectives to have ever demonstrated such a wide range of targets within a single high-profile vertical. While the value of aggressively sabotaging some of these sources is debatable (particularly in the case of an organization like NPR, for instance), the SEA saw things differently. "We will not say why we attacked NPR," the group scoffed on its website in mid-2013. "They know the reason and that's enough."[28]

While the SEA spoke frequently about the "lies" of Western media, it had an even less charitable view of media coverage in the Arab world, which could often be even more critical of the Syrian government. The Al-Jazeera network, famously funded by the Qatari government, offered non-stop focused reporting on the Arab Spring uprisings that prominently featured the voices of democratic protesters and other adversaries of the Assad regime. In January 2012, just as the SEA would later do to the AP, a prominent figure within the SEA known as The Pro (a.k.a. Th3 Pro) succeeded in using spear-phishing attacks to infiltrate Al-Jazeera's corporate email system by penetrating the account of a network supervisor.[29] Instead of simply defacing Al-Jazeera's social media accounts, The Pro and his colleagues began allegedly sending fake messages from the hijacked account to various Al-Jazeera journalists trying to bait them into falsely exaggerating their reporting on Syria with the goal of subsequently smearing their credibility in a scheme reminiscent of American right-wing activist James O'Keefe and his Project Veritas.[30] The SEA insisted that it had "discovered many facts related to the fabrication of news about Syria"[31] as a result of the attack on Al-Jazeera and that it would "continue to expose every traitor who sold his honor in exchange for Western and Wahhabi money."[32]

Some of the SEA attacks on media organizations were juvenile and, in certain cases, even counterproductive to the group's stated goals. In May

2013, the SEA hardly helped its credibility in Western circles by hijacking and defacing the Twitter and Facebook accounts for satirical publication *The Onion* as payback for it distributing "news that harms the reputation of Syria and its leader."[33] During the same month, the SEA also seized control of the social media accounts of E! Entertainment News and posted a series of trolling Tweets, including "Exclusive: Justin Bieber to E! online: I'm a gay" and "E! News Breaking: Justin Bieber arrested in Dubai due to false tweets with him coming out situation developing."[34] While the SEA had perhaps demonstrated how far its phishing attacks could reach, these antics did not convey the impression of a sophisticated and professional group of actors. They also raised questions as to how closely the SEA was being controlled by the Syrian government, whose international reputation hardly stood to benefit from the incidents.

Picking a fight with the amorphous (and mostly symbolic) Anonymous online movement did not particularly help either. Perhaps clearer now in retrospect, Anonymous was composed of a very small handful of skilled hackers surrounded by a much larger group of nameless trolls whose talents did not extend far beyond issuing dire threats on the internet. Responding to the meaningless taunts of Anonymous gained the SEA nothing other than added irritation. This should have been obvious to the SEA, as it had borrowed many of its own tactics directly from the Anonymous playbook. In early 2012, actors associated with the Anonymous movement began hinting through media leaks that they had acquired copies of sensitive Syrian government online communications, including personal emails from Assad and his wife.[35] On July 6, 2012, these actors issued an online communique in the name of "Anonymous Operation Syria" claiming responsibility for leaking 2 million such emails to WikiLeaks in order to deal "a mighty blow to the Assad regime." According to the statement, former LulzSec hackers affiliated with Anonymous "succeeded in creating a massive breach of multiple domains and dozens of servers inside Syria" and this was proof that Anonymous was "waging a relentless information and psychological campaign against Assad."[36]

The scale and complexity of the data made it hard to easily parse through, and journalists were only able to identify a single immediate "scoop" from the stolen "Syria Files" data released through WikiLeaks, namely evidence that an Italian industrial enterprise had offered telecommunications systems to Syria and Iran.[37] Nonetheless, the leak was personally embarrassing to Assad and quickly drew the ire of the SEA. On July 16, the SEA issued its own bellicose communiqué threatening Anonymous with "complete annihilation":

> *We have received your message and have prepared our reply. In our country we have a saying 'follow the liar to the end of the door' and we have been waiting for months for you to implement your various threats. You first said that you will shut down the internet for the entire world, then you threatened to shut down the social networking website Facebook and yet you have no[t] taken any steps towards that until now. Today you are promising threats to the Syrian Electronic Army. Your record is becoming hilarious even to children amongst us. ... If you were a virtual army, you should know that we are a real army who believes in the victory of their country and that no one can stop us. If you want to remember who the Syrian Electronic Army is, you should recall how many times we have infiltrated your systems.*[38]

To validate its threats, the SEA "hacked and defaced" a vulnerable Anonymous website based in the Netherlands and leaked "approximately 700 username and password for members of the Anonymous organization as a punishment for them to conspire against the Syrian people."[39] Getting such an emotional rise out of the SEA and being taken so seriously seems to have only encouraged Anonymous trolls to pursue a feud with the Syrian government. In hindsight, punching down at Anonymous was clearly not worth the trouble.

ANALYZING SEA OPERATIONS: FROM SMALL TO LARGE

As can perhaps be inferred from the pointless clash with Anonymous, many of the SEA's hacking attempts (especially early in its existence) did not display a great deal of technical sophistication or ingenuity. Rather, it was using fairly basic, off-the-shelf methods to attack any available target that could even remotely be connected with its ideological mission. Aside from spear-phishing attacks, one of the SEA's initial go-to tactics was mass-searching the internet for poorly administered, unpatched websites running the popular WordPress software package, and probing them for well-known and publicly reported vulnerabilities. Fittingly, this same tactic has been widely used by the Anonymous movement and other lower-level hacktivists for many years.

In October 2011, the SEA triumphantly announced "the success of the THE SHADOW & Ph03nix battalions in penetrating a number of Israeli websites and left the following message: .... 'We hacked your sites to spread our message... The Syrian Arab Army promises you and promises the entire world of the demise of Israel from the occupied territories. As for us, we promise you that Israel will disappear from the virtual world.'"[40] The list of targeted websites released by the SEA included many completely insignificant sites with no link to Israel whatsoever, including the homepages of an obscure Mexican canvas artist, a German tattoo parlor, and a discussion forum for fans of house electronica music with a total of seven registered users.[41] Quite clearly, these sites had been chosen simply because they were vulnerable to commonly known WordPress exploits and not for any other fathomable reason. Likewise, in the wake of Israeli airstrikes targeting Syrian government facilities near Damascus, the SEA attempted to retaliate "in our way" by allegedly "hack[ing] dozens of the Zionist entity websites."[42] The list of hacked websites included, among other things, an Israeli teen entertainment magazine, a carpenter selling wooden garden furniture, a database of jokes, and a site that displays the current time in various locations around the world.[43]

Nonetheless, it is also true that the SEA has gradually carried out more advanced operations, particularly later in its existence. This evolution toward more sophisticated and thoughtful hacking attempts may be evidence of how the SEA has evolved over time from a frequently amateurish hacktivist group into a more contemporary-style APT actor. In May 2013, the SEA used its classic spear-phishing tactics to target Sky News in the U.K., but rather than merely take control of its Twitter and Facebook accounts, it hijacked the Sky News Google Play account with stolen software developer credentials, manipulating the Sky News Android application on the Google Play store to feature its logo and tagline.[44] While the extent of the SEA's access to application user data is unclear, Sky News immediately sent out a warning via Twitter advising anyone who had downloaded the app to immediately uninstall it.[45]

In July 2013, SEA members targeted at least two popular VoIP services — Viber and Tango — in a combination of WordPress vulnerability scanning and phishing attacks aimed at company employees, defacing their public websites and allegedly seizing large databases of customer data.[46] While the group did not comment on why it had specifically targeted Tango, in the case of Viber, it accused the company of "spying and tracking of its users."[47] However, it should be noted that, at the time, such VoIP services were providing critical communications bridges for Arab Spring dissident activists and rebel groups (among others) who were seeking to avoid possible government surveillance.

In the case of Tango, the SEA claimed to have confiscated databases containing "millions of the app users phone numbers and contacts and their emails" — in addition to "more than 1,5 TB of the daily-backups of the servers network."[48] Screenshots of alleged Tango log information released by the SEA does appear to show some short-lived session identifier tokens and nondescript account names, but nothing very sensitive per se.[49] The SEA further published a screenshot showing 9.9TB of uncompressed "network backup" data that was allegedly stolen from Tango, but a list of subfolders within the "network backup" archive did little to further establish the significance of its theft or its potential value to cybercriminals and/or hostile state actors.[50] Likewise with the Viber hack, the SEA leaked screenshots of an app management system, along with the names and phone numbers of system administrators.[51] The screenshots included a view of a table from a database containing IP addresses, user agent information, and a few temporary authentication tokens, but once again offered nothing that would substantiate the SEA's claims to have taken a valuable motherlode of information.[52]

During the same month, the SEA also claimed to have exploited a WordPress vulnerability with the goal of hijacking the website of global phone directory/caller ID service Truecaller.com and seizing databases that purportedly contained "a handred [sic] of millions of phone numbers and its owners in addition [to] millions of Facebook/Twitter/Linkedin/Gmail accounts."[53] According to the SEA, the cache included almost half a terabyte of data, including Truecaller API data, Truecaller "profiles," and admin information.[54] However, since much of this information was arguably already available in the public domain, it is not clear what critical use case this data would fill for the Syrian government or any other rogue state.

A more focused and thoughtful purpose for the SEA's trademark spear-phishing attacks emerged in November 2013, when the group admitted to using the compromised email account of an American organizer for Syrian dissidents to gain access to the private communications of a variety of other key associates within the Syrian opposition. An alleged SEA representative later bragged to journalists that it had simply brute-forced its way into the organizer's account through trial-and-error due to his use of "easy and weak" passwords.[55] The SEA was able to document its claims to journalists by producing what appeared to be copies of dissident passports, email exchanges involving U.S. and British government officials, and even discussions "regarding military assistance."[56] According to SEA member The Pro, "We were watching their moves, and what they were planning."[57] On its own website, the SEA began boasting of having "infiltrated the email servers of countries that have actively participated in the blood shedding of the Syrian nation: it has acquired proofs, files and secret correspondence that clarify the extent of the conspiracy against our country and the involvement of these criminal nations in it."[58]

In late 2014 through mid-2015, the SEA launched several attacks on high-profile websites through an unusual backdoor: targeting their content delivery networks (CDNs). High-traffic sites like media organizations, online retail, and even the U.S. military rely on CDNs as a signal amplifier to help deliver their web content to users around the world in a fast and reliable flow. In November 2014, the SEA targeted an Israeli marketing company known as Gigya that has provided embedded advertisement delivery and user management services to a wide range of major sites, including *The Chicago Tribune*, CNBC, *Forbes Magazine*, and even the official website of the U.S. National Hockey League.[59]

Likely once again by means of phishing, the SEA was able to gain access to the password credentials for Gigya's account on GoDaddy.com, which controls where Gigya's domain name (i.e. Gigya.com) routes visitors to.[60] According to an official statement later released by Gigya, "the WHOIS record of gigya.com [was] modified to point to a different DNS server. That DNS server had been configured to point Gigya's CDN domain (cdn.gigya.com) to a server controlled by the hackers, where they served … an alert claiming that the site had been hacked by the Syrian Electronic Army."[61] Visitors to a range of media websites were suddenly greeted with an unsettling popup message reading, "You've been hacked by the Syrian Electronic Army (SEA)."[62] All available evidence suggests that site visitors were not, in fact, hacked by anyone (other than receiving the harmless popup), and Gigya was quick to insist that "neither Gigya's platform itself nor any user, administrator or operational data has been compromised and was never at risk of being compromised. Rather, the attack only served other JavaScript files instead of those served by Gigya."[63] Nonetheless, domain hijacking was a new twist in the SEA's playbook, and the technique offered many more advanced possibilities for a sophisticated hacker than just posting nasty taunts on Twitter.

In May 2015, the SEA pursued another CDN provider, this time the Instart Content Delivery Network (which has since been acquired by Akamai).[64] In an email to a journalist at *Motherboard*, The Pro admitted "hack[ing] InStart CDN service, and we were working on hacking the main site of *Washington Post*, but they took down the control panel. ... We just wanted to deliver a message on several media sites like *Washington Post*, *US News* and others, but we didn't have time :P."[65] Visitors to sections of *The Washington Post* online were suddenly forwarded without warning to an SEA website instead. A statement from *Washington Post* Chief Information Officer Shailesh Prakash insisted that "the situation has been resolved and no customer information was impacted."[66]

A month later, the SEA upped the stakes by targeting Limelight Networks, a major CDN provider being used by the official website of the U.S. Army.[67] As with the Gigya and Instart CDN breaches, the SEA employed basic JavaScript files to deliver trolling pop-up messages to web users attempting to browse www.army.mil, including "Your commanders admit they are training the people they have sent you to die fighting."[68] According to a later message posted by the SEA, the group "was able to intercept the content paths after discovering an exploit in the Control Panel that provide the ability to edit the protected content paths."[69] The SEA also posted screenshots purportedly showing the identities of active website users — "including the entire email addresses of military members" — and vowed that it would "qualify [sic] the data obtained from this attack and other old-attacks, to be published later if that was necessary."[70]

As the nature of the conflict in Syria has shifted, so have the tactics and targets of the SEA. With the U.S. and its allies entirely focused on the battle against ISIS and previous Western support for the removal of Assad stuck either on life support or entirely abandoned, by 2018, there was no longer a pressing justification for the SEA to chase unfriendly foreign media outlets. While the U.S. military retained outposts in eastern Syria, the added presence of Russian troops nearby made it unlikely that the American military would do anything significant to jeopardize the rule of the Assad regime. High-profile online hacks blasted out over social media and intended to intimidate a Western audience became pointless — and the drumbeat of audacious public claims of responsibility from the SEA have since come to a halt.

Meanwhile, as the main electronic threat to the Syrian regime has shifted back to internal opposition members and dissidents quietly using online communications systems, there are indications that the SEA is evolving into a more silent model of operations focused on sophisticated digital espionage instead of wasting cycles trolling websites like *The Onion*'s. A presentation by private analysts at the London Blackhat Conference in December 2018 tied metadata taken from an Android malware package to the SEA, including its most prominent member The Pro.[71] The malware was being disguised as software updates to WhatsApp or Telegram, and appeared to be targeted specifically at Syrian Android phone users. Circulating since at least mid-2016, once installed, it was able to secretly record audio streams, take photos, download executable files, scrape phone calls and messages, and track a user's location.[72] The same group of analysts recently reported that this and related malware packages all linked to the SEA are now even being baited using COVID-19 lures, including in downloads of fake personal thermometer software.[73]

UNMASKING THE SEA

From the earliest days of the SEA's existence, there has been widespread speculation about the real identities of its leadership and members. The SEA has been coy about offering much detail, acknowledging to journalists that the group's "special operations division" consists of "more than ten specialists … we are all based in Syria."[74] In a separate interview with ABC News, another SEA member described his colleagues as "university students [who] live in Syria … majority of us live in Syria."[75] As of mid-2012, the official SEA website identified the major players within that division by their online pseudonyms: Hwaks, The Shadow, ViCt0R, and The Pro.[76] From this list of four, the two who have featured most prominently in claiming responsibility for attacks and giving media interviews are The Shadow and The Pro.

In July 2011, the Al-Arabiya News Network published an article naming the founder of the SEA as Ammar Ismail, the director of the Damascus News Network page on Facebook.[77] The article appears to have been based on idiosyncratic "metaphorical" language Ismail used on his Facebook page and, according to the SEA, "these channels and websites then tried to use this writing to link Mr. Ismail to the Syrian Electronic Army." In an official statement on its website, the group insisted, "We deny here any link to us, Mr. Ismail, and any activity that he undertakes. Mr. Ismail is a friend of the Army, he along with all the administrators of [Facebook] pages that work together for the benefit of Syria, and each of us works in his own role and in the way we might agree or disagree with."[78]

During the late summer of 2013, a variety of different sources began claiming that they had unearthed the real identities of the SEA leadership, including The Pro. Based on interviews with other Syrian hackers, credit card receipts, and domain registry information, a journalist at *Motherboard* published an article identifying The Pro as a then 19-year-old Syrian national named Hatem Deeb.[79] Other similar exposes were released online that named "Mohamad Abd AlKarem" a.k.a. "Mohammed Osman" as a member of the group.[80] While it remains possible that some of these individuals may have performed website or graphics work on behalf of the SEA and/or its leadership, based on what we know now, it is unlikely that any of these individuals are actually The Pro or his SEA colleagues. Commenting to another journalist, an unnamed SEA representative scoffed, "The story has been the source of amusement and laughter for all of us. Neither Hatem Deeb nor Mohammed Osman are hackers, but are both friends of ours that they are trying to intimidate in order to blackmail us. What they're doing is actually illegal and irresponsible, they even posted a photograph of a random guy that none of us could identify and called him the leader of the SEA. ... We don't know anything about Osman nor [Mohamad] Abd Alkarem."[81] Nonetheless, within a short period of time, the SEA found a backdoor into the website of *Motherboard*'s parent Vice.com — once again by spear-phishing several key email accounts, including one belonging to the website's developer — allowing them to seize control of the site's content management system. The SEA hackers deleted the article *Motherboard* had published in August naming Hatem Deeb, and left behind a message threatening, "This time we just deleted the article that you claimed in it that you exposed 'Th3Pro' identity. But you didn't. You published names of innocent people instead."[82]

As it turns out, the SEA may have been telling the truth about Hatem Deeb and the others who were named at the time. In March 2016, the U.S. Justice Department unsealed federal computer hacking conspiracy charges against two Syrian nationals as "members of the Syrian Electronic Army," unmasking the real names of The Pro and The Shadow, respectively, as 22-year-old Ahmad Umar Agha from Damascus and 27-year-old Firas Dardar from Homs.[83] Both Agha and Dardar were added to the list of the FBI's most wanted cybercriminals and a reward of up to $100,000 was offered for information leading to the arrest of either suspect.[84]

Evidence cited in the complaint filed against both Agha and Dardar reveals additional color about the activities of the two men behind the scenes of their messy public wars on social media. One of the more eye-opening aspects is how aggressively they attempted to penetrate Obama's White House. According to the complaint, shortly after Obama first openly called upon Assad to step down, Agha and Dardar used LinkedIn.com to send an email lure to a former employee at the Executive Office of the President (EOP) and unsuccessfully requested to be connected over the service.[85] The next summer, the two men allegedly sent multiple email spear-phishing lures from what appeared to be White House email addresses to other employees at the EOP, which also failed. Once again, in July 2013, the men created a sock puppet email account that appeared to belong to an EOP employee and sent emails from this account to the personal and work email addresses of several other EOP employees. This time, according to the complaint, "at least one of the current employees of the EOP … clicked on a link and provided actual email credentials to the Conspiracy through the fraudulent website. A member of the Conspiracy thereafter accessed, without authorization, [their] personal email account and used that account to send emails to other EOP employees, at least one of which requested the password to a White House social media account. No official EOP email account was successfully compromised."[86]

Another interesting fact relayed by the criminal complaint was that Dardar (a.k.a. The Shadow) had been moonlighting all along as a financially motivated cyber extortionist, breaching various websites and web-based services and then demanding a ransom in exchange for not leaking their data or worse — and using the widespread notoriety of the SEA to convince his targets to comply.[87] Between July 2013 and December 2014, Dardar demanded a total of more than $500,000 in various ransom payments from 14 separate unnamed victims, including a Chinese online gaming website, four web hosting services based in Europe and the U.S., an American online media company, and an online entertainment service.[88] In order to evade U.S. sanctions on Syrian banks, Dardar partnered with another Syrian national affiliated with the SEA living in Germany, Peter Romar, who helped launder the ransom payments, and who pled guilty six months later to criminal charges of hacking and extortion.[89]

One of the remaining questions about the SEA is the degree to which it has been sponsored or directed by the Syrian government. Certainly, the SEA has received at least tacit approval from the Assad regime, as the group has itself acknowledged in media interviews that it has been permitted to take actions from Syrian territory that anywhere else would land its members in prison. In the aftermath of at least two major SEA attacks on the Tango VoIP service and Truecaller.com in July 2013, the group boasted that "much of the information that were [sic] stored in the databases has been delivered to the Syrian government."[90] In an interview with ABC News, The Shadow (a.k.a. Dardar) conceded, "We may deliver some sensitive information only for the security apparatus in Syria."[91]

However, during the same interview, The Shadow nonetheless insisted that "we do not have any relationship with the Syrian government."[92] The SEA has officially long maintained that its leaders do not come from "any governmental [sic] entity" and merely "took on the initiative of protecting the homeland and supporting the reforms of President Bashar al-Assad, who we see as the right option for our aspirations as youth."[93] The group has claimed that it has been able to operate solely on the basis of "self-funding ... because our work only requires access to a computer line, internet and set targets for the attacks. ... The Syrian youth have power and experience so we don't need funding."[94] In public statements, the U.S. Justice Department and the FBI have taken pains to note that the SEA's criminal actions were carried out "in support of the Syrian Government and President Bashar al-Assad" but have not (yet) charged the SEA as operating under the explicit direction of the Assad regime.[95] As of today, the precise nature and extent of their relationship remains somewhat of a mystery.

CONCLUSION

The history of the SEA offers more than one lesson for observers. In one sense, it is a needed reality check that, for all its dramatic successes, the group mostly used relatively basic social engineering tactics, and by no means should be conceived as some sort of nexus of technical wizardry. As reflected in the criminal complaint filed against Agha and Dardar, the genius of the SEA was in how it managed to devise schemes and draft email lures that were credible enough for at least one unsuspecting person to fall for — over and over and over again. Remarkably, it was able to do so in some cases even despite its targets receiving specific warnings in advance that they were being targeted. It is a cautionary tale about how far such spear-phishing tactics can extend, and the sweeping impact that even relative amateurs were able to achieve with mostly symbolic attacks.

Although the SEA has mostly been silent in recent years, the group still maintains social media accounts that regularly post news articles along with a "greatest hits" tour of major SEA hacking attacks from years past. Researchers who analyzed recent malware packages tied back to the SEA and Agha reportedly found references to the names of new SEA "personas" like "Medo CoDeR" and "Raddex," suggesting that the group is perhaps continuing (and even expanding) its activities, albeit in a less provocative and far more stealthy manner.[96] While the days of Facebook wars and populist hacktivism may have passed, the SEA is operating now more in the style of contemporary APT actors. As long as it continues to deliver cyberintelligence to the Syrian government and receives sanctuary on Syrian soil, there is reason to believe that the SEA will find success in pursuing this path.

Endnotes

1. "SEA Story," Syrian Electronic Army, Wayback Machine, September 2014, https://web.archive.org/web/20140901205100/http://www.sea.sy/index/en#story.
2. Ibid.
3. Ibid.
4. "About Us," Syrian Electronic Army, Wayback Machine, August 2011, http://web.archive.org/web/20120111093139/http://www.syrian-es.org:80/about-us.html.
5. Ibid.
6. Ibid.
7. Ibid.
8. Ibid.
9. Ibid.
10. Ibid.
11. "11 Twitter Accounts of the Guardian Hacked," Syrian Electronic Army, Wayback Machine, April 29, 2013, http://web.archive.org/web/20150509042112/http://sea.sy/article/id/1951/en.
12. Ibid.
13. "E! News Twitter Account and SMS Service Hacked," Syrian Electronic Army, Wayback Machine, May 5, 2013, http://web.archive.org/web/20150509064817/http://sea.sy/article/id/1955/en.
14. "بيان هام من الجيش السوري الإلكتروني إلى جميع مستخدمي الفيسبوك في سوريا," طارق, Syrian Electronic Army, Wayback Machine, June 4, 2011, http://web.archive.org/web/20110625144545/http://syrian-es.org/2011-05-10-18-40-09/151-2011-06-04-21-35-06.html.
15. "طارق, هل للجيش السوري الإلكتروني صفحة احتياطية أو صفحات وهل صفحته الحالية مخترقة," Syrian Electronic Army, Wayback Machine, August 8, 2011, http://web.archive.org/web/20120109064930/http://www.syrian-es.org/2011-05-10-18-41-22/269-2011-08-08-16-46-19.html.
16. Jim Romenesko, "AP Warned Staffers Just Before @AP Was Hacked," Jim Romenesko, Wayback Machine, April 23, 2013, http://web.archive.org/web/20130423223514/https://jimromenesko.com/2013/04/23/ap-warned-staffers-just-before-ap-was-hacked/.
17. Max Fisher, "Syrian Hackers Claim AP Hack That Tipped Stock Market by $136 Billion. Is It Terrorism?" *The Washington Post*, April 23, 2013, https://www.washingtonpost.com/news/worldviews/wp/2013/04/23/syrian-hackers-claim-ap-hack-that-tipped-stock-market-by-136-billion-is-it-terrorism/.
18. "AP Twitter Feed Hacked," Syrian Electronic Army, Wayback Machine, April 23, 2013, http://web.archive.org/web/20150709212722/http://sea.sy/article/id/1945/en. See also: Fisher, "Syrian Hackers Claim AP Hack That Tipped Stock Market by $136 Billion. Is It Terrorism?"
19. "Latest Hacks," Syrian Electronic Army, Wayback Machine, July 31, 2014, http://web.archive.org/web/20140731182707/http://sea.sy/Latest_Hacks_EN.
20. Ibid.
21. Israeli Defense Forces (@IDF), Twitter post, July 3, 2014, 3:51 p.m., https://twitter.com/IDF/status/484801563760680960. See also: "Hackers Took Over the Israeli Army's Twitter Account and They Tried Freaking Everyone Out About a Nuclear Leak," *The Times of Israel* for *Business Insider*, July 3, 2014, https://www.businessinsider.com/syrian-electronic-army-hacks-israeli-defense-forces-twitter-2014-7.
22. "Microsoft Official Blogs/Twitter Account Hacked," Syrian Electronic Army, Wayback Machine, March 12, 2014, http://web.archive.org/web/20150508204518/http://sea.sy/article/id/2026/en.
23. "Skype Blog/Twitter/Facebook Accounts Hacked," Syrian Electronic Army, Wayback Machine, January 3, 2014, http://web.archive.org/web/20150509102743/http://sea.sy/article/id/2024/en.
24. Fran Berkman, "Syrian Hackers Target Obama's Twitter, Facebook Posts," *Mashable*, October 28, 2013, https://mashable.com/2013/10/28/syrian-electronic-army-obama/.
25. Ibid.
26. "Barack Obama Social Media Accounts/Website Attacked," Syrian Electronic Army, Wayback Machine, October 29, 2013, http://web.archive.org/web/20150524112907/http://sea.sy/article/id/2009/en.
27. Syrian Electronic Army, "About Us."
28. "Syrian Electronic Army Hacked NPR Website and Social Media Accounts," Syrian Electronic Army, Wayback Machine, April 16, 2013,

http://web.archive.org/web/20141128233302/https://sea.sy/article/id/1938/en.

29. "تسريبات," Syrian Electronic Army, Wayback Machine, August 5, 2012, http://web.archive.org/web/20120805042144/http://syrian-es.org/section.php?id=1&lang=ar. See also: "تقرير الجيش السوري الإلكتروني - قسم العمليات الخاصة -, شبكة الجزيرة," Syrian Electronic Army, Wayback Machine, March 02, 2012, http://web.archive.org/web/20120302131751/http://www.syrian-es.com/02/jazop/index.html.

30. Ibid.

31. Ibid.

32. Syrian Electronic Army, "تسريبات."

33. "Syrian Electronic Army Hacked Today Twitter Accounts and Facebook Pages of The Onion Satirical Newspaper," Syrian Electronic Army, Wayback Machine, May 7, 2013, http://web.archive.org/web/20141129014905/https://sea.sy/article/id/1957/en.

34. Syrian Electronic Army, "E! News Twitter Account and SMS Service Hacked."

35. Robert Booth, Mona Mahmood, and Luke Harding, "Exclusive: Secret Assad Emails Lift Lid on Life of Leader's Inner Circle," *The Guardian*, March 14, 2012, https://www.theguardian.com/world/2012/mar/14/assad-emails-lift-lid-inner-circle.

36. "Anonymous Operation Syria – Press Release," Anonymous, Pastebin, July 8, 2012, https://pastebin.com/snj63PtF.

37. Andy Greenberg, "WikiLeaks Announces Massive Release With The 'Syria Files': 2.4 Million Emails From Syrian Officials And Companies," *Forbes*, July 5, 2012, https://www.forbes.com/sites/andygreenberg/2012/07/05/wikileaks-announces-its-largest-release-yet-in-the-syria-files-2-4-million-emails-from-syrian-officials-and-companies/#149bc3615081.

38. "Our Reply to Anonymous," Syrian Electronic Army, Wayback Machine, July 6, 2012, http://web.archive.org/web/20141129015044/https://sea.sy/article/id/417/en.

39. "One of Anonymous Website Got Hacked and Defaced by Us," Syrian Electronic Army, Wayback Machine, July 17, 2012, http://web.archive.org/web/20141129015039/https://sea.sy/article/id/420/en. See also: Syrian Electronic Army, "تسريبات."

40. "ابراهيم," اختراق عدد من المواقع الإسرائيلية | كتيبتي شادو وفينيكس," Syrian Electronic Army, Wayback Machine, October 6, 2011, http://web.archive.org/web/20111010024145/http://www.syrian-es.org/2011-05-26-16-21-27/317-2011-10-06-17-11-17.html.

41. Ibid.

42. "Dozens of Zionist Entity Websites Hacked by the Syrian Electronic Army," Syrian Electronic Army, January 31, 2013, http://web.archive.org/web/20141129015533/https://sea.sy/article/id/1889/en.

43. Ibid.

44. "Sky News Android Apps Hacked," Syrian Electronic Army, Wayback Machine, May 26, 2013, http://web.archive.org/web/20141129015126/https://sea.sy/article/id/1968/en.

45. https://twitter.com/SkyHelpTeam/status/338450352145850368, May 2013.

46. "Exclusive: Tango App Website Hacked, More Than 1.5 TB Daily Database Backup Compromised," E Hacking News, July 20, 2013, https://www.ehackingnews.com/2013/07/exclusive-tango-website-hacked-more.html. See also: Armando Orozco, "Syrian Electronic Army Hacks Tango and Viber Servers," Malwarebytes Labs Blog, July 24, 2013, https://blog.malwarebytes.com/cybercrime/2013/07/syrian-electronic-army-hacks-tango-and-viber-servers/.

47. Syrian Electronic Army, Viber SY, electronic, May 2015, http://web.archive.org/web/20150504052232/http://sea.sy/uploaded_files/articles/viber_sy.png.

48. "Tango App Website/Databases Hacked," Syrian Electronic Army, Wayback Machine, July 20, 2013, http://web.archive.org/web/20150910004510/http://www.sea.sy/article/id/1981/en.

49. Syrian Electronic Army, Tango App Log, electronic, May 2015, http://web.archive.org/web/20150513202850/http://sea.sy/uploaded_files/articles/tangoapplog.png.

50. Syrian Electronic Army, Tango App BU Folder Size, electronic, May 2015, http://web.archive.org/web/20150513202845/http://sea.sy/uploaded_files/articles/tangoappbufoldersize.png. See also: Syrian Electronic Army, Tango BU Folder, Electronic, May 2015, http://web.archive.org/web/20150513203002/http://sea.sy/uploaded_files/articles/tangobufolder.png.

51. "Viber App Website/Databases Hacked," Syrian Electronic Army, Wayback Machine,

July 23, 2013, http://web.archive.org/web/20150604154039/http://sea.sy/article/id/1983/en.

52. Syrian Electronic Army, Viber SY.

53. "True Caller Website/Database Hacked," Syrian Electronic Army, Wayback Machine, July 17, 2013, http://web.archive.org/web/20150710024828/http://sea.sy/article/id/1979/en. See also: http://sea.sy/uploaded_files/articles/1979.jpg, August 2013.

54. Ibid.

55. "FSA/'Syrian Opposition' Leaders Hacked," Syrian Electronic Army, Wayback Machine, April 3, 2015, https://web.archive.org/web/20150725165236/http://sea.sy/article/id/2078/en.

56. Lorenzo Franceschi-Bicchierai, "The Syrian Electronic Army's Most Dangerous Hack," *Motherboard*, Vice News, April 3, 2015, https://www.vice.com/en_us/article/nze5nk/the-syrian-electronic-armys-most-dangerous-hack.

57. Ibid.

58. Syrian Electronic Story, "SEA Story."

59. "New Attack on the Western Media Websites," Syrian Electronic Army, Wayback Machine, November 28, 2014, https://web.archive.org/web/20150711081741/http://sea.sy/article/id/2050/en. See also: Andrew Griffin, "Syrian Electronic Army Hacks Global Websites Including The Independent," *The Independent*, November 27, 2014, https://www.independent.co.uk/life-style/gadgets-and-tech/news/syrian-electronic-army-hacks-global-websites-including-the-independent-9887176.html.

60. Griffin, "Syrian Electronic Army Hacks Global Websites Including The Independent."

61. http://blog.gigya.com/regarding-todays-service-attack/, December 2014.

62. Griffin, "Syrian Electronic Army Hacks Global Websites Including The Independent."

63. http://blog.gigya.com/regarding-todays-service-attack/, December 2014.

64. "Washingtonpost Mobile Site Hacked," Syrian Electronic Army, Wayback Machine, May 15, 2015, https://web.archive.org/web/20150710005516/http://sea.sy/article/id/2082/en.

65. Lorenzo Franceschi-Bicchierai, "This Is How the Syrian Electronic Army Hacked the Washington Post," *Motherboard*, Vice News,

May 14, 2015, https://www.vice.com/en_us/article/mgbn58/this-is-how-the-syrian-electronic-army-hacked-the-washington-post.

66. Brian Fung, "The Syrian Electronic Army Just Hacked the Washington Post (Again)," *The Washington Post*, May 14, 2015, https://www.washingtonpost.com/news/the-switch/wp/2015/05/14/the-syrian-electronic-army-just-hacked-the-washington-post-again/.

67. Polly Mosendz, "Syrian Electronic Army Claims to Have Hacked U.S. Army Website," *Newsweek*, June 8, 2015, https://www.newsweek.com/syrian-electronic-army-claims-have-hacked-us-army-website-340874.

68. Ibid.

69. "US Army Official Website Hacked," Syrian Electronic Army, Wayback Machine, June 9, 2015, http://web.archive.org/web/20150717092952/http://sea.sy/article/id/2083/en.

70. Ibid.

71. Michael Flossman and Kristin Del Rosso, "Under the SEA: A Look at the Syrian Electronic Army's Mobile Tooling" (Presentation, BlackHat Europe 2018, London, England, December 2018). https://i.blackhat.com/eu-18/Wed-Dec-5/eu-18-DelRosso-Under-the-SEA.pdf. See also: Thomas Brewster, "Syrian Electronic Army Hackers are Targeting Android Phones with Fake WhatsApp Attacks," *Forbes*, December 5, 2018, https://www.forbes.com/sites/thomasbrewster/2018/12/05/syrian-electronic-army-hackers-are-targeting-android-phones-with-fake-whatsapp-attacks/#6c517abb6ce4.

72. Danny Palmer, "These Hackers are Using Android Surveillance Malware to Target Opponents of the Syrian Government," ZDNet, December 10, 2018, https://www.zdnet.com/article/these-hackers-are-using-android-surveillance-malware-to-target-opponents-of-the-syrian-government/.

73. Kristin Del Rosso, "Nation-state Mobile Malware Targets Syrians with COVID-19 Lures," Lookout Blog, April 15, 2020, https://blog.lookout.com/nation-state-mobile-malware-targets-syrians-with-covid-19-lures.

74. Lorenzo Franceschi-Bicchierai, "Syrian Electronic Army: If U.S. Attacks 'We Will Target All of It,'" *Mashable*, August 30, 2013, https://mashable.com/2013/08/30/syrian-electronic-army-interview/.

75. Lee Ferran, "Interview With Alleged Member

76. "كتائب في الجيش السوري الإلكتروني," Syrian Electronic Army, Wayback Machine, August 2012, http://web.archive.org/web/20120805045735/http://syrian-es.org/battalions.php?lang=ar.

77. "The 'Electronic Army' Encourages Attacks Against Artists Opposed to the Syrian Regime," Al-Arabiya, July 20, 2011.

78. "طارق," رد على خبر قناة العربية حول الفنانين ومؤسس الجيش," Syrian Electronic Army, Wayback Machine, July 20, 2011, http://web.archive.org/web/20120111094143/http://www.syrian-es.org/2011-05-12-12-15-11/2011-05-12-17-03/234-2011-07-20-21-49-03.html. See also: "'Bashar or Chaos': Syrian Regime's New Mantra," *Middle East Online*, June 5, 2011, https://middle-east-online.com/en/bashar-or-chaos-syrian-regimes-new-mantra.

79. Brian Merchant, "Is This the 19-Year-Old Leader of the Syrian Electronic Army?" *Motherboard*, Vice News, August 29, 2013, https://www.vice.com/en_us/article/4w7gmg/is-this-the-19-year-old-leader-of-the-syrian-electronic-army.

80. Fran Berkman, "Syrian Graphic Designer Denies Link to Syrian Electronic Army," *Mashable*, August 29, 2013, https://mashable.com/2013/08/29/syrian-denies-syrian-electronic-army/.

81. Franceschi-Bicchierai, "Syrian Electronic Army: If U.S. Attacks 'We Will Target All of It.'"

82. "Vice Website Hacked," Syrian Electronic Army, Wayback Machine, November 9, 2013, http://web.archive.org/web/20150524115424/http://sea.sy/article/id/2018/en.

83. "Computer Hacking Conspiracy Charges Unsealed Against Members of Syrian Electronic Army," United States Department of Justice Office of Public Affairs, March 22, 2016, https://www.justice.gov/opa/pr/computer-hacking-conspiracy-charges-unsealed-against-members-syrian-electronic-army.

84. "Cyber's Most Wanted," United States Federal Bureau of Investigation, https://www.fbi.gov/wanted/cyber.

85. *United States of America v. Ahmad Agha and Firas Dardar*, 1:14-mj-00292-TRJ (United States District Court for the Eastern District of Virginia, June 12, 2014). https://www.justice.gov/opa/file/834271/download.

86. Ibid.

87. *United States of America v. Peter Romar and Firas Dardar*, 1:15-mj-00498-MSn (United States District Court for the Eastern District of Virginia, September 29, 2015). https://www.justice.gov/opa/file/834276/download.

88. Ibid.

89. "Syrian Electronic Army Hacker Pleads Guilty," United States Department of Justice Office of Public Affairs, September 28, 2016, https://www.justice.gov/opa/pr/syrian-electronic-army-hacker-pleads-guilty.

90. Syrian Electronic Army, "True Caller Website/Database Hacked." See also: Syrian Electronic Army, "Tango App Website/Databases Hacked."

91. Ferran, "Interview With Alleged Member of Syrian Electronic Army."

92. Ibid.

93. Syrian Electronic Army, "SEA Story."

94. Ibid.

95. United States Department of Justice Office of Public Affairs, "Computer Hacking Conspiracy Charges Unsealed Against Members of Syrian Electronic Army."

96. Flossman and Del Rosso, "Under the SEA: A Look at the Syrian Electronic Army's Mobile Tooling." See also: Brewster, "Syrian Electronic Army Hackers are Targeting Android Phones with Fake WhatsApp Attacks."

CHAPTER SIX

DISINFORMATION IN THE GULF

JAMES SHIRES

INTRODUCTION

The flow of information is a fundamental part of politics. Democratic theory holds up a free and open public sphere — or as near to it as possible — as a central pillar of popular sovereignty, while studies of authoritarianism highlight domination of national narratives as well as political processes, and the suppression of alternative voices and individual freedoms. But such a stark dichotomy is misleading, as political actors in all forms of polity use information strategically. They seek to uncover information about their opponents and constituencies while keeping their own secrets, improvising within local contexts and constraints. New media technologies, and the new organizational ecologies they create, change these contexts, upsetting — or at least reshuffling — existing hierarchies. This is certainly the case for the internet, as global many-to-many communication and ubiquitous content creation have funneled capital into new arenas, and opened new spaces of identity and community.

However, internet content is a distorted mirror of society. This is not least due to individual "users," whose careful curation makes simple judgements of inauthenticity ring hollow, layered on a landscape of influencers, advertising, PR, and strong social pressure to conform. More recently, a powerful undercurrent of lies swirling under the foundations of political debate, with irregular eruptions of scandal and corruption, has become the norm.

Traditional media organizations, especially respected print journalism, have not been the bulwark against this tide that they were expected to be. While decrying the hegemony of media orthodoxy is nothing new — Antonio Gramsci's concept of "organic" intellectuals presaged the preference of contemporary political groups for their own experts or none — labels such as "mainstream media" are designed to discount and divide, not analyze. Appearance in a trustworthy source for one observer thus becomes proof of a conspiratorial lie for another. At the peak of this "post-truth" moment lies the concept of disinformation: deliberately created false information, sown to reap compliance or chaos.[1]

This chapter examines disinformation in the context of the Gulf crisis — the ostracization of Qatar led by the United Arab Emirates (UAE), Saudi Arabia, Bahrain, and Egypt that began in 2017 and continues to this day — to shed greater light on these issues. This is an important case for two reasons.

First, neo-patrimonial political systems, with elected assemblies wielding limited influence and social contracts premised on "rentier" distributions, present a stark contrast to European or U.S. fears of disinformation undermining democracy.[2] In the Gulf, hereditary royals seek to control and manipulate information flows, occupying multiple government and private sector positions while negotiating family and class dynamics.[3] At the same time, young, internet-connected populations have developed their own voices and identities, largely online.

Second, the Gulf crisis has revolved around both new social media networks and influential "traditional" media organizations, with Al-Jazeera and Saudi-owned alternatives entrenched across platforms, highly professionalized, and very partisan. The crisis also presents a political dilemma for multinational social network companies that regard themselves as defenders of free expression — technologies of liberation, even — especially after the Arab Spring.[4] Within the Gulf states, this chapter focuses on the key protagonists in the crisis: Qatar, Saudi Arabia, and the UAE. Disinformation — and in a strictly metaphorical sense, information warfare[5] — during the Gulf crisis promises to tell us not only about politics in the Gulf, but also about the challenges of defining and regulating internet content in the context of politics worldwide.

THE GULF CRISIS

The Gulf crisis took place in the context of wider tensions between Qatar and its surrounding states. From a historical perspective, interlaced familial and tribal relations across what is now Qatar and its neighbors have been the source of shared ties and disagreements for hundreds of years. In the process of British imperial retreat and modern state formation in the early 1970s, these differences crystalized into state borders, as Qatar and Bahrain remained separate from the consolidation of former Trucial states into the UAE. Tensions between Saudi Arabia and Qatar were prominent as alleged coup attempts in the 1990s and 2000s led to the removal of citizenship rights from thousands of Qataris under former Amir Hamad bin Khalifa al-Thani.[6] At the turn of the millennium, Qatar's independent media policy was a particular source of contention, with Al-Jazeera setting a new tone for political coverage of the region.[7] Al-Jazeera's dramatic reporting and sympathetic stance toward the Muslim Brotherhood appeared to contribute to revolutionary change in the 2011 Arab Spring protests in Tunisia and Egypt, leading to the station's characterization as a threat to the stability of the other Gulf monarchies, some of which also responded violently to protests in 2011.[8]

The central point of the Gulf crisis was the blockade or siege (*hisār*) led by Bahrain, Egypt, Saudi Arabia, and the UAE — known as the quartet states — imposed on June 5, 2017, during Ramadan. This blockade (referred to as a "rift" or "boycott" [*qaṭīʿah, maqāṭaʿa*] by the quartet states) was ostensibly in response to Qatar's support for terrorism, Iran, and general instability in the region. Some media reports suggested that this blockade was intended as a prelude to planned military action against

Qatar, and the swift approval of a Turkish military base in Qatar two days after the blockade was imposed lends some support to this theory — at least from the perspective of the Qatari Amir Sheikh Tamim bin Hamad al-Thani.[9] In addition to the blockade's significant effects on the domestic politics and economy of Qatar, and on the lives of individuals on both sides, it also ruptured the Gulf Cooperation Council (GCC) as an organization itself.

The U.S. was a key international participant in and audience for the Gulf crisis, specifically President Donald Trump, who visited Saudi Arabia from May 20-22, 2017. This visit, which was his first foreign trip as president, revolved around the opening of the Global Center for Combating Extremist Ideology (also known as *Etidal* or "moderation"), and Trump's speech focused on the dangers of terrorism to both the region and the U.S. On June 6, the day after the blockade was imposed, Trump tweeted that "During my recent trip to the Middle East I stated that there can no longer be funding of Radical Ideology. Leaders pointed to Qatar - look!"[10] Here Trump diverged from the foreign policy positions of both the legislative bodies of the U.S. government and his own appointed staff, in this case then-Secretary of State Rex Tillerson. Trump's other tweets suggest that the leaders he spoke to — including senior Saudi, Egyptian, and Emirati figures — raised Qatar's activity with him and potentially a planned response.[11] Of course, Trump's tweets are themselves a frequent source of disinformation, and therefore cannot necessarily be taken at face value.

The Gulf crisis has continued until the time of writing. There have been occasional indications of a thaw in relations, including a direct flight to Qatar by the Saudi Arabian soccer team, the restarting of postal services between Qatar and the UAE, and repeated attempts to engineer discussions between heads of state or senior ministers at GCC meetings, none of which has so far led to a restoration of relations.[12] The length of the dispute, its repercussions for regional stability and international alliances, and the depth of feeling it has engendered on both sides, notably including increased nationalism, distinguish it from many smaller diplomatic disagreements. The Gulf crisis is therefore a rich soil for disinformation, beginning with the events leading up to the blockade.

CYBER CATALYST

The Gulf crisis was catalyzed by a story about Sheikh Tamim on the website of Qatar News Agency (QNA) in May 2017, based on comments he purportedly made at an official ceremony on May 23. These included several controversial remarks, including a recognition of the "regional and Islamic prominence of Iran."[13] A speech purporting to be from the ceremony accompanied by the same comments on scrolling text aired on Saudi outlets Al-Arabiya and Al-Jazirah; however, there is no record of the video itself.[14]

The story was also disseminated by QNA-linked social media accounts, including alleged quotes from the Qatari foreign minister accusing Arab nations of a plot and withdrawing ambassadors from Bahrain, Egypt, Kuwait, Saudi Arabia, and the UAE.[15] QNA and the Qatari government quickly stated that the news story was not true, and around an hour after its first appearance it was removed from both the website and social media pages. However, media in the quartet states — especially Saudi newspapers *Al-Arabiya*, *Al-Riyadh*, *Al-Jazirah*, and *Okaz* — were swift to criticize the Qatari amir for these statements.[16]

This story was planted on the QNA website by a cyber operation, in an extreme case of what I have called elsewhere "hack-and-leak operations," with several stages.[17] The first stage was reconnaissance: enumerating the public areas of the QNA servers and seeking vulnerabilities in the webpages hosted on those servers, which — according to a Qatari investigation supported by the U.S. and U.K. government cybersecurity agencies — began on April 19 and was conducted through virtual private networks.[18] The next stage of the operation was to gain persistent access to QNA networks, which reportedly occurred on April 22. At 5:45am on April 22, a vulnerability enabling this access was "shared with another person through Skype from an iPhone with an IP address of one of the siege countries." The next stage was to escalate privileges and collect information. The end result was the collection of QNA employee credentials on April 28, which were shared over Skype with the same device that received the vulnerability details. The Qatari Ministry of Interior claimed that responders contained the intrusion by around 3:00am on May 24.

The QNA operation has been publicly attributed to the UAE government. In July 2017, *The Washington Post* reported that "senior members of the UAE government" met on May 23 to discuss a planned leak operation against QNA.[19] Further anonymous comments from two "Western officials" to a separate journalist indicated that these meetings were conducted by Mohammed bin Zayed, crown prince of Abu Dhabi.[20] Circumstantial technical details offer only limited support to this conclusion. On May 23, the usually low number of visits to the QNA website increased significantly, with most visits from IP addresses in the UAE. A different report, based on server logs, suggested that around 80 percent of visits originated in the UAE. One iPhone user — possibly the same one involved in the hack — was the first to access the story and returned to it repeatedly.[21] Further investigation identified a request for vulnerability scanning of the QNA website received by three Turkish companies from a UAE-registered company before the operation, leading to several arrests in Turkey.[22]

The QNA operation illustrates how disinformation lay at the heart of the Gulf crisis. If the attribution of the cyber operation to the UAE government is correct, then the deliberate dissemination of false news was designed to provide a pretext for diplomatic action. Furthermore, its coordinated reinforcement by sympathetic media, maintained even after Qatari efforts to correct the record, caused this disinformation to spread rapidly. The story grew further due to its resonance with already inflammatory issues and a receptive international audience in Trump. This case also demonstrates that disinformation overlaps significantly with other forms of adversarial information politics, including network intrusions.[23]

MEDIA CONTESTS

The political economy of Gulf media plays a crucial part in the production and spread of disinformation. Since the last decades of the 20th century, the Gulf states have exercised significant influence on media production in the region more broadly, in terms of both content — partly due to the revenues media companies collect from viewers in the Gulf — and ownership.

Large regional media conglomerations operate with varying degrees of independence depending on their connections to the ruling families and location (often outside the Gulf, in Beirut, Cairo, or London). These configurations change with political pressures and relationships; for example, in Saudi Arabia ownership of some outlets remains unclear following arrests of elite figures in November 2017.[24] Such relationships provide a crucial conduit for political influence on content. One Saudi editor has described how officials used a mobile phone messaging group to instruct journalists on how to shape coverage of the Gulf crisis, saying that such instructions "are orders, not suggestions."[25]

The Gulf states have also exploited the difference between placid local media and aggressive state-supported foreign channels to project regional standing and maintain domestic narratives of authority.[26] This has had a perceptible impact on public trust in media in the Gulf: A survey asking if people benefit from consuming news from foreign organizations saw a steep decrease in Qatar, from 51 percent agreement in 2015 to 40 percent in 2017 and 27 percent in 2019. In the UAE and Saudi Arabia, there was a similar dip in 2017, although the percentage of those agreeing recovered in 2019. General views of credibility of media *in that country* were more stable, although Qatari agreement was lower on average than that in the UAE or Saudi Arabia.[27]

Traditional media outlets have been enveloped by social media networks such as Twitter, WhatsApp, and Snapchat, which have high participation rates in the Gulf. Journalists — along with key political, religious, and cultural figures — promote themselves and their views on these networks, interacting with followers in a relatively spontaneous manner that is far removed from the dry pages of local broadsheets, with some limited space for criticism.[28] However, Gulf governments, like other authoritarian states worldwide — and, increasingly, democracies — have found many ways to manipulate the online world. Twitter in the Gulf is permeated by political interference, ranging from the completely artificial ("bot" networks of specially created or repurposed accounts) to the merely corralled (real people, paid or otherwise incentivized to act together), in addition to genuine supporters. This manipulation shapes what goes viral, who is influential, and — just as importantly — what is *not* said and *not* shared. Such suppression, amplification, and distraction has a complicated relationship with the economic interests of platform companies such as Facebook and Twitter: On one hand, their revenue and share price depend on user numbers and usage statistics, which at best do not discriminate against artificial manipulation and at worst encourage it; on the other hand, their liberal values and political pressure following interference in the 2016 U.S. presidential election have led to massive efforts to stem flows of disinformation on their platforms.

Social media manipulation occurred throughout the Gulf crisis.[29] As Jones has shown, a high proportion of all Twitter accounts that mentioned Qatar on May 27, 2017 were created that month, with other indications of a bot network also present, such as poor-quality profile images, few prior interactions, and use of Twitter's web client rather than mobile platform.[30] Most of these accounts retweeted anti-Qatar hashtags, artificially inflating their popularity and generating suspicion and misguided engagement from Qatari Twitter users. Some even masqueraded as Qatari public opinion despite a recorded location in Saudi Arabia. Many viral hashtags revolved around implausible news stories, and some bot accounts persisted for at least another year (some anti-Qatar networks were also observed by Jones in 2020).[31]

Other scholars have argued that the content of such Twitter storms — territorial disputes, Qatar's hosting of the World Cup in 2022, and gender discrimination — lasts far longer than the accounts themselves, with longer-term effects on political discourse.[32] In particular, Abrahams and Leber have traced the relationship between genuine support and artificial influence in the case of Saud al-Qahtani, former advisor to Saudi Crown Prince Mohammed bin Salman.[33] They argue that al-Qahtani's influential role on Twitter among Saudi users was just as important as artificial amplification in fomenting anti-Qatar sentiment. Finally, supposedly leaked content assists disinformation, as it provides an important source of propaganda and adds to its credibility. The Gulf crisis saw the creation of several websites designed to support the position of the quartet states, notably "The Qatar Insider" and "Qatarileaks," as well as "Emiratesleaks," a mirror site hosting leaked and negative stories about the UAE.

The shaping of public opinion through favorable news coverage and suppression of alternative perspectives is not new in the Gulf; the novelty here is in the range of techniques deployed to manufacture and disseminate disinformation, especially on social media, and the willingness of political actors to improvise and experiment, repeating what works and ignoring criticism. However, the efforts of regulatory actors to define disinformation as *verifiably* false information are likely to run aground in this volatile environment, because a common standard of verification is almost impossible to achieve. In the final section of this chapter, I examine one such instance.

SATELLITE SIGNALS

The case of beIN sports is instructive for studies of disinformation, as it involves false information on both sides of the Gulf divide and represents a concerted technical and policy effort to verify the facts of the case. beIN is a subsidiary of Al-Jazeera, which was banned in Saudi Arabia after the imposition of the blockade. beIN owns the rights to a wide range of international sporting events, including the 2018 World Cup in Russia. The blocking of Al-Jazeera applied also to beIN, leaving Saudi audiences without a popular source of entertainment including European soccer and Formula 1 racing.

At the start of the blockade, an alternative channel named PBS Sports was advertised by prominent Saudi figures, including Saud al-Qahtani, with rumors of negotiations with Egyptian media and a reported location at the Saudi Media City in Riyadh.[34] Al-Qahtani and sports journalist Abdulaziz al-Mriseul also tweeted oblique suggestions that Saudi audiences should stream pirated versions of sports matches (these tweets were later deleted).[35] In August 2017, the channel "beoutQ" — an apparent reference to the Qatar split — appeared, streaming the same content as beIN over the internet for the first few months and then offering its own set-top boxes with satellite reception, which al-Mriseul offered as prizes on Twitter.[36] beoutQ provided beIN content for two years until August 2019, including the 2018 World Cup. Social media engagement with beoutQ was high and very polarized, with disbelief and anger from Qataris and mocking humor from supportive — mainly Saudi — users, as well as extensive rumors and disinformation.

beIN attempted to prove that beoutQ was connected to the Saudi government in several ways. First, it identified an Arabsat satellite as the source of beoutQ broadcasts by commissioning technical reports of tests with beoutQ set-top boxes in Saudi Arabia. Arabsat, although an Arab League organization, is headquartered in Saudi Arabia, which is also its largest investor. A French court ruled in 2019 that Arabsat was the source of beoutQ broadcasts, based on these technical reports, but did not find Arabsat responsible.[37] Second, beIN identified payments made by Raed Khushaim, head of Saudi company Selevision, for U.S. servers used by beoutQ, while documents shown on an Al-Jazeera investigative documentary suggested that Selevision had a contract with the Saudi government to operate the Saudi Media City Company.[38] Third, beIN used further technical reports to argue that beoutQ was a sophisticated operation aimed solely at Saudi Arabia, using several layers of geofencing to prevent users outside Saudi Arabia from accessing streamed content, with specific beIN set-top boxes exploited to obtain codes to access beIN content.[39] However, none of these methods succeeded. The Saudi government denied any involvement in June 2018, claiming that it obeys all relevant copyright legislation, as well as highlighting its seizure of beoutQ set-top boxes and denouncing the accusations as a "smear campaign."[40]

beIN and the Qatari government then resorted to multiple legal and policy avenues to connect the Saudi Arabian government to beoutQ. Qatar brought a World Trade Organization claim against Saudi Arabia and an international arbitration for $1 billion in damages.[41] Friendly governments highlighted the issue, including those of the E.U., the U.K., and the U.S.[42] Commercial pressures also mounted, as copyright and IP bodies joined recipients of beIN's large license fees to highlight beoutQ's relationship to Saudi Arabia.[43] Qatar then arrested three employees of beIN, accusing them of espionage with a senior Saudi intelligence official and media figures linked to Egyptian intelligence agencies.[44] This pressure was eventually successful, as in June 2020 the World Trade Organization ruled in favor of Qatar. The tribunal dismissed Saudi Arabia's argument that the case concerned only national security matters and therefore was not properly a trade dispute at all, and instead found that Saudi Arabia had infringed international trade agreements by not permitting legal action against beoutQ in Saudi Arabia.[45]

However, the campaign against beoutQ itself tipped into disinformation. On the legitimate side of the fine line between biased, strategically produced content and disinformation were the glossy technical reports cited above. Closer to the edge is the website beoutq.tv, which aggregates information about the case with hyperbolic language but generally transparent sourcing. The Al-Jazeera documentary fits in the same bracket: partisan, but with clear sourcing and unsurprisingly close access to candid Qatari interviews and documents. But the publicity campaign against beoutQ also included what disinformation detection company Graphika called "Operation Red Card," a group of accounts across platforms operated by an Indian PR firm that used disinformation techniques such as false content and artificial accounts.[46] Soccer was among a variety of pro-Qatar and anti-Saudi Arabia themes in this campaign, including the 2022 World Cup and "TV soccer piracy in Saudi Arabia."

Overall, efforts across multiple Qatari government agencies, media organizations, and other supportive commercial actors to counter beoutQ and maintain an internationally recognized — and favorable — standard of truth eventually included disinformation tactics mirroring those of their opponents. This risks undermining Qatar's carefully constructed and expensive — in terms of both political and financial capital — coalition against information manipulation, and demonstrates the difficulty of finding common factual ground and a clear distinction between disinformation creators and those they target.

CONCLUSION

Politics in the Gulf states, especially around the Qatar split, is an important case for disinformation studies. This chapter has traced how the Gulf crisis began with a cyber operation designed to spread disinformation as a pretext for the blockade. It then argued that media contests in the Gulf display innovative and improvisational uses of disinformation as part of efforts to exert control over a volatile information sphere. Finally, it examined the internationalization of disinformation, with a sports piracy disagreement morphing into an international test of truth claims, and an opportunity for both sides to exploit the grey area between paid publicity and disinformation. Overall, this chapter has suggested that the extensive effects of the Gulf crisis may partly be due to the persistent presence of disinformation, especially the extent to which such content first divided and then cemented public opinion on both sides.

However, it is necessary also to recognize what this chapter has left unaddressed. It has not considered the relationship between disinformation and surveillance, even though internet monitoring is a key component of information controls. It has also not analyzed the development of legal structures to combat disinformation in the Gulf, such as cybercrime and media laws, nor their appropriation and misuse.[47] Finally, and to return to the metaphorical concept of information warfare invoked at the start of this chapter, the political impacts of disinformation in the Gulf crisis pale in comparison to the damage, suffering, and loss caused by severe conflicts elsewhere in the region, including in Yemen, Iraq, Syria, and Libya. A less metaphorical analysis of information warfare would focus instead on the use of social media in these conflicts, in which the Gulf states are central players. However, these exclusions were in service of the central argument of this chapter: that the concept of disinformation is both necessary, because it depicts an empirically well-documented phenomenon with substantial political effects in the Gulf, but also problematic, because it implies shared standards of verifiability and factual agreement not evident in entrenched political divides, and is itself open to cooption and manipulation.

Endnotes

1. European Commission, "A Multi-Dimensional Approach to Disinformation: Report of the Independent High Level Group on Fake News and Online Disinformation" (Luxembourg: European Commission Directorate-General for Communication Networks, Content and Technology, March 2018), pp.10-11.
2. For a more nuanced examination of these political systems see the recent special issue of the *British Journal of Middle East Studies*, 47, no.1 (2020), edited by Makio Yamada and Stefan Hertog, on "Revisiting rentierism: the changing political economy of resource-dependent states in the Gulf and Arabian Peninsula."
3. Adam Hanieh, *Money, Markets, and Monarchies: The Gulf Cooperation Council and the Political Economy of the Contemporary Middle East* (New York: Cambridge University Press, 2018).
4. Gholam Khiabany, "Technologies of Liberation and/or Otherwise," *International Journal of Middle East Studies* 47, no. 2 (2015): 348–53; for further discussion, see Neil Ketchley, *Egypt in a Time of Revolution* (Cambridge, England; New York: Cambridge University Press, 2017), pp.158-159.
5. Tarek Cherkaoui, "A New Kind of Information Warfare? Cyber-Conflict and the Gulf Crisis 2010-2017," *The Political Economy of Communication* 6, no.1 (2018); Ahmed Al-Rawi, "Cyberconflict, Online Political Jamming, and Hacking in the Gulf Cooperation Council," *International Journal of Communication* 13 (2019): 1301–22.
6. Mehran Kamrava, *Qatar: Small State, Big Politics* (Ithaca: Cornell University Press, 2013), p.111.
7. Marc Lynch, *Voices of the New Arab Public: Iraq, Al-Jazeera, and Middle East Politics Today* (New York, NY: Columbia University Press, 2007); Mohamed Zayani and Sofiane Sahraoui, *The Culture of Al Jazeera: Inside an Arab Media Giant* (Jefferson, N.C: McFarland & Co, 2007).
8. Toby Matthiesen, *Sectarian Gulf: Bahrain, Saudi Arabia and the Arab Spring That Wasn't* (Stanford, California: Stanford University Press, 2013).
9. Alex Emmons, "Saudi Arabia Planned to Invade Qatar Last Summer. Rex Tillerson's Efforts to Stop It May Have Cost Him His Job," *The Intercept*, August 1, 2018, https://perma.cc/A2LK-QUJV; Gulsen Solaker and Tom Finn, 'Turkey Throws Support behind Qatar in Rift with Gulf Arabs," *Reuters*, June 7, 2017, https://perma.cc/D8AB-2P2E.
10. Donald J. Trump, "During My Recent Trip to the Middle East I Stated That There Can No Longer Be Funding of Radical Ideology. Leaders Pointed to Qatar - Look!," Tweet, @realDonaldTrump, June 6, 2017, https://perma.cc/A7TG-ZKTV.
11. Karen DeYoung and Sudarsan Raghavan, "Trump Seems to Undercut Tillerson's Remarks on Qatar." *Washington Post*, June 9, 2017, https://perma.cc/PU6M-BUJG.
12. Alexander Cornwall, "Saudi-Qatar Talks to End Lengthy Gulf Dispute Falter: Sources," *Reuters*, February 11, 2020, https://www.reuters.com/article/us-gulf-qatar-idUSKBN2050Z8.
13. Staff Report, "*qaṭar tashuqqu al-ṣaf wa tanḥāzu al-'idā' al-'umma*" [Qatar breaks ranks and sides with enemies of the people]," *Okaz*, May 24, 2017, https://perma.cc/AXR4-SN89.
14. Zahraa Alkhalisi, "Qatar 'Fake News' Spat Divides Arab Media." *CNN Money*. May 25, 2017. https://perma.cc/8ET9-URUP.
15. Jon Gambrell, "Hack, Fake Story Expose Real Tensions between Qatar, Gulf," *AP News*, May 24, 2017, https://perma.cc/G4JF-BPGN.
16. MEMRI, "Uproar In The Gulf Following Alleged Statements By Qatari Emir Condemning Gulf States, Praising Iran, Hizbullah, Muslim Brotherhood And Hamas," Middle East Media Research Institute Inquiry and Analysis Series No.1315, May 25, 2017, https://perma.cc/SUK8-YHDK.
17. James Shires, "Hack-and-Leak Operations: Intrusion and Influence in the Gulf," *Journal of Cyber Policy* 4, no. 2 (2019): 235–56; James Shires, "The Cyber Operation against Qatar News Agency" in *The Gulf Crisis: Origins, Implications, Repercussions*, ed. Mahjoob Zweiri (Berlin Heidelberg: Springer Nature, forthcoming).
18. Ayman Adly, "Qatar presents proof of UAE role in QNA website hacking," *Gulf Times*, July 20, 2017, https://perma.cc/KFK9-DR3P.
19. Karen DeYoung and Ellen Nakashima, "UAE Orchestrated Hacking of Qatari Government Sites, Sparking Regional Upheaval, According to U.S. Intelligence Officials," *Washington Post*, July 16, 2017, https://perma.cc/TJ8D-8ZSE.

20. Peter Salisbury, "The Fake-News Hack That Nearly Started a War This Summer Was Designed for One Man: Donald Trump," *Quartz*, October 20, 2017, https://perma.cc/4ZA2-7JZA.

21. The Qatari Ministry of Interior press conference suggested that they located the iPhone in the UAE due to not only the IP address, which can be misleading, but also the details of the network (i.e. a UAE mobile carrier) and the type of iPhone itself. For further details see Adly and Salisbury, above.

22. Sean Gallagher, "UAE Buys Its Way toward Supremacy in Gulf Cyberwar, Using US and Israeli Experts," *Ars Technica*, February 1, 2019, https://perma.cc/Q89F-Y6FC.

23. James Shires, "Cybersecurity Governance in the GCC" in *Rewired: Cybersecurity Governance*, ed. Ryan Ellis and Vivek Mohan (Wiley-Blackwell, 2019).

24. Kristin Smith Diwan, "Mohammed Bin Salman's Media Obsession – and What It Means for Dissent," *Arab Gulf States Institute in Washington*, October 30, 2018, https://agsiw.org/mohammed-bin-salmans-media-obsessed-and-what-it-means-for-dissent/

25. Ahmed Al Omran, "Gulf Media Unleashes War of Words with Qatar," *Financial Times*, August 4, 2017, https://perma.cc/Q4DE-G8NB.

26. Mohamed Zayani, "Transnational Media, Regional Politics and State Security: Saudi Arabia between Tradition and Modernity," *British Journal of Middle Eastern Studies* 39, no.3 (2012): 307–27.

27. Survey conducted by Northwestern University in Qatar. http://www.mideastmedia.org/survey/2019/

28. Robert Uniacke, "Authoritarianism in the Information Age: State Branding, Depoliticizing and 'de-Civilizing' of Online Civil Society in Saudi Arabia and the United Arab Emirates," *British Journal of Middle Eastern Studies*, 2020, 1–21.

29. Ben Nimmo, "Robot Wars: How Bots Joined Battle in the Gulf," *Journal of International Affairs* 71, no.1.5 (2018): 87–96.

30. Marc Owen Jones, "Propaganda, Fake News, and Fake Trends: The Weaponization of Twitter Bots in the Gulf Crisis," *International Journal of Communication* 13 (2019): 27.

31. Marc Owen Jones, "Saudi Arabia's Bot Army Flourishes as Twitter Fails to Tame the Beast," *Middle East Eye*, January 20, 2020. https://www.middleeasteye.net/opinion/despite-twitter-culls-riyadhs-disinformation-network-still-going-strong

32. Jocelyn Sage Mitchell, "#Blockade: Social Media and the Gulf Diplomatic Crisis," *Review of Middle East Studies* 53, no.2 (2019): 200–220.

33. Andrew Leber and Alexei Abrahams, "A Storm of Tweets: Social Media Manipulation During the Gulf Crisis," *Review of Middle East Studies* 53, no.2 (2019): 241–58.

34. Dima Muhammad, "*iṭlāq 'awwalīi qanawāt "PBS Sports" al-riyaḍiyya al-jadida* [First launch of new sports channel 'PBS Sports']," *Al-'ain*, June 20, 2017, https://perma.cc/2Z6M-P3G9.

35. Staff Report, "*munāfis "beIN sports" yuwaddi'u… 'ighlāq qanāa "PBS Sports" al-sa'ūdiyya qabla bid'iha* [Rival to 'beIN Sports' leaves… closure of Saudi 'PBS Sports' channel before it starts]," *Raṣd*, June 22, 2017, https://perma.cc/7N67-UV9K; Staff Report, "'*beoutQ'… qarṣana 'i'lāmiyya mafḍūḥa lidawl al-ḥisār tastahdifu 'beIN Sports*' ['beoutQ'… scandalous media piracy by the siege countries targets 'beIN Sports']," *Al-'arabī*, August 7, 2017, https://perma.cc/9DD3-9ABA.

36. See various tweets from his account @almriseul7 (in Arabic) at https://perma.cc/7T5S-8XV6. His other account @almriseul only tweeted an official denial in September 2017: https://perma.cc/Z72U-MDZV.

37. Gwenaelle Barzic et al, "French Court Sees No 'Clear and Illegal Disruption' in Gulf Sports Piracy Case," *Reuters*, June 28, 2019, https://perma.cc/3XFC-BG3F.

38. Philip H. Kang and Ash Nagdev, "Declaration of [Redacted] Case No. 17CV316099, BeIN IP Ltd., Plaintiff, vs. BeoutQ, Saudi Selevision Company LLC, Raed Reda Hassan Khusheim and DOES 1-20, Inclusive, Defendants." (Superior Court for the State of California for the County of Santa Clara, 2018); "*al-qiṣat al-qarṣanat al-sa'ūdiyya liqanāa 'beIN Sports'* [The story of Saudi piracy of 'beIN Sports']," *mā khafīi 'a'ẓam [What Lies Beneath]* (Qatar: Al-Jazeera, September 22, 2019).

39. MarkMonitor, "BeoutQ Investigation," April 2019.

40. Staff Report, "GCAM Rejects Wimbledon's Accusations That BeoutQ Is Based in Saudi Arabia," *Okaz*, July 7, 2018, https://perma.cc/2PXC-7S87; Staff Report, "Ministry of Media

Rejects UEFA's 'Irresponsible Accusations' of BeoutQ Being Based in Saudi Arabia," *Arab News*, June 23, 2018, https://perma.cc/4RZK-TWDH.

41. State of Qatar, "Saudi Arabia — Measures Concerning the Protection of Intellectual Property Rights (WT/DS567). Qatar's First Written Submission" (World Trade Organization, 2019); Sidley Austin LLP, "Notice of Arbitration: BeIN Corporation v. Kingdom of Saudi Arabia," October 1, 2018.

42. Staff Report, "Report on the Protection and Enforcement of Intellectual Property Rights in Third Countries," working document (Brussels: European Commission, March 8, 2020), p.42; Alistair Carmichael, "Intellectual Property Rights - Hansard" (UK Parliament, April 25, 2019), Volume 658, Column 910514, House of Commons Hansard; Office of the US Trade Representative, "Special 301 Report" (Washington, D.C: USTR, April 2019), p.10.

43. Press Release, "Joint Statement by FIFA, the AFC, UEFA, the Bundesliga, LaLiga, the Premier League and Serie A Regarding the Activities of BeoutQ in Saudi Arabia," Lawinsport, July 31, 2019, https://perma.cc/P2PS-646B.

44. Staff Report, "*kaif altaqaṭat al-sulṭāt al-qaṭariyya al-khaiṭ alladhī ʾasqaṭa khaliyya qarṣana beIN Sports* [how the Qatari authorities followed the thread that brought down the cell pirating beIN Sports]," *Al-Shārq*, September 23, 2019, https://perma.cc/L67X-UFHT.

45. Murad Ahmed, "WTO Piracy Ruling Raises New Doubt over Saudi Takeover of Newcastle," *Financial Times*, June 16, 2020, https://perma.cc/5DSU-Q7X5.

46. Ben Nimmo et al, "Operation Red Card" (Graphika, March 2020). An example of anti-piracy content is in Facebook's February 2020 Coordinated Inauthentic Behaviour (CIB) report, p.6.

47. James Shires, "Ambiguity and Appropriation: Cybercrime in Egypt and the Gulf" in *Responsible Behaviour in Cyberspace*, ed. Dennis Broeders (London: Rowman & Littlefield Publishers, Inc., forthcoming).

CHAPTER SEVEN

OPERATION GLOWING SYMPHONY:

THE MISSING PIECE IN THE US ONLINE COUNTER-ISIS CAMPAIGN

MICHAEL MARTELLE AND AUDREY ALEXANDER

INTRODUCTION

The U.S. government has leveraged a range of mechanisms to combat the influence of ISIS in the digital sphere. One that deserves further discussion and analysis is the support from the U.S. Cyber Command (USCYBERCOM) for Operation Inherent Resolve (OIR) via Joint Task Force Ares (JTF Ares) and Operation Glowing Symphony. Most interagency efforts to counter the proliferation of extremist messaging online over the last few years have received significant attention from policymakers, practitioners, and scholars who scrutinized methods, debated effectiveness, and highlighted good practices. To some degree, this discourse was possible because initiatives unfolded in clear view of the public. Meanwhile, USCYBERCOM developed concurrent efforts behind closed doors in support of OIR.

Due to the sensitivity of operations to target ISIS' networks, publicly available information about the work was comparatively limited. Consequently, the process of evaluating such measures was restrained. Now, as details about JTF Ares and Operation Glowing Symphony become publicly available, researchers can work to understand USCYBERCOM efforts, and examine how they align with other contemporary approaches attempting to curb the influence of ISIS online, and produce a more complete picture of U.S. efforts to counter extremism on the internet.

THE HISTORICAL BACKDROP OF CONTEMPORARY CHALLENGES AND PRIOR INTERAGENCY EFFORTS

Although ISIS undoubtedly presented unique challenges for counterterrorism policymakers and practitioners in the digital arena, the U.S. government already faced issues concerning terrorist exploitation of the internet and communications technologies before its rise. While the American far-right pioneered the use of computer networks to promote its worldview, a variety of groups have embraced the potential of various platforms.[1]

These tools have proven attractive to violent extremist groups because of their potential to cheaply enhance an organization's capabilities in content production and dissemination, recruitment, fundraising, and planning.[2] The benefits afforded to terrorists through information and communications technologies were a growing cause for concern in the eyes of the U.S. government by the mid-to-late 2000s. In addition to the challenges arising from wars in Iraq and Afghanistan, groups like al-Shabaab and al-Qaeda in the Arabian Peninsula also posed distinct dangers.[3] Although U.S. military, intelligence, and law enforcement were critical to detecting and disrupting terrorist plots, there was a growing desire to leverage other methods to curb recruitment internationally.[4] Strategic communications, an essential instrument that the U.S. wielded in past conflicts, became a more prominent part of the government's counterterrorism toolkit.

Interagency efforts between the U.S. Department of Defense (DoD) and the State Department on the matter of counterterrorism communications lacked cohesion from the start. This issue — fueled by competing perspectives between the agencies, legal limitations, and inconsistent funding — led to the recasting and rebranding of the entity intended to counter terrorism with strategic messaging every few years.[5] One analyst synthesizes this process, explaining that "each manifestation signaled the failure of the previous version to achieve meaningful gains or survive bureaucratic infighting."[6] In 2011, as the State Department's Center for Strategic Counterterrorism Communications (CSCC) came onto the scene, concerns about the role of information and communications technologies were still mounting quickly.[7] By that point, several designated terrorist groups were developing more pronounced messaging efforts, promoting propaganda featuring U.S. persons, catering to Western audiences, and experimenting with social media.[8] These factors and the supposed effects they had on the mobilization of sympathizers, including "homegrown violent extremists," fueled calls for a stronger policy response.[9]

The government's multi-administration effort to use counter-speech and influence operations to alter the attitudes of foreign audiences faced several limitations, including bureaucratic constraints, as it grew online. Between 2012 and 2014, the CSCC experimented with a range of messaging efforts to influence non-English-language foreign audiences online.[10] By then, however, ISIS and other terrorist organizations were using English-language content to reach Western and American audiences.[11] When the CSCC used English in its efforts to respond to this problem, like the "Think Again, Turn Away" counter-messaging campaign on social media, it drew a deluge of attention and criticism.[12] The downward trajectory of earlier iterations of the body became an inevitable path for the CSCC and its "Think Again, Turn Away" campaign, at least in part because bureaucratic limitations affected the scope and agility of its counter-messaging efforts. The U.S. government still lacked a comprehensive response to extremist use of the internet as the threat posed by ISIS escalated.

At this point in the chronology, from around 2013-16, it is essential to deconstruct the capabilities of ISIS and its members to better contextualize developments in U.S. policies to counter the group in cyberspace. This chapter will consider three facets of ISIS' online activities: (1) the production and distribution of propaganda; (2) the mobilization of recruits and facilitation of physical operations; and (3) the posturing, planning, and execution of network attack operations.

The following paragraphs detail the scope of each category, then turn back to the evolution of policy responses to these issues.

The production and distribution of propaganda are among ISIS' most notorious and distinguishable lines of effort. Even before the organization formally declared the caliphate in 2014, it used promotional materials to engage a global audience.[13] Recognized for its professionalized but jarring content, which made it a fierce competitor for entities trying to counter the group's influence, ISIS' messaging efforts required significant resources and planning.[14] An analysis of internal documents captured from the group casts ISIS' media organization as a bureaucratic entity focused on creating quality products and controlling ISIS' image while simultaneously emphasizing the operational security of its operatives.[15] Entities within ISIS' formalized media apparatus have delivered content in a variety of formats including videos, photo reports, audio releases, and text-based publications such as newsletters and magazines over the years.[16] In doing so, ISIS attracted a global base of sympathizers that consumed, redistributed, and engaged with said material.

In addition to propaganda production and dissemination, ISIS leveraged information and communications technologies to mobilize recruits and facilitate terrorist operations. Whether issuing guidance to foreigners on traveling to ISIS-controlled territory, or coordinating plans for an attack, logistics-related uses of information and communications technologies were troubling for counterterrorism policymakers and practitioners. The cases of so-called "virtual entrepreneurs," meaning operatives in jihadist-held territory with links to external terrorist plots, offer poignant illustrations of this phenomenon.[17] Among the handful of well-known virtual entrepreneurs, ISIS member Junaid Hussain was known for his efforts to compel sympathizers in the U.S. to conduct attacks.[18] Other notable facilitators sought to mobilize supporters in Europe and South-East Asia.

The third category of ISIS cyber capabilities discussed in this chapter relates to the posturing, planning, and execution of network attack operations. On this point it is critical to note that a disconnect emerges between ISIS' projection of its abilities compared to its demonstrated skills.[20] In some scenarios, alleged ISIS members conducted activities made to look more technically advanced than they were, though such actions were still concerning.[21] On several occasions, members of the group defaced websites and doxxed individuals by publishing personally identifiable information (PII) on "kill lists."[22] At least one of these lists was populated using more sophisticated techniques, as Ardit Ferizi, a Kosovar national and hacker, illegally accessed a server for a U.S.-based company and stole the PII of store patrons, including mailing addresses, email addresses, phone numbers, and passwords.[23] Ferizi created a list of 1,351 U.S. government and military personnel by searching the PII for .gov and .mil accounts.[24] Ferizi sent the file to Hussain, who published the list online "in the name of the Islamic State Hacking Division."[25] In a 2017 interview, the National Counterterrorism Center's former acting director for intelligence, Lora Shiao, explained that ISIS' hacking ability was relatively limited. She noted that ISIS members "deface[d] websites" and disseminated "hit lists" of PII on Westerners, primarily for the sake of intimidation.[26] ISIS members are ultimately adept at stoking fear online, even though their technical capabilities are not typically particularly advanced.[27]

With this overview of ISIS' online capabilities established, it is easier to reflect on the scale of the problem, the nature of the U.S. government's response, and security gaps that likely contributed to subsequent policy developments, including USCYBERCOM support to OIR. By 2015 the law enforcement and intelligence communities faced a variety of challenges associated with ISIS' exploitation of internet technology, and they worked to detect and disrupt efforts to support ISIS in the U.S. and abroad.[28] The State Department's CSCC, meanwhile, was not suited to confront ISIS messaging online. Counter-speech efforts alone were not likely to adequately address the facilitation of terrorist operations or the execution of network attack operations. The tumultuous year ended with attacks on Western targets, including in November 2015 in Paris, France and in December 2015 in San Bernardino, California.[29] These events pushed the U.S. government to take a more offensive posture against ISIS online.

In the wake of these attacks, the CSCC was retooled and transformed into the Global Engagement Center (GEC).[30] The Obama administration, along with the State Department and other government agencies, sought alternative means to combat the persistent threat of violent extremism online. The GEC supported two complementary lines of effort, which included shifting toward government-sponsored, not government-run, counterterrorism communications for foreign audiences, and integrating the private sector to help counter violent extremist messaging and ideologies abroad. Concerning the former, the GEC aimed to promote more credible, non-governmental actors to reach their audiences with more persuasive messaging. As an example, the GEC sought to "counter ISIS propaganda by creating a network of regional messaging centers," like the Sawab Center in the United Arab Emirates, to position more compelling voices against radicalization in the digital sphere and beyond.[31] To further the impact of said communications, the Obama administration, along with the GEC and other government entities, reached out to the technology, advertising, and entertainment industries for help.[32] An initiative called the Madison Valleywood Project encouraged these industries to assist in the fight against terrorism by producing and promoting counter-speech, and enforcing terms of services.[33]

While facets of the U.S. government developed the measures discussed above, the DoD had already started thinking about how to curb threats emanating from ISIS-controlled territory, particularly in cyberspace. Despite efforts to leverage counter-messaging and private industry against ISIS, practitioners in law enforcement, intelligence, and the military had enduring concerns about the influence of ISIS operations online.[34] Since existing initiatives did not target all the ways ISIS exploited the digital sphere, it was necessary to develop supplementary methods to mitigate these threats. Details about such developments are still coming to light, but behind the scenes the DoD discussed the prospect of USCYBERCOM support to OIR in March 2015. That month, according to a presentation by two FBI employees, Hussain released the "names, photos, unit assignments, and addresses of 100 US military members" under the banner of the "Islamic State Hacking Division."[35] Although it is unclear whether Hussain's March 2015 "kill list" played a role in early discussions about USCYBERCOM support to OIR at the DoD, Hussain and his affiliates' subsequent publication of additional lists and links to several U.S.-based terrorist plots were not inconsequential.[36] Evidence indicates that actions by Hussain's network, which were closely monitored by the FBI because of the cohort's efforts to mobilize Americans, led the FBI to "[press] the military to focus on the group."[37] In August 2015, Hussain was killed in a drone strike, but one FBI official said in a 2016 interview, "We are still dealing with the repercussions of that development" and the "recruitment of that network."[38] When high-profile attacks in Europe and the U.S. persisted, along with a range of other threats, the U.S. began to shift its footing to more proactively combat ISIS online by the start of 2016.

USCYBERCOM "CLEARED HOT"

The increased role of the DoD in countering online extremism began in March 2015, when USCYBERCOM issued Operation Order (OPORD) 15-0055 outlining for the first time plans to provide direct military cyber support[39] to OIR. This order sought to address ISIS' use of cyberspace "as a means to maintain situational awareness, direct and support combat forces and disseminate propaganda and media." The language of the declassified order did not explicitly call for offensive cyber operations at that point, but ordered general support to the goals of OIR and U.S. Central Command commanders with measures including defensive cyber operations, force protection, and command and control capabilities. The last of these could be interpreted to encompass offensive cyber operations targeting ISIS internal communications, but OPORD 15-0055 stopped short of calling for cyber operations beyond direct support to other military actions.[40]

ISIS' escalation in attacks and associated online media campaigns throughout 2015 led to increased pressure on and from U.S. leadership to counter ISIS activity. Members of a joint USCYBERCOM/National Security Agency (NSA) team, formed in 2014 to gather intelligence from ISIS networks, began developing a plan to disrupt the systems they had been observing. In a podcast interview a USCYBERCOM mission commander who worked on the initiative said they "were ready at a tactical level" to execute more independent disruptive operations in cyberspace, but "there wasn't that appetite at higher levels." Appetite grew for USCYBERCOM to take a more prominent role in the nation's response to ISIS after Secretary of Defense Ashton Carter called a meeting around Christmas 2015 and asked for options in response to the escalating challenge.[41]

Planning for what would become Operation Glowing Symphony started in February 2016 after the USCYBERCOM mission commander began noticing critical vulnerabilities in the ISIS media enterprise. The same officer began to convince his superiors that the ISIS media network was "a house of cards" because the entire network could be affected if an entity targeted just a few critical nodes.[42] To execute this mission under the military's Title 10 authorities[43] USCYBERCOM recommended the formation of a JTF.[44]

In May 2016, USCYBERCOM issued Tasking Order 16-0063 ordering the establishment of JTF Ares. This force was formed from the cyber components of each military service and placed under the command of the U.S. Army's top cyber commander (Gen. Edward Cardon at the time, and Gen. Paul Nakasone as of October of the same year). The task force was assigned "to counter the Islamic State in Iraq and the Levant in cyberspace."[45] In keeping with the scope outlined in OPORD 15-0055, JTF Ares was not limited to the OIR battleground regions of Iraq and Syria. In other words, this would be an international campaign.

During the summer of 2016, JTF Ares successfully executed a small-scale attack on a portion of an ISIS network to prove the viability of the counter-media concept. After this trial operation Gen. Timothy Haugh, the deputy commander of JTF Ares, asked the team for the next steps. The mission commander was confident: "Let's go global."[46] A concept of operations for Operation Glowing Symphony was issued by September.[47] According to the mission commander, "What we saw with GLOWING SYMPHONY was an opportunity to give a massive blow to their operation, to take down everything that we could as fast as we could in one go, and then see what's left, and then pick apart the little pieces that were left, the remnants that remained [...] and then maintain engagement with the enemy through until they were no longer."[48]

Debates raged at the national level before the mission could be approved, worrying the operators whose hard-earned access to target networks could disappear at any moment. The late-2015 call for escalation against ISIS came as USCYBERCOM's Cyber Mission Force was approaching, but had not yet reached, the milestone of initial operational capability,[49] and more than two years before reaching full operational capability. Questions persisted as to whether USCYBERCOM was up to what would be the largest Title 10 offensive cyber operation to date so early in the command's development.[50] There were also concerns over providing notification to governments before attacking ISIS targets hosted on infrastructure within their borders.

Two needs were in tension: maintaining operational security and tempo versus minimizing political fallout. USCYBERCOM and the DoD argued that OPORD 15-0055 already granted the authority to operate against such targets without notification, allowing for rapid execution, and that maintaining secrecy maximized the likelihood of mission success. Other members of the National Security Council (NSC), still reeling from the impact the Edward Snowden leak had on intergovernmental trust, feared the risk to the multinational partnerships on which their own counter-ISIS missions relied should news of U.S. cyber operations in other countries once again become public.[51] The question was ultimately settled in favor of notification, but not until it had delayed the launch of Operation Glowing Symphony by two months.[52]

As the operation neared execution, preparations had been made for four teams[53] to disrupt 10 to 15 targets each as quickly as possible.[54] The rapidity at the outset of the operation was crucial in preventing ISIS operators from being able to react, recover, and prevent further USCYBERCOM assaults.[55] Each team had four members. One member was the operator working at the keyboard to communicate with and control the team's malware and tools on target systems. A signal intelligence development analyst supported the operator, and served as an expert in how target networks are configured and used. This pair's technical expertise was supplemented by an intelligence analyst, who studied the target organization and individuals, and "[got] to know these guys down to such detail that they can anticipate what these guys are going to do before they actually do it." These three members, likely senior-enlisted with several years of expertise, were led and coordinated by a team leader, likely an officer.[56]

Once the teams were assembled and given their assignments, they waited for final approval to come through their chain of command from the NSC. In November 2016, the order to begin taking down targets that had been under observation for up to a year and a half was given on an operations floor in Ft. Meade, Maryland. Operation Glowing Symphony was functional.[57] The first inkling of success came quickly for the USCYBERCOM mission commander. He said, "We had control and we knew at that point that they couldn't stop us and we stayed on for the next two to four hours going through the rest of the target list but at that point … we could take our time and we knew that they couldn't take it back from us. It was like, they were totally pwned after ten minutes." Glowing Symphony would maintain a cycle of target discovery, submission, validation, and disruption for seven months,[58] and the sustained scale of the operation taxed the command to its limits. It was clear from the outset that Glowing Symphony was going to provide an opportunity to validate or modify existing untested procedures, including the targeting processes and deconfliction with other government agencies, a learning process which would impact USCYBERCOM's models for operating in the future.[59]

To those involved with Operation Glowing Symphony, evidence of impact on ISIS media was demonstrated in changes to one of ISIS' flagship periodicals, *Rumiyah* magazine. A continuation of *Dabiq* magazine, one of ISIS' most important English-language products, *Rumiyah* was published by media operatives at the beginning of each month in the Islamic calendar. Issues typically contained 50-60 pages of feature articles, slick graphics, how-to guides, and inspirational content aimed at ISIS members and sympathizers. The first issue after the opening of Glowing Symphony was delayed by nearly a week. Delays began to stack up until the publication ceased in 2017.[60] By the end of *Rumiyah* the publication's degradation was apparent in more than delays. Issue 12 of the magazine contained inconsistencies, and fell short of the high-level media products ISIS had become known for.[61]

Over time JTF Ares expanded to supporting further aspects of the multi-pronged counter-ISIS campaign. Fundraising and recruitment efforts were targeted in partnership with the State Department, Treasury, Department of Homeland Security, and the FBI to enable diplomatic pressure, sanctions, and domestic prosecution through information found during Glowing Symphony operations.[62] As the coalition ground fight against ISIS progressed, particularly in Mosul, cyber operations against ISIS media producers and enablers were executed in coordination with kinetic operations on the ground.[63] During the span of Operation Glowing Symphony, seven senior ISIS propagandists and facilitators — reliant on the internet and likely targets of the operation — were killed in precision airstrikes by coalition forces. These included Bassam al-Jayfus, chief coordinator for funding to international terror attacks; Rayaan Meshaal, the founder and head of the terror group's official Amaq media outlet; and Abu Sulayman al-Iraqi, a senior official and advisor on topics of propaganda and recruitment.[64]

CONCLUSION

Operation Glowing Symphony represented a new component of a multi-pronged approach to combat terrorist exploitation of the internet. The rise of ISIS invited new challenges to the U.S. government's response to terrorists in the digital arena, and it evolved the toolkit available to policymakers and practitioners for challenges ahead. Beyond interagency efforts to improve counter-messaging, and leverage private industry, USCYBERCOM's support to OIR supplemented efforts and enhanced capabilities for fighting ISIS online. JTF Ares used targeted attacks to disrupt the operations of an extremist media and recruitment enterprise, and used information gathered during these attacks to provide intelligence support to existing arms of the nation's counterextremism apparatus. This addition was made possible by a newfound willingness and heightened demand within the U.S. government to more readily use computer network attack (to be contrasted with computer network exploitation, or espionage) as a tool of national power.

While Operation Glowing Symphony will certainly inform future counterterrorism operations or efforts to counter online extremism, this model has also been adopted to address other aspects of the "grey zone challenge" as it is presented through cyberspace. The Congressional Research Service in 2016 likened the ISIS challenge to the hybrid threat posed by Russia's tactics in Ukraine,[65] and in 2019 Gen. Nakasone revealed that the Russia Small Group, an NSA/USCYBERCOM team formed to counter Russian political interference, was in part inspired by the experiences of JTF Ares.[66] The U.S. continues to add offensive cyber options to toolkits built for the nation's most vexing security challenges, a trend which began with the campaign to counter ISIS.

Endnotes

1. For more on this topic, see: Levin, Brian. 2002. "Cyberhate: A Legal and Historical Analysis of Extremists' Use of Computer Networks in America." *American Behavioral Scientist* 45(6), 977-978, https://doi.org/10.1177/0002764202045006004; Weimann, Gabriel. 2004. "Www.Terror.Net: How Modern Terrorism Uses the Internet." Special Report. United States Institute for Peace. https://www.usip.org/sites/default/files/sr116.pdf; Zelin, Aaron. 2003. *The State of Global Jihad Online*. New America Foundation. https://www.washingtoninstitute.org/uploads/Documents/opeds/Zelin20130201-NewAmericaFoundation.pdf.

2. Weimann, Gabriel. 2004. "Www.Terror.Net: How Modern Terrorism Uses the Internet." Special Report. United States Institute for Peace. https://www.usip.org/sites/default/files/sr116.pdf.

3. Shane, Scott. 2017. "Inside Al Qaeda's Plot to Blow Up an American Airliner." *New York Times*. https://www.nytimes.com/2017/02/22/us/politics/anwar-awlaki-underwear-bomber-abdulmutallab.html; See also, Shane, Scott. 2015. *Objective Troy: A Terrorist, A President, and the Rise of the Drone*. Tim Duggen Books, New York.

4. Weimann, Gabriel. 2004. "Www.Terror.Net: How Modern Terrorism Uses the Internet." Special Report. United States Institute for Peace. https://www.usip.org/sites/default/files/sr116.pdf; Homeland Security Project. 2012. "Countering Online Radicalization in America," Bipartisan Policy Center. https://bipartisanpolicy.org/wp-content/uploads/2019/03/BPC-_Online-Radicalization-Report.pdf.

5. In *Messing with the Enemy*, Clint Watts discussed this cycle, highlighting the key iterations of the entity, starting with the Counterterrorism Communication Center (CTCC), which was launched in 2006. By 2008, the Global Strategic Engagement Center (GSEC) replaced the CTCC. Then, in 2011, the Center for Strategic Counterterrorism Communication (CSCC) took the place of the GSEC. "Watts, Clint. 2018. *Messing with the Enemy*. Harper Collins: New York, p.203; See also, Ingram, Haroro. 2020. "Persuade or Perish: Addressing Gaps in the U.S. Posture to Confront Propaganda and Disinformation Threats." GW Program on Extremism. https://extremism.gwu.edu/sites/g/files/zaxdzs2191/f/Ingram%20Persuade%20or%20Perish.pdf.

6. Watts, Clint. 2018. *Messing with the Enemy*. Harper Collins: New York, p.203.

7. Watts, Clint. 2018. *Messing with the Enemy*. Harper Collins: New York, p.203.

8. For more on different aspects of these dynamics, see: Zimmerman, Katherine. 2010. "Expanding the Campaign of Violence: Al Qaeda in the Arabian Peninsula's English Language Magazine." Critical Threats. American Enterprise Institute. https://www.criticalthreats.org/analysis/expanding-the-campaign-of-violence-al-qaeda-in-the-arabian-peninsulas-english-language-magazine; Brachmann, Jarett and Alix Levine. 2011. "You too can be Awlaki!" Fletcher Forum on World Affairs. http://www.fletcherforum.org/home/2016/9/13/you-too-can-be-awlaki; "Meleagrou-Hitchens, Alexander. 2012. "Lights, Camera, Jihad: Al-Shabaab's Western Media Strategy." International Centre for the Study of Radicalisation. https://icsr.info/wp-content/uploads/2012/11/ICSR-Report-Lights-Camera-Jihad-al-Shabaab%E2%80%99s-Western-Media-Strategy.pdf; Anzalone, Christopher. 2012. "The Evolution of an American Jihadi: The Case of Omar Hammami." *CTC Sentinel*, 5(6), https://ctc.usma.edu/the-evolution-of-an-american-jihadi-the-case-of-omar-hammami/; Prucha, Nico and Ali Fisher. 2013. "Tweeting for the Caliphate: Twitter as the New Frontier for Jihadist Propaganda." *CTC Sentinel*, 6(6), https://ctc.usma.edu/tweeting-for-the-caliphate-twitter-as-the-new-frontier-for-jihadist-propaganda/; Watts, Clint. 2018. *Messing with the Enemy*. Harper Collins: New York.

9. Homeland Security Project. 2012. "Countering Online Radicalization in America." Bipartisan Policy Center. https://bipartisanpolicy.org/wp-content/uploads/2019/03/BPC-_Online-Radicalization-Report.pdf.

10. Watts, Clint. 2018. *Messing with the Enemy*. Harper Collins: New York, p.204; Fernandez, Alberto. 2014. "Confronting the Changing Face of Al-Qaeda Propaganda." Washington Institute (blog). February 25, 2014. https://www.washingtoninstitute.org/policy-analysis/view/confronting-the-changing-face-of-al-qaeda-propaganda.

11. Homeland Security Project. 2012. "Countering Online Radicalization in America." Bipartisan Policy Center. https://bipartisanpolicy.org/

wp-content/uploads/2019/03/BPC-_Online-Radicalization-Report.pdf.

12. Critiques of the campaign suggest its products were offensive, and aggrandized the organizations they sought to counter. Others argued its contents were not professionalized or persuasive. Katz, Rita. 2014. "The State Department's Twitter War With ISIS Is Embarrassing." *Time*. September 16, 2014. Miller, Greg. 2015. "Panel Casts Doubt on U.S. Propaganda Efforts against ISIS." *Washington Post*. December 2, 2015. https://www.washingtonpost.com/world/national-security/panel-casts-doubt-on-us-propaganda-efforts-against-isis/2015/12/02/ab7f9a14-9851-11e5-94f0-9eeaff906ef3_story.html?utm_term=.021256fdeb04.

13. Take, for example, the popular "Clashing of Swords" video series produced by al-Furqan media starting in June 2012. For more context, see: Whiteside, Craig. "Lighting the Path: the Evolution of the Islamic State Media Enterprise (2003-2016)." International Centre for Counter-Terrorism, p.16-17. https://icct.nl/wp-content/uploads/2016/11/ICCT-Whiteside-Lighting-the-Path-the-Evolution-of-the-Islamic-State-Media-Enterprise-2003-2016-Nov2016.pdf.

14. Milton, Daniel, "Communication Breakdown: Unraveling the Islamic State's Media Efforts." Combating Terrorism Center. October 2016. https://ctc.usma.edu/app/uploads/2016/10/ISMedia_Online.pdf.

15. Milton, Daniel. "Pulling Back the Curtain: An Inside Look at the Islamic State's Media Organization." Combating Terrorism Center. August 28, 2018. https://ctc.usma.edu/pulling-back-the-curtain-an-inside-look-at-the-islamic-states-media-organization/.

16. Bindner, Laurence and Raphael Gluck, "Wilayat Internet: ISIS' Resilience across the Internet and Social Media." *Bellingcat*. September 1, 2019. https://www.bellingcat.com/news/mena/2017/09/01/wilayat-internet-isis-resilience-across-internet-social-media/; Milton, Daniel. "Communication Breakdown." Combating Terrorism Center. October 2016, p.49. https://ctc.usma.edu/app/uploads/2016/10/ISMedia_Online.pdf.

17. Meleagrou-Hitchens, Alexander and Seamus Hughes. 2017. "The Threat to the United States from the Islamic State's Virtual Entrepreneurs." *CTC Sentinel*. https://ctc.usma.edu/the-threat-to-the-united-states-from-the-islamic-states-virtual-entrepreneurs/.

18. Meleagrou-Hitchens, Alexander and Seamus Hughes. 2017. "The Threat to the United States from the Islamic State's Virtual Entrepreneurs." *CTC Sentinel*. https://ctc.usma.edu/the-threat-to-the-united-states-from-the-islamic-states-virtual-entrepreneurs/.

19. Nesser, Petter, Anne Stenersen, and Emilie Oftedal. 2016. "Jihadi Terrorism in Europe: The IS-Effect." Perspectives on Terrorism, 10:6, http://www.terrorismanalysts.com/pt/index.php/pot/article/view/553; Gartenstein-Ross, Daveed and Madeleine Blackman. 2017. "ISIL's Virtual Planners: A Critical Terrorist Innovation." *War on the Rocks*. https://warontherocks.com/2017/01/isils-virtual-planners-a-critical-terrorist-innovation/; Cragin, Kim and Ari Weil. 2018. "'Virtual Planners' in the Arsenal of Islamic State External Operations." *Orbis*, 62:2. https://www.sciencedirect.com/science/article/pii/S0030438718300127.

20. Bernard, Rose. 2017. "These are not the terrorist groups you're looking for: an assessment of cyber capabilities of Islamic State." *Journal of Cyber Policy*, 2:2. https://www.tandfonline.com/doi/abs/10.1080/23738871.2017.1334805.

21. One example includes the 2015 hack of the United States Central Command's (CENTCOM) Twitter and Youtube accounts: Lamothe, Dan. 2015. "U.S. military social media accounts apparently hacked by Islamic State sympathizers." *Washington Post*, https://www.washingtonpost.com/news/checkpoint/wp/2015/01/12/centcom-twitter-account-apparently-hacked-by-islamic-state-sympathizers/?utm_term=.55daf919edf8; Gompert, David and Martin Libicki. 2015. "Decoding the Breach: The Truth About the CENTCOM Hack." RAND Blog. https://www.rand.org/blog/2015/02/decoding-the-breach-the-truth-about-the-centcom-hack.html; A second example includes Junaid Hussain's March 2015 publication of a list of U.S. military personnel, which Hussain acquired using open-source methods, not hacking. For more, see: Alexander, Audrey and Bennett Clifford. 2019. "Doxing and Defacements: Examining the Islamic State's Hacking Capabilities." *CTC Sentinel*, 12:4. https://ctc.usma.edu/doxing-defacements-examining-islamic-states-hacking-capabilities/.

22. "Special Report: Kill Lists from Pro-IS Hacking Groups." SITE Intelligence. 2016. http://sitemultimedia.org/docs/SITE_

Analysis_of_Islamic_State_Kill_Lists.pdf; Alexander, Audrey and Bennett Clifford. 2019. "Doxing and Defacements: Examining the Islamic State's Hacking Capabilities." *CTC Sentinel*, 12:4. https://ctc.usma.edu/doxing-defacements-examining-islamic-states-hacking-capabilities/.

23. Alexander, Audrey and Bennett Clifford. 2019. "Doxing and Defacements: Examining the Islamic State's Hacking Capabilities." *CTC Sentinel*, 12:4. https://ctc.usma.edu/doxing-defacements-examining-islamic-states-hacking-capabilities/.

24. "Criminal Complaint." USA v. Ardit Ferizi. United States District Court for the Eastern District of Virginia. Case: 1:15-mj-515, 2015. See also "ISIL-Linked Kosovo Hacker Sentenced to 20 Years in Prison." Department of Justice. September 23, 2016.

25. "Criminal Complaint." USA v. Ardit Ferizi. United States District Court for the Eastern District of Virginia. Case: 1:15-mj-515, 2015. See also "ISIL-Linked Kosovo Hacker Sentenced to 20 Years in Prison." Department of Justice. September 23, 2016.

26. Starks, Tim. 2017. "How the Islamic State is doing in cyberspace." *Politico*. https://www.politico.com/newsletters/morning-cybersecurity/2017/12/07/how-the-islamic-state-is-doing-in-cyberspace-044112.

27. Theohary, Catherine, Kathleen McInnis, and John Rollins. 2016. "Information Warfare: DOD's Response to the Islamic State Hacking Activities." *CRS Insight*. Congressional Research Service. https://fas.org/sgp/crs/natsec/IN10486.pdf.

28. In the following transcript, national security officials articulate some of the challenges their respective agencies faced by that point: Transcript of a hearing before the Committee on Homeland Security. U.S. House of Representatives. "Worldwide threats to the homeland: ISIS and the new wave of terror." July 14, 2016. https://www.govinfo.gov/content/pkg/CHRG-114hhrg25265/html/CHRG-114hhrg25265.htm.

29. Please note, although the San Bernardino attack was initially attributed to ISIS, the FBI has not confirmed that there are links between the attackers and the organization.

30. Matthew Weed. 2017. "Global Engagement Center: Background and Issues." *CRS Insight*. Congressional Research Service. https://fas.org/sgp/crs/row/IN10744.pdf.

31. Levitt, Matthew. 2016. "A Counterterrorism Restructuring That Can't Work Without Funding." Washington Institute. January 16, 2016. https://www.washingtoninstitute.org/policy-analysis/view/a-counterterrorism-restructuring-that-cant-work-without-funding.

32. Harris, Gardiner, and Cecilia Kang. 2016. "Obama Shifts Online Strategy on ISIS." *New York Times*. https://www.nytimes.com/2016/01/09/world/middleeast/white-house-officials-to-meet-with-tech-leaders-on-thwarting-terrorists.html; Kang, Cecilia and Matt Apuzzo. 2016. "U.S. Asks Tech and Entertainment Industries Help in Fighting Terrorism." *New York Times*. https://www.nytimes.com/2016/02/25/technology/tech-and-media-firms-called-to-white-house-for-terrorism-meeting.html; Svetand, Oleg and Elissa Miller. 2016. "What the real takeaway should be from White House engagement with Silicon Valley." *The Hill*. https://thehill.com/blogs/congress-blog/technology/273610-what-the-real-takeaway-should-be-from-white-house-engagement.

33. "Remarks by Assistant Attorney General John Carlin Opening of Madison Valleywood Project." 2016. Department of Justice. https://epic.org/foia/MadisonValleywood_2.pdf; Kang, Cecilia and Matt Apuzzo. 2016. "U.S. Asks Tech and Entertainment Industries Help in Fighting Terrorism." *New York Times*, https://www.nytimes.com/2016/02/25/technology/tech-and-media-firms-called-to-white-house-for-terrorism-meeting.html.

34. In the following transcript, national security officials articulate some of the challenges their respective agencies faced by that point: Transcript of a hearing before the Committee on Homeland Security. U.S. House of Representatives. "Worldwide threats to the homeland: ISIS and the new wave of terror." July 14, 2016. https://www.govinfo.gov/content/pkg/CHRG-114hhrg25265/html/CHRG-114hhrg25265.htm.

35. Please note that according to this presentation, Hussain published the kill list on March 20, 2015: Barghouty, Ammar and Erin Joe. 2018. "Understanding Cyberterrorism: The Ardit Ferizi Case." https://www.rsaconference.com/industry-topics/presentation/understanding-cyberterrorism-the-ardit-ferizi-case.

36. Meleagrous-Hitchens, and Seamus Hughes. 2017. "The Threat to the United States from the Islamic State's Virtual Entrepreneurs." *CTC*

Sentinel. https://ctc.usma.edu/the-threat-to-the-united-states-from-the-islamic-states-virtual-entrepreneurs/; Alexander, Audrey and Bennett Clifford. 2019. "Doxing and Defacements: Examining the Islamic State's Hacking Capabilities." CTC Sentinel, 12:4. https://ctc.usma.edu/doxing-defacements-examining-islamic-states-hacking-capabilities/.

37. Goldman, Adam and Eric Schmitt. 2016. "One by One, ISIS Social Media Experts Are Killed as Result of FBI Program." *New York Times.* https://www.nytimes.com/2016/11/24/world/middleeast/isis-recruiters-social-media.html.

38. Goldman, Adam and Eric Schmitt. 2016. "One by One, ISIS Social Media Experts Are Killed as Result of FBI Program." *New York Times.* https://www.nytimes.com/2016/11/24/world/middleeast/isis-recruiters-social-media.html.

39. Readers should assume that other cyber operations had already occurred under Title 50 intelligence authorities.

40. "USCYBERCOM Operations Order (OPORD) 15-0055 Operations Order in Support of Operation Inherent Resolve." Operations Order, United States Cyber Command. 2015. https://nsarchive2.gwu.edu//dc.html?doc=5751043-National-Security-Archive-COS-MEMO-11-FEB-19.

41. *Darknet Diaries.* Episode 50. "Operation Glowing Symphony." Jack Rhysider (2019). Podcast. https://darknetdiaries.com/episode/50/.

42. *Darknet Diaries.*

43. For more on Title 10 vs Title 50 authorities in cyberspace, see: Chesney, Robert. 2018. "Title 10 and Title 50 Issues When Computer Network Operations Impact Third Countries." Lawfare. 2018. https://www.lawfareblog.com/title-10-and-title-50-issues-when-computer-network-operations-impact-third-countries.

44. "Mission Analysis Brief: Cyber Support to Counter ISIL." Briefing, United States Cyber Command. 2016. https://nsarchive2.gwu.edu/dc.html?doc=4311638-United-States-Cyber-Command-Mission-Analysis.

45. "TASKORD 16-0063 to Establish Joint Task Force (JTF) -ARES to Counter the Islamic State of Iraq and the Levant (ISIL) in Cyberspace." Task Order, United States Cyber Command. 2016. https://nsarchive2.gwu.edu/dc.html?doc=3678213-Document-07-USCYBERCOM-to-CDRUSACYBER-Subj#document/p23.

46. *Darknet Diaries.*

47. "United States Cyber Command Concept of Operations (CONOP): OPERATION GLOWING SYMPHONY." Concept of Operations, United States Cyber Command. 2016. https://nsarchive2.gwu.edu/dc.html?doc=4638018-USCYBERCOM-JTF-ARES-United-States-Cyber-Command.

48. *Darknet Diaries.*

49. Martelle, Michael. "Preparing for Computer Network Operations: USCYBERCOM Documents Trace Path to Operational Cyber Force." National Security Archive. 2019. https://nsarchive.gwu.edu/news/cyber-vault/2019-05-03/preparing-computer-network-operations-uscybercom-documents-trace-path-operational-cyber-force.

50. *Darknet Diaries.*

51. Nakashima, Ellen. "U.S. Military Cyber Operation to Attack ISIS Last Year Sparked Heated Debate over Alerting Allies." *Washington Post.* 2017. https://www.washingtonpost.com/world/national-security/us-military-cyber-operation-to-attack-isis-last-year-sparked-heated-debate-over-alerting-allies/2017/05/08/93a120a2-30d5-11e7-9dec-764dc781686f_story.html.

52. "USCYBERCOM 30-Day Assessment of Operation Glowing Symphony." United States Cyber Command. 2016. Page 17. https://nsarchive2.gwu.edu/dc.html?doc=6655596-National-Security-Archive-5-USCYBERCOM.

53. Temple-Raston, Dina, "How The NSA And U.S. Cyber Command Hacked ISIS's Media Operation." NPR. 2019. https://www.npr.org/2019/09/26/763545811/how-the-u-s-hacked-isis.

54. *Darknet Diaries.*

55. *Darknet Diaries.*

56. *Darknet Diaries.*

57. Temple-Raston.

58. *Darknet Diaries.*

59. This learning process is tangential to the focus of this paper, but further details can be found in: Martelle, Michael. 2020. "USCYBERCOM After Action Assessments of Operation GLOWING SYMPHONY." National Security Archive. 2020. https://nsarchive.gwu.edu/briefing-book/cyber-vault/2020-01-21/uscybercom-after-action-assessments-

operation-glowing-symphony.

Martelle, Michael. 2019. "Targeting in Cyber Operations: FOIA Release Discusses Considerations of US Military Targeting Doctrine." National Security Archive. 2019. https://nsarchive.gwu.edu/briefing-book/cyber-vault/2019-09-05/targeting-cyber-operations-foia-release-discusses-considerations-us-military-targeting-doctrine.

Martelle, Michael. 2019. "Preparing for Computer Network Operations: USCYBERCOM Documents Trace Path to Operational Cyber Force." National Security Archive. 2019. https://nsarchive.gwu.edu/news/cyber-vault/2019-05-03/preparing-computer-network-operations-uscybercom-documents-trace-path-operational-cyber-force.

60. *Darknet Diaries*.
61. Ingram, Haroro J. "Islamic State's English-Language Magazines, 2014-2017: Trends & Implications for CT-CVE Strategic Communications." *Terrorism and Counter-Terrorism Studies*, March (2018): 1-46. https://doi.org/10.19165/2018.1.03.
62. Temple-Raston.
63. "USCYBERCOM 30-Day Assessment of Operation Glowing Symphony." Page 5.
64. "Coalition Removes ISIS Leaders from Battlefield." US Central Command. 2017. https://www.centcom.mil/MEDIA/PRESS-RELEASES/Press-Release-View/Article/1259744/coalition-removes-isis-leaders-from-battlefield/.
65. Theohary, Catherine A, Kathleen J McInnis, and John W Rollins. 2016. "Information Warfare: DOD's Response to the Islamic State Hacking Activities." https://fas.org/sgp/crs/natsec/IN10486.pdf.
66. Temple-Raston, Dina. "Task Force Takes On Russian Election Interference NPR." NPR. 2019. https://www.npr.org/2019/08/14/751048230/new-nsa-task-force-takes-on-russian-election-interference.

CHAPTER EIGHT

THE RISE OF DIGITAL AUTHORITARIANISM IN THE MIDDLE EAST

MOHAMMED SOLIMAN

INTRODUCTION

There were signs of the power of digital authoritarianism in the early 2010s in China's utilization of the internet as a tool to control and maintain political stability.[1] Now, as we enter the 2020s, the term has a more comprehensive definition: the use of digital information technology by authoritarian regimes to surveil, repress, and manipulate domestic and foreign populations.[2]

In the first wave of the Arab Spring, protesters utilized social media and the internet to self-organize, to successfully take down old, established authoritarian regimes in Cairo, Tunis, and Sana'a, and to spark mass movements in almost every Arab capital. The pre-Arab Spring states had acted almost as cults of personality. Moammar Gadhafi ruled Libya for 42 years, Ali Abdullah Saleh was president of Yemen for 34 years, and Hosni Mubarak ran Egypt for 30 years.

The pre-Arab Spring authoritarians were men in their 70s and 80s who were in total denial that their multi-decade rule could end because of a tool called the internet that they did not understand. In 2009, when a journalist asked Mubarak's son and likely successor, Gamal Mubarak, about online activism, specifically the April 6 Youth Movement,[3] he brushed the question aside. Mubarak's entire security apparatus did not take online activism and the cybersphere seriously, which explains their incompetent online messaging during the 2011 revolution.

Egypt's longest-serving president, Mubarak was the first Arab leader to try to exert significant digital authoritarianism in the region. His security apparatus imposed a week-long, state-wide internet blackout that angered Egypt's middle class and led to them taking to the streets[4] — a strategic mistake that Mubarak likely regretted after his ousting.

In the past decade, authoritarian regimes came to an understanding that their security and stability lie in controlling online public opinion to avoid another 2011 moment. Therefore, the regimes tried to quell public anger and frustration through basic disinformation techniques, such as using fake Facebook accounts to manipulate presidential polls and Twitter bots to amplify government messages. Due to disinformation campaigns, the region's rulers, aside from in Tunisia, successfully absorbed the shock of the Arab Spring starting from 2013. Thus began the period known as the Arab Winter, the five years between 2013 and 2018, when Arab authoritarian regimes defeated the emergent revolutions and turned most of them into endless civil wars.[5]

Authoritarian governments across the region had always expressed their aspiration to implement a local version of the Great Firewall of China to assert their dominance in cyberspace, despite originally not having the necessary technical capabilities. Between 2018 and 2019, a new wave of the Arab Spring swept across Algeria, Sudan, and Lebanon. However, this time, authoritarian governments were equipped with state-of-the-art technology to control the flow of information inside and outside their countries using disinformation operations to affect public opinion and hacking activists' accounts. This wave of protests provides an example of how authoritarian governments in the region are highly capable of imposing internet curfews and creating firewalls during times of turmoil.

Over the past decade, governments in the Middle East have forged systems of digital authoritarianism that include authoritarian digital laws, online censorship, digital surveillance, and disinformation operations. This chapter will examine country-specific examples of each of the core principles of digital authoritarianism.

AUTHORITARIAN DIGITAL LAWS

Middle Eastern governments have been extremely invested in controlling crowd-sourced information by making any online activism from their own domestic populations or from meddling foreign powers illegal. There has been an increasing number of invasive cyber laws and government actions to criminalize and stop a wide range of online activities.

Qatar

During the Arab Spring, Qatar embraced the growing protest movements across the region. Traditional conservative Arab actors (e.g., Saudi Arabia and the United Arab Emirates [UAE]) viewed Qatar's foreign policy as interventionist, supportive of regime change, and potentially destabilizing to their own governments.[6] Therefore, Saudi Arabia and the UAE pursued an assertive foreign policy of supporting military leaders across the region in their efforts to assume power and take down various Muslim Brotherhood factions, as the latter played a major role in protests in several countries.[7]

Qatar was forced into a defensive position in 2017, when Saudi Arabia, Egypt, the UAE, and Bahrain led a diplomatic boycott of Doha, banning Qatari airplanes from using their airspace and its ships from using their regional waters, closing the Saudi land border with Qatar, and expelling Qatari citizens.[8] The Saudi-led quartet had previous grievances against Qatar's foreign policy; however, they first made the case to boycott the country after a news story appeared on the website of the Qatar News Agency (QNA). The story attributed comments to Qatari Amir Sheikh Tamim bin Hamad that described Iran as "a regional and Islamic power that cannot be ignored [and that deemed] it ... unwise to face up against it."[9] In addition, QNA's Twitter account posted accusations of Arab states' potential plots against Qatar and said the government of Qatar had recalled its ambassadors from Saudi Arabia, the UAE, Kuwait, Bahrain, and Egypt as a result.[10]

Qatar quickly denounced the statements and the news story, deeming them "fake" and declaring that it was the victim of a hack. The U.S. intelligence community came to the same assessment — that the story on the QNA website was fake.[11] Despite the external backing, the Qatari announcement cut no ice with the quartet countries, which weaponized the story and Twitter comments to mobilize their population and Arab allies to boycott Qatar.[12]

This crisis was a turning point for both Qatar's foreign policy and, more importantly, its media influence through TV channel Al-Jazeera. The station and its associated websites became inaccessible in the quartet and other Arab states, depriving Qatar of its traditionally influential narrative amplifier that usually swung public opinion in Doha's favor.[13] The Saudi-led quartet started online campaigns aimed at destabilizing Qatar's internal politics through state-sponsored disinformation operations. The UAE and Saudi Arabia swamped Twitter with bots to "manipulate Twitter trends, promote fake news, increase the ranking of anti-Qatar tweets from specific political figures, present the illusion of grassroots Qatari opposition to the Tamim regime, and pollute the information sphere around Qatar, thus amplifying propaganda discourses beyond regional and national news channels."[14]

In direct response to the continuation of the Gulf crisis and anti-Qatar cyber activities, Qatar passed a harsh cyber security law in 2020 that was deemed authoritarian in nature and is similar to laws in the UAE, Saudi Arabia, and Egypt. This amendment authorized the imprisonment of individuals involved in circulating "false or biased rumors, statements, or news, or inflammatory propaganda, domestically or abroad" that could harm national security, influence public opinion, or destabilize the public order of the state.[15] The amendment means that violators can be punished with up to five years in prison and a fine of $25,000.[16]

Qatar shares similarities with other Gulf monarchies in terms of the media immunity that the monarch, the royal family, and the government enjoy. However, the country has tried to portray its commitment to democracy to the wider Arab world through Al-Jazeera. The new cyber security law, which targets anti-Qatar and foreign-originated content as well as domestic dissidents, is a stain on Qatar's self-proclaimed reputation as a defender of democracy in the Middle East.

Egypt

In Egypt, the government has a long and mixed history of digital authoritarianism that includes implementing restrictive cyber laws, imposing taxes on social media, and blocking websites without legal basis. The country's digital infrastructure was created in the mid-2000s, when technocrats and a businessmen-led government sponsored the Computers for Homes Initiative to increase the number of Egyptian families that had internet access in their homes.

In 2009, in an attempt to limit young people's access to the global network, the Ministry of Interior tried to coerce internet cafés into recording the names and national identity numbers of every customer, and later tried to create a nationwide registration system to access the internet.[17] While the Egyptian police were focusing on internet cafés in Cairo and Giza, around two-thirds of households in urban areas were sharing DSL internet connections.[18] When the protests unfolded in 2011, the security apparatus finally realized the high level of internet penetration in Egyptian society and decided that the only solution to quell the protests was to shut down all internet access by forcing internet service providers (ISPs) to cut their connections. Eventually, this tactic became one of the mistakes that cost Mubarak his presidency.

Egypt's security apparatus used the 2003 Telecommunication Regulation Law as the legal basis for instructing telecoms companies and ISPs to shut down their networks.[19] The ISPs faced a nationwide backlash and calls to boycott their services because they had honored the security apparatus' legal request to shut down the internet during the revolution.[20]

Following Mubarak's fall, political parties and civil society legally challenged the internet shutdown, and Egypt's highest administrative court, the Council of State, ruled that the internet and telecoms closure threatened the lives of Egyptians and that the shutdown went against the constitutional protections for freedom of expression and the right to access information.[21] Despite this historic court ruling, the security apparatus maintained its legal hold over the internet and telecoms. Currently, the telecoms law mandates that the security apparatus protect the state's interests, provides access to private information and encrypted systems, and gives the National Telecommunications Regulatory Authority (NTRA) wide licensing powers.[22]

ONLINE CENSORSHIP

Governments have been obsessed with controlling online content, especially content that opposes political decision-making or touches on sensitive issues such as religion or sexuality. This obsession is based on the need and desire to control narratives in their respective countries, to reshape the world views of their constituents, and to prevent outside influence that poses threats to the ruling regimes. This is what makes online censorship important to Saudi Arabia, Qatar, and Egypt.

Egypt

In the summer of 2013, the Egyptian military, led by then Gen. Abdel-Fattah el-Sisi, ousted former President Mohamed Morsi and launched a nationwide crackdown on the Muslim Brotherhood. This created societal tension among military supporters, the Islamists, and, to some extent, the pro-democracy camp. Therefore, the newly established Sisi government needed to control the political narrative surrounding the military takeover of power, especially given that the country had experienced a slight increase in freedom of expression after the 2011 revolution that people were eager to use.

Following his election as president in the summer of 2014, Sisi quickly moved to change the legislative landscape by passing the Terrorist Entities Law, which created a government procedure to designate organizations and individuals considered a "threat to national unity" as terrorists.[23] The law emerged as a core tool for Sisi in his crackdown on Islamist movements, and on liberal and leftist political groups.

The Sisi government flexed its muscles and exerted massive control over cyberspace by banning foreign-sourced news websites. In 2017, Egypt blocked at least 63 websites, including 48 news sites.[24] The banned websites included Mada Masr, Daily News Egypt, El Borsa, Masr Al Arabia, Albedaiah, Elbadil, Bawabit Yanair, Medium, Daily Sabah, Al-Jazeera, and The Huffington Post (now HuffPost).[25] The Egyptian security apparatus banned the websites based on their output, influence in cyberspace, investigations into government practices, and provision of a platform for the opposition to express views that conflicted with the government's position. However, the 2017 crackdown on news websites was specifically linked to controlling traditional media and social media around two specific events: the transfer of two Egyptian islands to Saudi Arabia[26] and the anticipated presidential elections in 2018.[27] A second round of censorship happened in 2018, which included the blocking of websites enabling the downloading of virtual private networks (VPN), and brought the total number of blocked websites to over 500.[28]

Even though the government, without legal basis, had blocked websites, the Egyptian NTRA denied having done so.[29] However, the security apparatus justified blocking the websites because of their affiliation "with the outlawed Muslim Brotherhood or for being funded by Qatar."[30] [31] In reality, most of them are independent, progressive websites. Mada Masr is a left-wing progressive platform that broke stories on the role of Egypt's General Intelligence Services in electing the Parliament[32] and on the Egypt-Israel gas deal.[33] Mada Masr's last report on the sidelining of Sisi's son from his position[34] eventually led to the Egyptian government's crackdown on the website's headquarters and the temporary detention of its staff.[35] Despite the website being blocked, Mada Masr has continued to publish on Facebook and other social media.

Websites like Masr Al Arabia, Albedaiah, Elbadil, and Bawabit Yanair have been targeted because of the space they offered prominent opposition figures to criticize government policies, and because of their reporting on controversial topics such as human rights abuses, the transfer of two Egyptian islands to Saudi Arabia, and the security apparatus' terrorism doctrine. Foreign-based websites such as Daily Sabah, Al-Jazeera, and The Huffington Post were targeted because they often purportedly produced stories that supported their backing states (Turkey and Qatar) against the Egyptian government's positions on the Muslim Brotherhood, Hamas, the Assad regime, and Israel.

Human rights groups deemed this government censorship unconstitutional because it violates Article 57 of Egypt's constitution, which stipulates the freedom of media and the public's right to know and access information. The government, however, was working with a loose interpretation of the Terrorist Entities Law to prosecute websites for "spreading lies"[36] and "supporting terrorism."[37] The government tacitly acknowledged the contradiction between the constitution and this law with its 2020 amendment to the Terrorist Entities Law, changing the list of "associations, organizations, or groups" that could be deemed as terrorists to include traditional and digital media.[38]

Following Egypt's unprecedented censorship campaign, there were massive investments in pro-government websites that circulated and amplified stories to rebuke independent and foreign media narratives. The security apparatus' strategy was to increase the presence of its media arm on social media to amplify pro-government stories, circulate conspiracy narratives, and defame the opposition. For example, the pro-government Youm 7 has almost 30 million followers on Facebook, Twitter, and Instagram collectively. Youm 7 is the most influential and vocal pro-government digital media organization today, both in Egypt and across the region.[39]

Saudi Arabia

Since the foundation of Saudi Arabia, its monarchs have been in control of the traditional media landscape in the kingdom. "Although in principle there is no legal restriction on freedom of expression, censorship is strict, and criticism of the government and Islam is automatically barred."[40] According to the BBC, despite newspapers operating as private companies, publishers and editors must be informally approved by the government.[41] This tacit supervision lets newspapers know that the government is watching. Unsurprisingly, the restrictive media environment forced Saudi Arabia's top channels to operate outside the kingdom in its neighbor, the UAE. It is noteworthy that Al-Arabiya, the MBC Network, and Rotana network all operate from Dubai. The controlled media environment allows the Saudi leadership to focus on banning foreign-sourced content that criticizes the kingdom's royal family or contradicts Islamic values.[42]

Certainly, the Arab Spring created an increasing fear of similar demonstrations in Saudi Arabia that might threaten the monarchy. Following the typical route for Arab authoritarian governments in the region, the Saudi authorities increased their control over cybersphere by banning content that mentions the killing of journalist Jamal Khashoggi, unfavorably describes Saudi involvement in Yemen, advocates for political reform in the kingdom, or criticizes the treatment of Saudi activists.

In 2018, the kingdom sent an official legal request based on Saudi law to media services provider Netflix to remove an episode of Hasan Minhaj's "Patriot Act." In the controversial episode, Minhaj criticized Saudi Crown Prince Mohammed bin Salman (MbS) over the killing of

Khashoggi inside the Saudi consulate in Istanbul, Turkey.[43]

According to the Saudi Communications and Information Technology Commission, the program violated the 2007 Anti-Cyber Crime Law. This law punishes the "production, preparation, transmission, or storage of material impinging on public order, religious values, public morals, and privacy, through the information network or computers" with up to five years in prison. Saudi Arabia uses the Anti-Cyber Crime Law to punish activists, especially female ones, for their online activism. Given the importance of the Saudi market, Netflix pulled the episode in Saudi Arabia while keeping it on YouTube.[44]

The provider's concession to the kingdom set a precedent both regionally and globally, allowing other authoritarian regimes to follow the same path regarding any content deemed problematic, unpatriotic, or critical of their leaders. This precedent could scare companies into self-censorship, as was the case when Disney's Indian subsidiary Hotstar blocked the HBO show "Last Week Tonight with John Oliver" because he criticized Prime Minister Narendra Modi.[45]

DIGITAL SURVEILLANCE

Digital surveillance is an evolution of the commonly used repressive measure of physical surveillance. The Nasserist regime in Egypt and the Ba'athist regimes in Syria and Iraq ensured their stability through mass surveillance of their populations to quell political opposition.[46] Even though Arab youth benefited from technology to organize their movements, Arab regimes also gained from new technologies to improve their surveillance capabilities in cyberspace. Today, digital surveillance in the Middle East has become a global issue because governments target human rights activists both in their countries and overseas. The killing of *Washington Post* columnist Khashoggi demonstrates how digital surveillance by a Middle Eastern government can have ripple effects across the world.

Saudi Arabia

Since the death of King Abdullah and the prolonged transition led by MbS to confine succession to the House of Salman instead of the broader House of Saud, MbS has led the kingdom into one international crisis after another and increased domestic dissent. In his effort to install himself as the de facto leader of Saudi Arabia, MbS has enacted major changes to cement his posture as a strongman inside and outside the kingdom. His actions have included the war in Yemen against the Iranian-backed Houthis, the arrest and detention of dozens of princes and businessmen in the Riyadh Ritz-Carlton, the forced resignation of Lebanese Prime Minister Saad Hariri during his visit to Riyadh,[47] and the arrest of prominent Sunni clerics[48] and female activists.[49] The increasing repression has led directly to an unprecedented degree of dissent among Saudi society, and unleashed a wave of Saudi online activists and dissidents in exile. The fear of persecution has also made Saudis turn Twitter into their own town hall, where they "meet to swap information and debate the latest issues."[50]

Saudi Arabia is "the most Twitter-crazy country in the world,"[51] according to Business Insider Intelligence, with 41 percent of its population actively using the platform.[52] Across the region, Twitter's penetration has led autocrats to utilize the platform to gain insights on the population, filter information, shape political and social narratives, and suppress dissidents and critics.[53] Twitter gave Saudi critics a voice and created online leadership in the growing dissident movement, which in turn motivated the new leaders in Riyadh to obtain surveillance tools to spy on dissidents.

Saudi Arabia acquired digital spying capabilities from the Israeli NSO Group, specifically its landmark spyware Pegasus, which secretly jailbreaks iOS and Android devices to track call history, read text messages, access locations, and collect passwords and data from installed applications.[54] There have been legal suits accusing Saudi Arabia of weaponizing NSO's Pegasus against Khashoggi, one of its most prominent online critics Omar Abdulaziz,[55] and *New York Times* journalist Ben Hubbard.[56] The kingdom and the NSO Group have actively denied these allegations and called them baseless.

Twitter users like Khashoggi and Abdulaziz are prominent voices and easy to identify; however, many of Saudi Arabia's dissidents tweet anonymously. The invisibility of anonymous Twitter users has even driven Saudi Arabia to recruit employees inside Twitter to obtain users' personal information, such as email addresses and phone numbers, to help the government to identify them.[57] The kingdom's infiltration of Twitter emphasizes the reemergence of human intelligence against digital platforms, the need to limit the accessibility of users' personal data internally, and the importance of constantly vetting employees who have access to personal data.

UAE

The UAE banned BlackBerry's services completely in 2010 because the company refused to provide the country's security services with its users' data. This set a precedent for the UAE's relationships with other technology companies: If they refused to cooperate, they would meet the same fate as BlackBerry.[58]

Following the Arab Spring, the rulers of the UAE, like those of most of the countries in the Gulf, were anxious that they would face a similar fate to those in Egypt, Tunisia, and Yemen.[59] Instead of engaging in political reform, the UAE's risk mitigation strategy focused on two pillars: 1) traditional fiscal incentives — providing more jobs, financing development projects, and offering more subsidies; and 2) digital control: expanding the ban on encrypted services, localizing data inside the UAE, and establishing state-run applications.

Rather than seeing it as a movement that sought political and economic reforms, the UAE diagnosed the Arab Spring as the result of mismanaged social contracts that were not providing enough to everyday people. The UAE also thought that the Arab Spring would embolden Islamists, particularly the Muslim Brotherhood, to seize power from autocrats in neighboring countries, as the Brotherhood did in Egypt.[60]

Following the first wave of the Arab Spring in 2011, the UAE launched generous fiscal packages to hire unemployed young people, finance development projects, and dole out more subsidies.[61] Toward the end of 2011 and after putting its new fiscal policy into effect, the UAE launched a crackdown on the local Muslim Brotherhood, eventually designating it as a terrorist group in 2014.[62]

The fact that the UAE saw the Muslim Brotherhood as a threat made any community organization a threat as well. To control growing online activism, the country blocked political websites, such as UAE Hewar, that offered space for Emiratis to debate politics and the status of freedoms in the UAE.[63] In addition, the government cracked down on political activists[64] and democracy promotion organizations.[65] Once the UAE eliminated the immediate threat of pro-democracy demonstrations in 2011, it shifted its focus to data sovereignty and solidifying its control of the digital sphere. Starting in 2013, the UAE blocked access to voice over internet protocol (VOIP) services. Skype was routinely blocked and unblocked over the years, and is currently unblocked because of the COVID-19 pandemic.[66]

After denying operating licenses to VOIP services, the UAE expanded its ban to include Facetime, Viber,[67] Snapchat voice and video calls,[68] and WhatsApp calls.[69] The main driver of this policy is the UAE's stance on restricting the flow of data outside of the country, and its emphasis on data security and localization will define the country's digital policy for years to come. The UAE's excessive policy of blocking VOIP services mainly affected expatriates, who make up more than 80 percent of its population and could use VOIP services to communicate with their families overseas. This led to the widespread use of VPNs by UAE residents and visitors, eventually resulting in a draconian new law. In 2016, the UAE amended the 2012 Information Technology Crimes Law to penalize subjects who use "a fraudulent computer network protocol address (IP address) by using a false address or a third-party address."[70] Using a VPN then became punishable by temporary imprisonment and a fine.[71]

Blocking VOIP services and criminalizing VPNs created another opportunity in the Emirati market for a state-backed app that could give the security apparatus ultimate data access.

In 2019, the UAE launched ToTok, a chat and voice calling app that was downloaded by millions from Apple and Google stores.[72] Like any other app, ToTok users are based all over the world; however, a majority are in the UAE.[73]

The New York Times revealed that ToTok is "used by the government of the United Arab Emirates to try to track every conversation, movement, relationship, appointment, sound and image of those who install it on their phones."[74] ToTok gave the Emirati security service access to millions of users' data, including contacts, messages, video chats, voice chats, and locations, around the globe and in the UAE, Saudi Arabia, the U.K., and India in particular. ToTok represents the UAE's transformation into a digital hegemon among authoritarian governments in the region; not only did it ban VOIP and other secure messaging services, it created a hold over its population's data in an unprecedented way.

DISINFORMATION

Following the Arab Spring, Middle Eastern governments developed state-backed disinformation warfare. The autocratic governments believed that the uprisings were fueled by propaganda, especially from the Qatar-based Al-Jazeera. In Tunisia and Egypt, Al-Jazeera showed footage of thousands of protesters, while Tunisian and Egyptian TV stations showed empty streets. The Arab autocrats lost the information war to Al-Jazeera and other international channels that reported on the Arab Spring. They were new to this world of social media, which is dominated by a new generation that seeks change. The 2011 optics defeat created a need for authoritarian governments to craft and amplify their political narrative and influence public opinion on the widely used digital platforms.

Egypt

Following Mubarak's resignation, Egypt's new rulers understood the power of the internet and its influence over the population. Consequently, the country's security apparatus created *Legan Electronyah*, or Electronic Committees. These committees are the online arm of security agencies or political groups, and they include both fake and actual users who amplify fake news against their opponents.[75] The Egyptian security apparatus started to be proactive in cyberspace through its Electronic Committees that supported the political decisions of the Supreme Council of the Armed Forces, whitewashed the old regime's policies and its figures, spread fake information targeting activists and opposition figures, and rigged online polls to show the increasing popularity of old regime figures.

Disinformation wars and Legan Electronyah's activities peaked between 2012 and 2013, because of increasing social and political tensions between opponents and proponents of Morsi and the Muslim Brotherhood.[76] The two camps circulated fake images on Twitter and Facebook that accused the other of treason and brutality. The Muslim Brotherhood accused the Egyptian military of committing war crimes in Cairo and Sinai, but the images they used were actually from the Syrian civil war.[77] Muslim Brotherhood accounts also circulated images of Christian citizens holding crosses among the opposition protests to portray the opposition movement as a conspiracy orchestrated by the Coptic Church to topple an Islamist president.[78] Disinformation was not limited to the Brotherhood, however. Security services bots also used pictures from Syria to accuse Islamist groups of killing protesters. Egypt's political factions began weaponizing disinformation in 2013. In the years following the military takeover and Gen. Sisi's ascension to the presidency, disinformation operations became more concentrated on Egyptian Twitter, where hashtag wars became a daily occurrence.

The pro- and anti-Sisi groups have been using similar hashtags with similar meanings but slightly different words to circulate their political narratives to the other camp and increase their number of followers.[79] For example, the anti-Sisi groups usually use "#Sisi_is_not_my_president." Consequently, the pro-Sisi groups use "#Sisi_is_my_president" and "#El-Sisi_is_my_president_and_I'm_proud."[80] Hashtag wars also take place using the same hashtag. The proponents and opponents of President Sisi both often use "#Sisi," "#Egypt," and "#LongLiveEgypt" to amplify their messages.[81]

These hashtag wars reflect the radical political and socioeconomic changes that have taken place in Egypt since President Sisi took office. The hashtags "#Sisi_Leave" and "#Leave" started as a response to Sisi's speech on his willingness to leave office if people asked.[82] He expressed his disapproval of the hashtag "#Sisi_Leave" during a later speech at the World Youth Forum (WYF) summit. When Sisi launched the WYF summit, he also started a digital campaign using the hashtag "#WeNeedtoTalk." The hashtag became a town hall between proponents and opponents of President Sisi, where the opponents focused on the number of political prisoners and security services bots, and proponents touted Sisi's achievements.[83]

The excessive use of disinformation operations provided business opportunities for marketing and PR firms based in Egypt, Saudi Arabia, and the UAE to launch paid disinformation against political dissidents or regional rivals such as Qatar, Turkey, and Iran. Since 2019, Twitter and Facebook have dismantled disinformation networks, as well as named and shamed the states that sponsor disinformation operations.[84] For example, Twitter dismantled a disinformation network targeting Qatar and Iran with hundreds of fake bots managed and created by "DotDev, a private technology company operating in the UAE and Egypt."[85] The Emirati-Egyptian company ran disinformation operations against

Qatar, Turkey, and Iran, and supported Gen. Khalifa Hifter in Libya, the independence of Somaliland, and the successes of the Saudi-Emirati coalition in Yemen.[86] Similarly, Facebook suspended disinformation networks associated with two PR firms, New Waves in Egypt and Newave in the UAE.[87]

Saudi Arabia

Saudi Arabia has been involved in many domestic, regional, and international disputes that have had an impact on the kingdom's reputation. From MbS' ascension to power to the imprisonment of powerful Saudi figures in the Riyadh Ritz-Carlton and from the war on Yemen to the killing of Khashoggi, Saudi Arabia has become a target for international media scrutiny.[88] This increasing focus prompted the kingdom to invest heavily in its information warfare capabilities to attack dissidents, amplify pro-Saudi propaganda, and attack its regional rivals: Iran, Turkey, and Qatar.

Following the killing of Khashoggi inside its consulate in Istanbul, Saudi Arabia launched disinformation operations against *The Washington Post*'s owner, Jeff Bezos, because of the newspaper's coverage of the affair. Saudi bots amplified the pro-Saudi narrative. They asked Saudis to unfollow anti-Saudi sources and to trust MbS through three main hashtags: "#We_all_trust_Mohammad_Bin_Salman," "#Saudis_boycott_Amazon," and "#Unfollow_enemies_of_the_nation."[89]

Like the Russian interference in the 2016 presidential elections in the U.S., the death of Khashoggi was a wake-up call for big tech companies to pay closer attention to authoritarian governments' disinformation networks, especially Saudi Arabia's. In September 2019, Twitter suspended a group of six accounts,[90] but by December 2019 it had removed 5,929 accounts for violating Twitter platform manipulation policies.[91] Similarly, Facebook has had a more coordinated response to Saudi disinformation operations on the platform recently. In August 2019, it removed hundreds of accounts, pages, and Instagram accounts that were circulating disinformation against Qatar, Turkey, and Iran.[92]

The lack of traditional media to mobilize the public behind its leadership made Saudi Arabia more dependent on disinformation operations. In response to increasing global scrutiny on the Saudi war in Yemen and the death of Khashoggi, Saudi Arabia increased its disinformation operations against political dissidents and regional rivals.

However, the kingdom's excessive use of disinformation operations brought more attention from online platforms to crack down on Arabic-language disinformation networks.

CONCLUSION

The rise of digital authoritarianism in the Middle East started in the 2010s at a slow pace. Egypt tried to register visitors to internet cafés, and the UAE banned BlackBerry over its refusal to share users' data with its security apparatus. The Arab Spring utilized the internet to organize protest movements across the region. Governments saw the internet as a threat to their security and stability, which accelerated their transformation and adoption of digital authoritarianism.

Digital authoritarianism is increasingly dependent on invasive laws, online censorship, digital surveillance, and disinformation operations. Governments laid the groundwork for controlling the sphere by issuing invasive digital laws or amending current ones to punish and ban content that threatens national security, which usually includes the government's security and stability. In Egypt, the years following the 2011 revolution saw greater freedom of speech and ability by citizens to criticize the government. When Sisi took office, his government used a terrorism law to persecute media outlets. Meanwhile, Qatar abandoned its self-proclaimed role as a champion of democracy in the region when it issued an invasive cyber law to prosecute anyone posting content critical of the government.

Invasive digital laws led to an increase in online censorship of media websites that publish content critical of governments and in the amount of banned content on international platforms about local leaders. Egypt banned hundreds of websites, and Saudi Arabia pressured Netflix to suspend content critical of MbS. Historically, authoritarian governments in the region have been dependent on mass surveillance to ensure the stability of their regimes. Therefore, these governments needed to develop or import their own cyber surveillance capabilities. The UAE banned VOIP services to divert traffic into its state-backed application ToTok. Saudi Arabia bought the cyber surveillance tool Pegasus from the NSO Group to gain access to dissidents' data.

The Arab Spring made governments in the Middle East more invested in crafting their own political narratives in cyberspace and in influencing other societies. In Egypt, the power struggle between the military and the Muslim Brotherhood resulted in a huge number of bots circulating fake news to tarnish the other camp's reputation. Because of the increasing scrutiny of Saudi Arabia due to its politics and foreign policy, the kingdom uses disinformation operations against regional rivals and political dissidents.

The last 10 years in the Middle East have been full of revolutions and coups d'etat. The region's governments thought that the Arab Spring had come to an end, but now there is another wave of protests starting in Algeria, Iraq, Lebanon, and Sudan that might be more successful. The more protests the region witnesses, the more digitally authoritarian Middle Eastern governments will become in the hope of avoiding the fate of fallen regimes.

Endnotes

1. Erixon, Fredrik and Hosuk Lee-Makiyama. "Digital Authoritarianism: Human Rights, Geopolitics and Commerce." European Centre for International Political Economy (ECIPE), 2011.
2. Polyakova, Alina, and Chris Meserole. "Exporting Digital Authoritarianism." Brookings Institution. August 2019. www.brookings.edu/wp-content/uploads/2019/08/FP_20190826_digital_authoritarianism_polyakova_meserole.pdf.
3. An online movement started in April 2008, when over 100,000 users joined a Facebook group to express solidarity with factories' workers protesting in the Delta industrial city of al-Mahalla al-Kubra.
4. Howard, Philip, Sheetal D. Agarwal, and Muzammil M. Hussain (August 9, 2011). "When Do States Disconnect Their Digital Networks? Regime Responses to the Political Uses of Social Media." Working Paper Series. SSRN 1907191.
5. Spencer, Richard. "Middle East Review of 2012: the Arab Winter." *The Telegraph*. December 31, 2012. www.telegraph.co.uk/news/worldnews/middleeast/9753123/Middle-East-review-of-2012-the-Arab-Winter.html.
6. Ulrichsen, Kristian Coates. "Qatar and the Arab Spring." Carnegie Endowment for International Peace. September 2014, pp. 99-120. doi:10.1093/acprof:oso/9780190210977.003.0005.
7. Ibid.
8. Soliman, Mohammed. "How the Gulf Crisis Complicates US Foreign Policy towards Iran?" Institute for the Study of Diplomacy. May 1, 2019.
9. Gambrell, Jon. "Hack, Fake Story Expose Real Tensions between Qatar, Gulf." *Associated Press*. May 24, 2017. apnews.com/f5da3293be18401a954d48249f75394e/Hack,-fake-story-expose-real-tensions-between-Qatar,-Gulf.
10. Ibid.
11. Browning, Noah. "Qatar Investigation Finds State News Agency Hacked: Foreign Ministry." *Reuters*. June 7, 2017. www.reuters.com/article/us-gulf-qatar-cybercrime/qatar-investigation-finds-state-news-agency-hacked-foreign-ministry-idUSKBN18Y2X4.
12. Gambrell, Jon. "Hack, Fake Story Expose Real Tensions between Qatar, Gulf." *Associated Press*. May 24, 2017. apnews.com/f5da3293be18401a954d48249f75394e/Hack,-fake-story-expose-real-tensions-between-Qatar,-Gulf.
13. Soliman, Mohammed. "How the Gulf Crisis Complicates US Foreign Policy towards Iran?" Institute for the Study of Diplomacy. May 1, 2019.
14. Jones, Marc Owen. "Propaganda, Fake News, and Fake Trends: The Weaponization of Twitter Bots in the Gulf Crisis." *International Journal of Communication*, vol. 1932, no. 8036, 2019: pp. 1389–1415. https://ijoc.org/index.php/ijoc/article/view/8994/2604.
15. "Qatar: Repressive New Law Further Curbs Freedom of Expression." Amnesty International, January 20, 2020, www.amnesty.org/en/latest/news/2020/01/qatar-repressive-new-law-further-curbs-freedom-of-expression/.
16. Ibid.
17. "Egypt: Increasing Curb over Internet Usage Harassments against Net Cafs Should Immediately End." The Arabic Network for Human Rights Information. February 23, 2005. www.anhri.net/en/reports/2005/pr0223.shtml.
18. "Egypt." OpenNet Initiative. August 6, 2009. opennet.net/research/profiles/egypt.
19. Arthur, Charles. "Egypt Blocks Social Media Websites in Attempted Clampdown on Unrest." *The Guardian*. January 26, 2011. www.theguardian.com/world/2011/jan/26/egypt-blocks-social-media-websites.
20. Shenker, Jack. "Fury over Advert Claiming Egypt Revolution as Vodafone's." *The Guardian*. June 3, 2011. www.theguardian.com/world/2011/jun/03/vodafone-egypt-advert-claims-revolution.
21. "Egypt: Legal Analysis of Telecommunications Law." ARTICLE 19. www.article19.org/resources/egypt-legal-analysis-telecommunications-law/.
22. Ibid.
23. "Egypt: Counterterrorism Law Erodes Basic Rights." August 19, 2015. Retrieved from https://www.hrw.org/news/2015/08/19/egypt-counterterrorism-law-erodes-basic-rights
24. "Dozens of News Sites Blocked as Egypt Ramps up Digital Censorship." Amnesty International. June 13, 2017. www.amnesty.org/en/latest/

25. Ibid.

26. In 2017, Egypt President Abdel-Fattah el-Sisi and King Salman of Saudi Arabia ratified a maritime border agreement. Under the agreement, Egypt ceded sovereignty over Tiran and Sanafir, two uninhabited Red Sea islands, to Saudi Arabia, leading to widespread public criticism and demonstrations.

27. "Egyptian Websites Try to Resist Blocking: Reporters Without Borders." Reporters Without Borders. July 13, 2017. rsf.org/en/news/egyptian-websites-try-resist-blocking.

28. "Egypt's Masr Al-Arabia Raided, Editor in Chief Arrested." *Egyptian Streets*. April 4, 2018. egyptianstreets.com/2018/04/04/egypts-masr-al-arabia-raided-editor-in-chief-arrested/.

29. Atef, Maged. "Here's Why Egypt Has Just Banned 21 Websites." *BuzzFeed News*. May 25, 2017. https://www.buzzfeednews.com/article/magedatef/egyptian-journalists-say-the-government-blocked-websites-to.

30. Aboulenein, Ahmed. "Egypt blocks 21 websites for 'terrorism' and 'fake news.'" *Reuters*. May 25, 2017. https://www.reuters.com/article/us-egypt-censorship/egypt-blocks-21-websites-for-terrorism-and-fake-news-idUSKBN18K307.

31. Atef, Maged. "Here's Why Egypt Has Just Banned 21 Websites." *BuzzFeed News*. May 25, 2017. https://www.buzzfeednews.com/article/magedatef/egyptian-journalists-say-the-government-blocked-websites-to.

32. Bahgat, Hossam. "Anatomy of an election." *Mada Masr*. March 14, 2016. https://madamasr.com/en/2016/03/14/feature/politics/anatomy-of-an-election/.

33. Bahgat, Hossam. "Who's buying Israeli gas? A company owned by the General Intelligence Service." *Mada Masr*. October 23, 2018. https://madamasr.com/en/2018/10/23/feature/politics/whos-buying-israeli-gas-a-company-owned-by-the-general-intelligence-service/.

34. "President's eldest son, Mahmoud al-Sisi, sidelined from powerful intelligence position to diplomatic mission in Russia." *Mada Masr*. November 20, 2019. https://madamasr.com/en/2019/11/20/feature/politics/presidents-eldest-son-mahmoud-al-sisi-sidelined-from-powerful-intelligence-position-to-diplomatic-mission-in-russia/.

35. Michaelson, Ruth. "Egypt's security forces raid online newspaper's office in Cairo." *The Guardian*. November 24, 2019. https://www.theguardian.com/world/2019/nov/24/egypts-security-forces-raid-online-newspapers-office-in-cairo.

36. "Egypt bans 21 websites for 'Supporting terrorism' and 'Spreading lies.'" *Reuters*. May 25, 2017. https://ara.reuters.com/article/topNews/idARAKBN18K30X.

37. Ibid.

38. "Egypt poised to add news media to list of 'terrorist entities.'" Reporters Without Borders. January 29, 2020. https://rsf.org/en/news/egypt-poised-add-news-media-list-terrorist-entities.

39. "RANKED: The Most Influential Arabic Newspapers (2020 Edition)." Industry Arabic. January 23, 2020. www.industryarabic.com/arabic-newspapers/.

40. "The press in Saudi Arabia." *BBC News*. December 13, 2006. http://news.bbc.co.uk/2/hi/middle_east/6176791.stm.

41. Ibid.

42. Ibid.

43. Griffiths, James and Euan McKirdy. "Netflix pulls 'Patriot Act' episode in Saudi Arabia after it criticized official account of Khashoggi killing." *CNN*. January 2, 2019. https://www.cnn.com/2019/01/01/middleeast/netflix-patriot-act-hasan-minhaj-jamal-khashoggi-intl/index.html.

44. Ibid.

45. Singh, Manish. "Disney blocks John Oliver's new episode critical of India's PM Modi." *TechCrunch*. February 25, 2020. https://techcrunch.com/2020/02/25/disney-hotstar-blocks-john-olivers-new-episode-critical-of-narendra-modi/.

46. Brooks, Risa. *Political-Military Relations and the Stability of Arab Regimes*. Oxford University Press for International Institute for Strategic Studies, 1998.

47. Matthiesen, Toby. "A Purge in Riyadh." *Foreign Affairs*. November 8, 2017. www.foreignaffairs.com/articles/saudi-arabia/2017-11-08/purge-riyadh.

48. "Saudi Arabia: Prominent Clerics Arrested." Human Rights Watch. September 15, 2017. www.hrw.org/news/2017/09/15/saudi-arabia-prominent-clerics-arrested#.

49. Beaumont, Peter. "Further Arrests of Saudi Women's Rights Activists in Escalating Crackdown." *The Guardian*. May 21, 2018. www.theguardian.com/global-development/2018/may/21/further-arrests-saudi-arabia-womens-rights-activists-driving-ban.
50. Hubbard, Ben. "Why Spy on Twitter? For Saudi Arabia, It's the Town Square." *New York Times*. November 7, 2019. www.nytimes.com/2019/11/07/world/middleeast/saudi-arabia-twitter-arrests.html.
51. "Saudi Arabia Is the Most Twitter-Crazy Country in the World: Business Insider." Ministry of Communications and Information Technology. February 28, 2018. www.mcit.gov.sa/en/media-center/news/91426.
52. Ibid.
53. Ibid.
54. Groll, Elias. "The Kingdom's Hackers and Bots." *Foreign Policy*. October 19, 2018. foreignpolicy.com/2018/10/19/the-kingdoms-hackers-and-bots-saudi-dissident-khashoggi/.
55. Kenyon, Miles. "The NSO Connection to Jamal Khashoggi." The Citizen Lab. October 24, 2018. citizenlab.ca/2018/10/the-nso-connection-to-jamal-khashoggi/.
56. Marczak, Bill, et al. "Stopping the Press: New York Times Journalist Targeted by Saudi-Linked Pegasus Spyware Operator." The Citizen Lab. January 28, 2020. citizenlab.ca/2020/01/stopping-the-press-new-york-times-journalist-targeted-by-saudi-linked-pegasus-spyware-operator/.
57. Hubbard, Ben. "Why Spy on Twitter? For Saudi Arabia, It's the Town Square." *New York Times*. November 7, 2019. www.nytimes.com/2019/11/07/world/middleeast/saudi-arabia-twitter-arrests.html.
58. Gross, Doug. "Experts: BlackBerry ban could affect privacy everywhere." *CNN*. August 4, 2010. https://www.cnn.com/2010/TECH/mobile/08/02/blackberry.uae/index.html
59. Forstenlechner, Ingo, Emilie Rutledge, and Rashed Salem Alnuaimi. (2012). The UAE, the "Arab Spring" and Different Types of Dissent. *Middle East Policy*, 19(4), 54-67. doi: 10.1111/j.1475-4967.2012.00559.x.
60. Baskan, Birol. "Turkey and the UAE: A Strange Crisis." The Middle East Institute. May 1, 2019. www.mei.edu/publications/turkey-and-uae-strange-crisis.
61. Forstenlechner, Ingo, et al. "The UAE, the 'Arab Spring' and Different Types of Dissent." *Middle East Policy*, vol. 19, no. 4, 2012, pp. 54-67., doi:10.1111/j.1475-4967.2012.00559.x.
62. Ibid.
63. "World Report 2011: Rights Trends in World Report 2011: United Arab Emirates." Human Rights Watch. April 16, 2015. www.hrw.org/world-report/2011/country-chapters/united-arab-emirates.
64. Habboush, Mahmoud. "UAE Sentences Activists to Jail for Insulting Leaders." *Reuters*. November 27, 2011. www.reuters.com/article/us-emirates-activists-jail-idUSTRE7AQ04320111127.
65. Admin. "UAE Closes Dubai Office of U.S. Pro-Democracy Group: March 30, 2012." National Democratic Institute. May 1, 2012. www.ndi.org/node/16709.
66. "Is Skype Blocked in the United Arab Emirates (UAE)?: Skype Support." Skype , support.skype.com/en/faq/FA391/is-skype-blocked-in-the-united-arab-emirates-uae.
67. "Viber Seeks Ways to Circumvent Ban in Middle East." *The National*. June 10, 2013. www.thenational.ae/uae/viber-seeks-ways-to-circumvent-ban-in-middle-east-1.296775.
68. Nagraj, Aarti. "Snapchat Voice and Video Calling Blocked in UAE." *Gulf Business*. July 10, 2016. gulfbusiness.com/snapchat-voice-and-video-calling-blocked-in-uae/.
69. Sankar, Anjana. "No WhatsApp Calls in the UAE, Authority Clarifies." *Khaleej Times*. June 23, 2017. www.khaleejtimes.com/technology/no-whatsapp-calls-in-the-uae-authority-clarifies.
70. "Dh500,000 Fine If You Use Fraud IP in UAE." *Emirates24*. October 3, 2018. www.emirates247.com/news/emirates/dh500-000-fine-if-you-use-fraud-ip-in-uae-2016-07-22-1.636441.
71. Ibid.
72. Mazzetti, Mark, et al. "It Seemed Like a Popular Chat App. It's Secretly a Spy Tool." *New York Times*. December 22, 2019. www.nytimes.com/2019/12/22/us/politics/totok-app-uae.html.
73. Ibid.
74. Ibid.
75. El Gendi, Yosra. (2020). "Social Media in Egypt's Transition Period." AUC Egypt. February 19, 2020, from http://schools.aucegypt.edu/huss/pols/Khamasin/Documents/Social%20

Media%20in%20Egypt%27s%20Transition%20Period%20-%20Yosra%20El-Gendi.pdf.

76. Kirkpatrick, David. "Morsi Turns to His Islamist Backers as Egypt's Crisis Grows." *New York Times*. December 7, 2012. www.nytimes.com/2012/12/08/world/middleeast/egypt-islamists-dialogue-secular-opponents-clashes.html.

77. "Altered Images: Egypt's Disinformation War." *BBC Monitoring*. July 27, 2013. www.bbc.com/news/blogs-news-from-elsewhere-23469516.

78. Ibid.

79. Karan, Kanishk. "Bots Are Dominating Political Debate in Egypt." *InfoTimes*. February 12, 2019. infotimes.org/bots-are-dominating-political-debate-in-egypt/.

80. Ibid.

81. Ibid.

82. Ibid.

83. Khalife, Leyal. "#WeNeedToTalk: Egyptians Are Calling out Violations of Human Rights." StepFeed. October 31, 2017. stepfeed.com/weneedtotalk-egyptians-are-calling-out-violations-of-human-rights-2149.

84. Sardarizadeh, Shayan. "BBC Monitoring – Essential Media Insight." *BBC*. October 7, 2019. monitoring.bbc.co.uk/product/c2015157.

85. "Disclosing New Data to Our Archive of Information Operations." Twitter Safety, September 20, 2019. blog.twitter.com/en_us/topics/company/2019/info-ops-disclosure-data-september-2019.html.

86. Ibid.

87. Gleicher, Nathaniel. "Removing Coordinated Inauthentic Behavior in UAE, Egypt and Saudi Arabia." Facebook. August 1, 2019. about.fb.com/news/2019/08/cib-uae-egypt-saudi-arabia/.

88. Hubbard, Ben and Nick Cumming-Bruce. "On Khashoggi Killing and Yemen, Saudis Cannot Avoid Fresh Scrutiny." *New York Times*. September 26, 2019. www.nytimes.com/2019/09/26/world/middleeast/mbs-khashoggi-killing-responsibility.html.

89. Burke, Samuel. "Twitter Shuts down Bots Pushing pro-Saudi Message." *CNN*. October 19, 2018. www.cnn.com/2018/10/19/tech/twitter-suspends-spam-khashoggi-accounts-intl/index.html.

90. "Disclosing New Data to Our Archive of Information Operations." Twitter Safety September 20, 2019. blog.twitter.com/en_us/topics/company/2019/info-ops-disclosure-data-september-2019.html.

91. "New Disclosures to Our Archive of State-Backed Information Operations." Twitter. December 20, 2019. blog.twitter.com/en_us/topics/company/2019/new-disclosures-to-our-archive-of-state-backed-information-operations.html.

92. "Removing Coordinated Inauthentic Behavior in UAE, Egypt and Saudi Arabia." Facebook. August 1, 2019. about.fb.com/news/2019/08/cib-uae-egypt-saudi-arabia/.

CHAPTER NINE

A BATTLE OF TWO PANDEMICS:

CORONAVIRUS AND DIGITAL AUTHORITARIANISM IN THE ARAB WORLD

SAHAR KHAMIS

INTRODUCTION

This chapter explores the current wave of coronavirus-related digital crackdowns in the Arab region, which are unfolding in multiple forms, and analyzes its causes, contexts, and consequences. It explores why and how the stifling of media freedom and freedom of speech online in the Arab region has been exacerbated in the midst of the coronavirus pandemic, and sheds light on the various tools and mechanisms of control being used by Arab regimes to ensure that the official, state-orchestrated narrative around the pandemic dominates all communication platforms, both online and offline. In doing so, the chapter unpacks a number of methods of control that are being deployed by Arab regimes to achieve this end, ranging from closing down websites to arresting local journalists and ousting international correspondents, as well as exploiting punitive legal codes and laws to tighten their grip on all communication outlets, under the mantle of countering disinformation. It also sheds light on a closely-intertwined dimension in these new cyberwars,[1] namely reliance on online surveillance and contact tracing tools and applications, which are justified by regimes as part of the effort to curb the spread of the deadly pandemic, but which simultaneously, and dangerously, open the door to threats to personal security, invasion of privacy, and government hacking of opposition. The chapter concludes with a discussion of the most important consequences and implications of these complex, and interconnected, phenomena, as well as the paradoxes and dilemmas they pose.

BATTLES OVER "MEDIATED NARRATIVES": LISTEN TO ONLY "ONE" VOICE!

Since the COVID-19 pandemic crisis began sweeping the world, it has been accompanied by a surge in interest in learning more about this unwelcome new guest. In the absence of a consistent flow of accurate, reliable, and credible information about the pandemic, many people resorted to rumors, as well as misinformation and disinformation, to fill some of the communication gaps.[2]

This new phenomenon was referred to as an "infodemic," a term coined by the World Health Organization (WHO) to describe the wave of fake claims that paralleled the spread of COVID-19.[3]

The spread of rumors and misinformation around the pandemic could also be attributed to a number of other reasons, including panic, coupled with people's desire to further distract themselves from the dire situation, and its negative implications, by relying on, oftentimes untrustworthy, social media sources and stories when seeking answers to their questions about the nature of the disease, its causes, symptoms, remedies, and cures.[4]

This surge in people's desire for information was alarming to many countries, especially those with authoritarian governments, for whom any window to gain access to non-state-controlled information was immediately perceived as a threat and promptly shut down. These efforts on the part of authoritarian regimes, which culminated in waves of internet shutdowns, were met by counterwaves of resistance.[5]

This was certainly true in the Arab world. According to the "Covid-19 and Press Freedom" map and report[6] produced by the Committee to Protect Journalists (CPJ), which document the types and locations of various COVID-19-related threats, including digital threats, and their impact on press freedom globally, restrictions and violations by Arab regimes against press freedom, including shutting down or restricting access to numerous websites, were widespread throughout the region.

Interestingly, resistance to the impact of governments' restrictive measures on access to news and information, in the midst of a pandemic, did not just come from professional journalists. Rather, there have been some attempts on the part of average citizens as well to resist such efforts. For example, residents in the United Arab Emirates (UAE) called for the governmental ban on internet-based calling applications, such as WhatsApp and Skype, to be lifted, especially as enforced restrictions impacted mobility and travel amid the coronavirus lockdown.[7] This could also be attributed to the increased need to have access to near constant news and information about the virus and its implications, in the midst of a devastating global health disaster.

Many countries in the Arab region were negatively affected, and hugely impacted, by the dire consequences of the pandemic, both socially and economically. The IMF has predicted an overall seven percent drop in real GDP in Arab economies, as well as a 14 percent fall in remittances throughout the region, with myriad political, economic, and social effects exacerbating the region's existing challenges.[8]

At the heart of the governmental clampdown on various media outlets in the Arab world is a relentless effort on the part of authoritarian regimes to control the mediated narrative around the pandemic, including infection, positivity, and death rates, in an attempt to minimize the negative effects, through damage control.

In doing so, different governments in the region struggled to control, and define, the official narrative around the virus, according to their own terms, interests, and agendas, using their manipulated, official media outlets, as their main communication avenues and platforms.

Oftentimes, these efforts to ensure "maximum narrative control" resulted in crackdowns on both local and international media outlets and journalists[9] who dared to challenge the state-manipulated narrative, through presenting an alternative, or amended, version.

This led to an overall deterioration in the margin of freedom of the press in the Arab region, with the spread of "weaponized censorship" resulting in the "demise of free expression"[10] — a trend reflected in the ranking of journalistic practices produced by Reporters Without Borders (RSF) in April 2020.[11]

Numerous examples could be cited throughout the Arab region to illustrate this point, as reported by organizations including CPJ, RSF, and Sky Line International.[12] The prevailing regional trend was one characterized by a lack of transparency and iron-fisted policies in dealing with both mainstream media and social media. For example, the CPJ reported several incidents of Arab governments cracking down on both local and foreign media outlets in March and April 2020, in retaliation for noncompliant COVID-19 reporting. These incidents included the Iraqi regulator suspending Reuters' license for three months; the Iraqi Kurdish authorities closing down NRT TV station; Jordan arresting two journalists; and Bahrain imprisoning several journalists, and placing one of them in solitary confinement.[13]

Egyptian security forces briefly detained Lina Attalah, the editor-in-chief of the website Mada Masr, described as Egypt's last independent media outlet, which was blocked by the regime in May 2017, along with at least 500 other websites. Her arrest came in the midst of a growing wave of crackdowns on press freedom linked to COVID-19 reporting.[14] Egyptian security forces also detained another journalist, Hassan Mahgoub, after reporting a series of stories about the virus, and an editor, Atef Hasballah, was arrested after questioning the government's official statistics about COVID-19 on his personal Facebook page.[15]

The crackdown also impacted foreign journalists and correspondents. One example is the infamous case of *Guardian* correspondent Ruth Michaelson: The British-German journalist had her press credentials revoked and she was expelled from Egypt after publishing an article citing a study by a Canadian research center, which estimated that the number of COVID-19 cases in Egypt had exceeded 19,000, at a time when the officially declared number was under 200.[16] After being accused of spreading false information, which undermines public order and causes panic, Michaelson stated: "Egypt in their response to this reporting has politicized that problem and it's made it a press freedom issue when it's simply a public health issue."[17]

The Egyptian regime did not only target Michaelson. The official State Information Service (SIS) also denounced tweets by the Cairo bureau chief of *The New York Times*, Declan Walsh, referencing the same figures, and censured him for "bad faith" reporting. Walsh later deleted the tweets following a backlash from Egyptians online.[18] A statement issued by SIS, which is responsible for foreign media accreditation, criticized this type of reporting on the part of both journalists, saying that, "It shows their intentional bad faith to harm Egyptian interests."

Ironically, the accusations made by the Egyptian authorities against these foreign correspondents included damaging Egypt's international reputation and hurting its image abroad; however, it can be argued that taking such actions against these renowned journalists was far more damaging in that regard.

These actions by the Egyptian government could be interpreted as an attempt on its part to save itself from further damage, taking into account the negative effects caused by this invisible new enemy in a number of domains, especially the economy, which has been suffering from the fall in oil prices and declining tourism.[19]

According to Sherif Mansour and Courtney Radsch from the CPJ, the exacerbation in the stifling of press freedom in the MENA region amid the pandemic created truly dire and dangerous situations for journalists, both in mainstream media and digital media. They are compelled to battle the parallel threats of being infected while covering coronavirus-related stories, on the one hand, and being punished by their own regimes, as a result of this coverage, especially if it does not comply with the official, governmental narrative, on the other hand.[20]

One of the recent, and most devastating, examples has been the infamous case of Egyptian journalist Mohamed Mounir, who was believed to have been "murdered by coronavirus."[21] The 65-year-old journalist, who suffered from multiple health conditions, was arrested and held in a crowded jail in Egypt, where it is believed he contracted COVID-19. Mounir was released when his health started to deteriorate, and he died a few days later from coronavirus-related complications in a hospital in Giza.

Among the accusations Mounir faced was spreading "false information," after giving a television interview to Al-Jazeera Mubasher, and publishing a column on the channel's website, criticizing the Egyptian government's handling of the coronavirus pandemic, especially the shortages of necessary medical supplies and equipment, including personal protective equipment for medical and health care professionals.[22] Therefore, it could be said that Mounir was killed by the coronavirus "twice," once by daring to write about it, and a second time by actually contracting it.

There is mounting fear that the continued crackdown on journalists in the region, including arrests and imprisonments in crowded jails, amid a deadly pandemic, could lead to the permanent silencing of crucial voices, as witnessed in Mounir's tragic case.

LEGAL CONTROL MECHANISMS: COUNTERING "DISINFORMATION" OR BLOCKING "INFORMATION"?

One of the major challenges that has negative effects on media credibility and professionalism in the Arab world is the legal challenge, which could be described as "two-fold." On the one hand, there are legal codes and laws that are meant to protect journalists, but these are not effectively enforced, leaving them vulnerable to pressure and retaliation. On the other hand, there is the exploitation of existing punitive measures, or even drafting of new ones, with the purpose of cracking down harder on journalists, many times with harsh consequences, such as imprisonment, long jail sentences, and closing down websites.[23]

An unfortunate example of the latter is the drafting, and enforcement, of so-called "Cybercrime Laws" (قوانين الجرائم الإلكترونية), which, as the name implies, are intended to punish those who are perceived by various Arab dictatorial regimes as crossing the line in the realm of cyberspace, by committing "online violations." The definition, and nature, of these violations is, of course, decided by the governments and their official regulatory bodies, leaving a lot of room for subjectivity, manipulation, and even retaliation.

One striking example of how such laws have been exploited is the issuance of new decisions by the Supreme Council for Media Regulation (المجلس الأعلى لتنظيم الاعلام), the main, state-run media regulatory body in Egypt, requiring all media to seek official approval before publishing stories on sensitive topics, including the Grand Ethiopian Renaissance Dam, the situation in Sinai and Libya, and the coronavirus pandemic. It even issued warnings against those who dare to violate such regulations when publishing about these topics, including coronavirus-related coverage.[24]

The danger of these new regulations is that they criminalize any reporting that falls outside the realm of state approval, and/or which contradicts the official, governmental narrative, in reporting about these topics, and investigates it as a "violation."[25] Those who spread so-called "false news" online about coronavirus, for example, could face up to five years imprisonment and steep fines, according to a warning from Egypt's top prosecutor.[26]

One recent example illustrating the exploitation of the "Cybercrime Laws" is the arrest of Sanaa' Seif, the sister of the jailed Egyptian blogger, Alaa' Abdel Fattah, under the pretense that she was spreading "disinformation" related to coronavirus on various social media outlets. In reality, all she was doing was alerting the public about the dire conditions in which her brother, and other prisoners, are being held; such unsanitary and inhumane conditions in crowded jails provide the ideal environment for the rampant spread of the virus. More importantly, her arrest could be interpreted as an official retaliation for the online campaign she, and her family, launched on Facebook and Twitter under the hashtag "#Iwantaletter #عايزة_جواب," which, as the name implies, demanded that they receive a letter from her brother Alaa' to make sure he is safe while in prison.[27]

Similar "Cybercrimes Laws" were issued and implemented in other Arab countries as well. For example, in Morocco at least a dozen people have been arrested for supposedly spreading rumors about the coronavirus. "Fake news is the first cause of panic among citizens," said Prime Minister Saadeddine el-Otmai, comparing the spread of misinformation with the contagion of the disease. On the same day, the government approved a draft law governing the use of social media, aiming to deter fake news and cybercrimes from undermining public order and the economy.[28]

One success story came out of Tunisia: In March 2020, a member of the Tunisian Parliament proposed a draft law to combat "disinformation" during the COVID-19 crisis, on the pretext of fighting "fake news" and controlling the flow of information on social media platforms that could impact "national security and order." Those who objected to this proposed new law perceived it as a direct threat to freedom of expression online; it would muzzle journalists and activists, as well as exercise control over them through intimidation and by limiting access to the information necessary to document any rights violations.[29] Fortunately,

Tunisian civil society took quick action. Only hours after the proposed bill was leaked to the press, the public responded with a wave of criticism on social media. This response led the MP who proposed the draft law to withdraw it, stopping it from moving forward in Parliament.[30]

Indeed, the greatest threat with such laws, as the Tunisians successfully realized, is that they can be exploited as tools to curb the spread of "information" about coronavirus, and other pressing and sensitive issues, via different media outlets, including internet-based communication. The justification of countering "disinformation" and "fake news" can be used to disguise persistent efforts to stifle all freedoms, both online and offline.

SURVEILLANCE AND CONTACT TRACING CONCERNS: THE "BIG BROTHER" SYNDROME AND ITS THREATS

Part of the international effort to curb the spread of this deadly virus includes putting in place more rigorous online surveillance mechanisms and utilizing digital contact tracing applications to monitor COVID-19 cases and identify the location, mobility, and social networks of those who tested positive, in an effort to slow down the spread of the pandemic.

However, there are numerous dangers posed by the spread of location-tracking and spyware tools, which are deployed by various regimes throughout the world, under the guise of tracing the spread of the virus, and, hence, protecting the public from the health hazards of this deadly disease. Undoubtedly, such dangers are exacerbated under authoritarian regimes, with their tendency to strive to maintain tight, and sometimes even total, control over the flow, and exchange, of information.

In fact, it is safe to say that the most salient trend witnessed in the context of the rise of authoritarian, technology-related, repressive tendencies by various governments amid the pandemic has been the spread of digital surveillance techniques. This is certainly true in the case of the Arab world.

According to Michael Sexton and Mohammed Soliman from the Middle East Institute (MEI) Cyber Program, the implementation of new surveillance applications and contact tracing tools pose serious threats to personal privacy and security, making civilians' use of the internet in the MENA region riskier, more hazardous, and, in some cases, life-threatening, especially taking into account the myriad ways in which such data could be gathered, exposed, and exploited by authoritarian regimes in the region.[31]

Some of the most advanced surveillance and contact tracing applications developed in the Arab world during the current health crisis, unsurprisingly, came out of the Gulf region. This is due to the higher levels of technical advancement and technological-savviness in these countries, compared to the rest of the Arab world, which are closely related to their greater economic affluence and better infrastructure.

The Gulf states have successfully developed an advanced technological infrastructure that is conducive to processing new digital data and has enabled them to keep pace with and take advantage of modern technological developments, increase efficiency and productivity, and improve government services.[32] The Gulf states' positive rankings on the eGovernment Readiness Index (EGDI) reflect the major ongoing efforts that regional governments have made to improve information and communications technology (ICT) infrastructure across all ministries and agencies in recent years.[33]

One of the recent examples of the contact tracing applications adopted in the Gulf is the UAE's "TraceCovid" app, aimed at slowing the spread of coronavirus by helping to trace people who have come into close proximity with an infected individual. Currently, the TraceCovid app can be downloaded and installed by anyone living in the UAE using a supported Bluetooth-enabled smartphone running on Android or iOS. Once downloaded, the user will receive a one-time password for verification, through the National Emergency Crisis and Disaster Management Authority.[34] The app requires access to location services in the phone to function effectively. The TraceCovid app augments the contact tracing process as it can automatically record all people who have been in proximity to a COVID-19 patient, including people the patient does not know. Although the adoption of the app is not compulsory, it is highly encouraged by the authorities, as the more people who download it, the more effective this contact tracing approach will be, significantly reducing the manpower required.[35]

In addition, the Abu Dhabi-based firm G42 Healthcare is set to work with Israeli company NanoScent to develop and manufacture a product they say will be capable of detecting suspected cases of COVID-19 from a sample of exhaled nasal air.[36] The fact that this company is working on developing counter-coronavirus products, while presenting itself as an artificial intelligence (AI)/cloud computing company raises questions as to its remit and the nature of the data it expects to collect.

In Qatar, a contact tracing app has been adopted that uses a mixture of GPS and Bluetooth technology to track COVID-19 cases and warn people who may have been exposed to an infectious person. It operates on a centralized model, allowing the country's Interior Ministry access to the information it gathers. A security flaw in this contact-tracing app put the sensitive personal details of its users at risk, according to an investigation by Amnesty International. The app, which is mandatory for Qatari residents to install, was configured in a way that would have allowed hackers "to access highly sensitive personal information, including the name, national ID, health status and location data of more than 1 million users," according to Amnesty International's security lab. Claudio Guarnieri, the lab's head, said the flaws, fixed following their discovery, "should act as a warning to governments around the world rushing out contact tracing apps that are too often poorly designed and lack privacy safeguards."[37]

It is fair to say that, due to their novelty, many of the long-term effects, implications, and threats of these new surveillance tools and contact tracing applications are only starting to become clear. One alarming example of such threats is a controversial Israeli cyber tool company called NSO Group marketing software that uses mobile phone data to monitor and predict the spread of the coronavirus. NSO Group says it is in talks with governments around the world, and claims some are already testing its new software.[38] There is arguably no worse company to navigate the thorny privacy challenges inherent in developing this software than NSO, which is under investigation by the FBI for facilitating the hacking of American residents,[39] and has been implicated countless times in the targeting of journalists and human rights activists from Mexico[40] to India.[41]

BETWEEN "DOWNPLAYING" AND THE "FEAR APPEAL": THE LEGITIMIZATION OF AUTHORITARIANISM?

When major crises erupt, they provide a unique opportunity for authoritarian regimes to tighten their grip on power, and to heighten their iron fist policy against all forms of dissent and opposition in all spheres, including mainstream media and new media. The COVID-19 pandemic has proven to be another example of how this authoritarian consolidation plays out in the Arab world.

In the case of the Arab world's battle against the COVID-19 pandemic, it could be said that the response of regimes in the region oscillated between two contradictory, yet equally detrimental, strategies, namely downplaying the danger of the deadly pandemic, on the one hand, and using the "fear appeal" strategy to monopolize the framing of the narrative around it, on the other.

The first strategy of downplaying the danger of the pandemic,[42] which has been adopted by a number of global leaders, including the current president of the United States, is intended to limit the damaging effects of the pandemic on the economic welfare of societies, oftentimes with detrimental impacts on people's health, and it is usually justified as an effort to keep people calm and to prevent them from panicking.

The second strategy rests on mastering the ability to play on people's worst fears, or even to amplify, and magnify, such fears, using the "fear appeal" strategy, as the primary tool. Ironically, in this particular case, the perceived, magnified, fear is not meant to be that of the pandemic itself, taking into account the governments' efforts to downplay its dangers, as previously mentioned. Rather, it is instilling fear of the danger of drifting away from the official, state-controlled narrative around the pandemic, through discouraging people from listening to or believing any alternative, or challenging, narratives. Labelling such alternative narratives as "fake news," and classifying them as part of the tide of COVID-19-related "misinformation" and "disinformation,"[43] has been one successful strategy used by these regimes in this regard.

This "fear appeal" strategy, which has been historically used by populist authoritarian leaders to advance their causes, through mobilizing the masses to rally behind their leadership and to support their agendas, oftentimes proves to be effective, albeit with devastating effects, as history has shown time and again.

By playing on people's worst fears, populist, authoritarian leaders succeed in painting themselves as the ultimate "saviors" and sole "rescuers" of their people. They position themselves as wise leaders who are providing their people with the best chance to survive, through conquering a common "enemy," whether it is a foreign power or a global pandemic.

The ultimate danger posed by these parallel, and equally harmful, phenomena is the legitimization of authoritarianism. In other words, feeding and catalyzing the dangerous tendency by people to ultimately defer to authority, or even to accept dictatorship, as a fair price to pay for ensuring their safety and survival.

The current wave of coronavirus-related, information-control wars, both in the real world and in cyberspace, opens the door for these alarming tendencies to flourish and these dangerous trends to grow and accelerate. This is especially true given the widespread admiration of East Asian success stories in containing the spread of the virus, which are largely attributed to authoritarian regimes' tight control mechanisms, including the use of highly effective surveillance and digital contact-tracing tools.[44]

Some echoes of such arguments could be heard throughout the Arab world by those who hail the efforts of Arab regimes to contain the virus, even if it means stifling all freedoms, including freedom of expression, and eliminating all forms of opposition and resistance, both online and offline.

However, it is ironic that these arguments are echoed throughout the Arab region, given that Arab countries are generally not classified among the best worldwide for their coronavirus response efforts.[45]

With this dubious track record, one has to wonder if the surveillance measures to ensure safety were truly worth the restrictions imposed upon individual and collective freedoms, both online and offline.

THE PARADOXES OF TECHNOLOGY AS A "DOUBLE-EDGED SWORD"

The latest tide of "digital authoritarianism"[46] has manifested itself in a number of aggressive ways throughout the Arab region during COVID-19, covering all 10 of the dangerous symptoms of curbing press freedom amid the pandemic that the CPJ warned against.[47] These include:

- Laws against "fake news"
- Jailing journalists
- Suspending free speech
- Blunt censorship, online and offline
- Threatening and harassing journalists, online and offline
- Accreditation requests and restricted freedom of movement
- Restricted access to information
- Expulsions and visa restrictions
- Surveillance and contact tracing
- Emergency measures[48]

This escalating and dangerous trend compels us to consider a number of important points. It is indicative of the shrinking margin of freedom in this troubled part of the world, in general, as well as the diminishing margin of freedom of expression in mainstream media and social media, in particular. If anything, this trend has only accelerated amid the devastating global pandemic.

It is safe to conclude that 10 years after the eruption of the Arab Spring uprisings, the dashed hopes for smooth political transitions to democratization and reform are paralleled by an unfortunate shift from "techno-euphoria,"[49] defined as highly optimistic expectations of the democratizing potential of social media, to escalating "digital authoritarianism."

When the uprisings erupted in 2011, the new phenomenon of "cyberactivism,"[50] or the use of new media to enact socio-political change online, was effectively utilized by young activists and protesters. They were many steps ahead of the dictatorial regimes in the region, which were mostly unprepared and taken by surprise.[51] A decade later, however, it is safe to say that many of the region's regimes have enhanced their technological savviness, and are now capable of not only matching, but oftentimes exceeding, the technical capabilities of dissidents and opponents.

However, it is important to acknowledge the fact that these attempts on the part of dictatorial regimes throughout the region to dominate and shape the official COVID-19 narrative have frequently been resisted and challenged by other voices from inside and outside the region, as witnessed in the case of local and foreign journalists, for example.

The various push and pull mechanisms between authoritarian regimes in the Arab region and those who dare to challenge them in the context of the coronavirus battles, both online and offline, compel us to pay attention to a number of important points.

Most importantly, in exploring why and how the relentless battles over who controls the mediated narratives around the coronavirus pandemic took different forms, used differing tools, and exhibited varying degrees of severity in various Arab countries, myriad factors have to be carefully considered. These include the degree of authoritarianism exercised by the regime in power, and its reflections on the media arena; the shifts and transformations in the socio-political landscape, and the accompanying shifts in the media landscape; the different forms of direct and indirect media control and digital manipulation exercised by various Arab regimes, ranging from censorship to sponsorship; and the varying levels of technological savviness, economic affluence, and digital literacy across these countries.

In other words, to effectively analyze the ongoing trends in the two parallel battles of the coronavirus pandemic and digital authoritarianism in the Arab region, it is important to take into account the overarching similarities, as well as the distinctive differences between different countries, in terms of their degree of openness (or lack thereof), political systems, economies, and levels of technological advancement.

We must also acknowledge the double-edged sword effect of these new technologies as tools for both liberation and repression, depending on who is using them, against whom, when, where, how, and why. This duality in the roles and effects of new technologies and modern means of communication stems from the fact that just as they provide regimes with strong tools to restrict freedoms and block the flow of information, both online and offline, they also provide activists, dissidents, opponents, and journalists with the needed tools and platforms to resist such restrictions and counter them, giving momentum to a never-ending tug of war.

It is realistic to conclude that as new technologies and techniques are developed, this tug of war will only strengthen, while taking on different forms and utilizing new platforms, in a vicious, interconnected, yet constantly shifting cycle, against the backdrop of a region in flux.

While the current crisis triggered by the COVID-19 pandemic did not create any of these complex processes and dynamics, it has certainly provided a suitable environment and a strong catalyst for them to be manifested and proliferated through a variety of tangled, and sometimes contradictory, push and pull mechanisms, the long-term effects and implications of which remain to be seen.

Endnotes

1. Evgeny Morozov, *The Net Delusion: The Dark Side of Internet Freedom* (New York: Public Affairs, 2011).

2. Jessica Weiss, "Sifting Through the Deluge of Covid-19 Information," Interview with Dr. Sahar Khamis, College of Arts and Humanities (ARHU), University of Maryland, April 13, 2020, https://arhu.umd.edu/news/sifting-through-deluge-covid-19-information.

3. Zoe Thomas, "WHO Says Fake Coronavirus Claims causing Infodemic," *BBC*, February 13, 2020, https://www.bbc.com/news/technology-51497800.

4. Laura Hazard Owen, "Why Do People Share Misinformation about Covid-19? Partly Because They're Distracted," NiemanLab, July 2, 2020, https://www.niemanlab.org/2020/07/why-do-people-share-misinformation-about-covid-19-partly-because-theyre-distracted/.

5. "Civil Society to WHO: Let's End Government-Ordered Internet Shutdowns," AccessNow, May 26, 2020, https://www.accessnow.org/civil-society-to-who-lets-end-government-ordered-internet-shutdowns/.

6. "Covid-19 and Press Freedom," Committee to Protect Journalists (CPJ), https://cpj.org/covid-19/.

7. Natasha Turak, "UAE Loosens Some VoIP Restrictions as Residents in Lockdown Call for End to WhatsApp and Skype Ban," *CNBC*, March 26, 2020, https://www.cnbc.com/2020/03/26/coronavirus-lockdown-uae-residents-call-for-end-to-whatsapp-skype-ban.html.

8. "Covid-19 Poses Formidable Threat for Fragile states in the Middle East and North Africa," International Monetary Fund, *IMF Country Focus*, May 13, 2020, https://www.imf.org/en/News/Articles/2020/05/13/na051320-COVID-19-poses-formidable-threat-for-fragile-states-in-the-middle-east-and-north-africa.

9. Middle East Eye Correspondent, "Fear is Overcoming Me: Egypt Cracks Down Harder on Media Amid Pandemic," *Middle East Eye*, June 21, 2020, https://www.middleeasteye.net/news/fear-overcoming-me-egypt-steps-crackdown-media-amid-pandemic.

10. Horriya Marzouk, "Weaponized Censorship: The Final Demise of Free Expression in Egypt's Media," *The New Arab*, July 2, 2020, https://english.alaraby.co.uk/english/indepth/2020/7/2/the-final-demise-of-free-expression-in-egypts-media.

11. مراسلون بلا حدود: التصنيف في زمن كورونا "Journalistic Ranking During the Corona Era," Reporters Without Borders (RSF), April 20, 2020, https://rsf.org/ar/news/-244.

12. تقرير لسكاي لاين يرصد انتهاكات حكومية ضد الصحفيين في خضم جائحة كورونا "A Report on Governmental Violations Against Journalists Amid the Covid-19 Pandemic," Sky Line International, April 13, 2020, http://skylineforhuman.org/ar/news/details/277/press_violations.

13. Sahar Khamis, Interview with "Voice of America Radio" (English), the International Edition, "Arab Governments' Responses to the Covid-19 Pandemic and Press Freedom," April 20, 2020, https://www.voanews.com/episode/countries-plan-ahead-ease-lockdowns-4247411.

14. Ruth Michaelson, "Egyptian Editor Briefly Detained in Covid-19 Reporting Crackdown," *The Guardian*, May 17, 2020, https://www.theguardian.com/world/2020/may/17/egyptian-editor-held-in-covid-19-reporting-crackdown.

15. Ibid.

16. Lewis Sanders IV, "Egypt Expels British Journalist Over Coronavirus Coverage," *DW*, March 27, 2020, https://www.dw.com/en/egypt-expels-british-journalist-over-coronavirus-coverage/a-52942136.

17. Ibid.

18. "Egypt Targets Guardian, NYT Journalists Over Coronavirus Reports, *Al-Jazeera*, March 18, 2020, https://www.aljazeera.com/news/2020/03/egypt-targets-guardian-nyt-journalists-coronavirus-reports-200318155434068.html.

19. Jared Malsin, "Egypt Gets 2.77 Billion IMF Loan as Coronavirus Hurts Economy," *Wall Street Journal*, May 11, 2020, https://www.wsj.com/articles/egypt-gets-2-77-billion-imf-loan-as-coronavirus-hurts-economy-11589219450.

20. Radio interview with Sahar Khamis in the program "The Bridge" on "U.S. Arab Radio," May 27, 2020, "Press Freedom in the Arab World in the Coronavirus Era," https://www.youtube.com/watch?v=61DpkZsqcrU&feature=youtu.be.

21. Elisabeth R. Myers, "Egyptian Journalist Mohamed Mounir Murdered by Coronavirus,"

    Inside Arabia, August 25, 2020, https://insidearabia.com/egyptian-journalist-mohamed-mounir-murdered-by-coronavirus/?fbclid=IwAR0bgj32CYLOiAuVQFpgNyJD7R_QVnpx9G_GKcxLqMrOp75WdKcqFws3bog.
22. Ibid.
23. Mohammed El Nawawy and Sahar Khamis, *Egyptian Revolution 2.0: Political Blogging, Civic Engagement and Citizen Journalism* (New York: Palgrave Macmillan, 2013).
24. توضيح وتحذير الأعلى للإعلام يصدر بيانا بشأن تغطية فيروس كورونا "The Supreme Council for Media Regulation Issues a Statement and a Warning about Corona Coverage," *AlMasry AlYoum*, March 9, 2020, https://www.almasryalyoum.com/news/details/1513648.
25. "الأعلى للإعلام يحقق في مخالفات تغطية كورونا The Supreme Council for Media Regulation Investigates the Violations in Covering Corona," *ElWatan*, May 19, 2020, https://www.elwatannews.com/news/details/4777322.
26. "Egypt Arrests Doctors, Silences Critics over Virus Outbreak," Associated Press, *The Washington Post*, July 6, 2020, https://www.washingtonpost.com/health/egypt-arrests-doctors-silences-critics-over-virus-outbreak/2020/07/06/65eb7984-bf50-11ea-8908-68a2b9eae9e0_story.html.
27. د ليلى سويف مرابطة امام سجن طرة للاطمئنان على ابنها علاء عبد الفتاح: عايزة جواب "Dr. Laila Souif Sits In By Tora Prison to Check on Her Son Alaa' Abdel Fattah: I Want A Letter," *Rai Al Youm*, June 21, 2020, https://www.raialyoum.com/index.php/%D8%AF-%D9%84%D9%8A%D9%84%D9%89-%D8%B3%D9%88%D9%8A%D9%81-%D9%85%D8%B1%D8%A7-%D8%A8%D8%B7%D8%A9-%D8%A3%D9%85%D8%A7%D9%85-%D8%B3%D8%AC%D9%86-%D8-%B7%D8%B1%D8%A9-%D9%84%D9%84%D8%A7%D8%B7%D9%85%D8%A6/.
28. "Morocco Makes a Dozen of Arrests Over Coronavirus Fake News," *Reuters*, March 19, 2020, https://www.reuters.com/article/us-health-coronavirus-morocco/morocco-makes-a-dozen-arrests-over-coronavirus-fake-news-idUSKBN2162DI.
29. Dima Samaro and Emna Sayadi, "Tunisia's Parliament on Covid-19: An Initiative to Fight Disinformation or an Opportunity to Violate Fundamental Rights? AccessNow, April 1, 2020, https://www.accessnow.org/tunisias-parliament-on-covid-19-an-initiative-to-fight-disinformation-or-an-opportunity-to-violate-fundamental-rights/.
30. Ibid.
31. Radio interview with Sahar Khamis in the program "The Bridge" on "U.S. Arab Radio," June 21, 2020, "Cybersecurity in the Middle East in the Covid-19 Era," https://www.youtube.com/watch?v=NUCfCNPGLZU.
32. Fatima AlSubaei, "Blockchain Adoption in the Gulf States," December 10, 2019, https://www.mei.edu/publications/blockchain-adoption-gulf-states.
33. Ibid.
34. Muhammed Nafei, "UAE's Coronavirus Tracing App-Is it Compulsory and Other Questions Answered," *Al Arabiya English*, April 20, 2020, https://english.alarabiya.net/en/coronavirus/2020/04/20/UAE-s-coronavirus-tracing-app-Is-it-compulsory-and-other-questions-answered-.
35. Ibid.
36. Ismaeel Naar, "UAE's G42 to Work with Israeli NanoScent to Develop Covid-19 Detector from Scent," *Al Arabiya*, August 19, 2020, https://english.alarabiya.net/en/coronavirus/2020/08/19/UAE-s-G42-to-work-with-Israeli-NanoScent-to-develop-COVID-19-detector-from-scent.
37. Alex Hern, "Qatari Contact-Tracing App Put 1M People's Sensitive Data at Risk," *The Guardian*, May 27, 2020, https://www.theguardian.com/world/2020/may/27/qatar-contact-tracing-app-1m-people-sensitive-data-at-risk-coronavirus-covid-19.
38. Rory Cellan-Jones, "Israeli Spyware Firm Pitches to be Covid-19 Saviour," *BBC News*, April 2, 2020, https://www.bbc.com/news/health-52134452.
39. Joseph Menn and Jack Stubbs, "Exclusive: FBI Probes Use of Israeli Firm's Spyware in Personal and Government Hacks – Sources," *Reuters*, Thomson Reuters, January 30, 2020, https://www.reuters.com/article/us-usa-cyber-nso-exclusive/exclusive-fbi-probes-use-of-israeli-firms-spyware-in-personal-and-government-hacks-sources-idUSKBN1ZT38B.
40. Sean Lyngaas, "NSO Group Spyware Used to Target Widow of Mexican Journalist, Researchers Say," *CyberScoop*, March 21, 2019,

https://www.cyberscoop.com/nso-group-spyware-targeted-widow-mexican-journalist-researchers-say/.

41. "Indian Journalists Reported among Targets of Alleged NSO Group WhatsApp Hack," Committee to Protect Journalists, October 31, 2019, https://cpj.org/2019/10/india-journalists-nso-group-whatsapp-php/.

42. Ryan Grace, "COVID-19 Prompts the Spread of Disinformation Across MENA," Middle East Institute, March 20, 2020, https://www.mei.edu/publications/covid-19-prompts-spread-disinformation-across-mena.

43. Ibid.

44. Yasheng Huang, Meicen Sun and Yuze Sui, "How Digital Contact Tracing Slowed Covid-19 in East-Asia," *Harvard Business Review*, April 15, 2020, https://hbr.org/2020/04/how-digital-contact-tracing-slowed-covid-19-in-east-asia.

45. Ian Bremmer, "The Best Global Responses to Covid-19 Pandemic," *Time*, June 12, 2020, https://time.com/5851633/best-global-responses-covid-19/.

46. Philip N. Howard, *The Digital Origins of Dictatorship and Democracy: Information Technology and Political Islam* (Oxford: Oxford University Press, 2011).

47. Katherine Jacobsen, "Amid Covid-19, the Prognosis for Press Freedom is Dim. Here Are 10 Symptoms to Track," Committee to Protect Journalists (CPJ), https://cpj.org/reports/2020/06/covid-19-here-are-10-press-freedom-symptoms-to-track/.

48. Ibid.

49. Sahar Khamis, "The Online Public Sphere in the Gulf: Contestation, Creativity, and Change," *Review of Middle East Studies* (RoMES) 53, no. 2 (December 2019): 190–199, https://doi.org/10.1017/rms.2019.41.

50. Sahar Khamis, Paul B. Gold, and Kathryn Vaughn, "Beyond Egypt's 'Facebook Revolution' and Syria's 'YouTube Uprising': Comparing Political Contexts, Actors and Communication Strategies. *Arab Media & Society*, 15 (Spring 2012), https://www.arabmediasociety.com/beyond-egypts-facebook-revolution-and-syrias-youtube-uprising-comparing-political-contexts-actors-and-communication-strategies/.

51. Marc Lynch, *The New Arab Wars: Uprisings and Anarchy in the Middle East* (New York: Public Affairs, 2016).

CONCLUSION

TOWARD A SAFER REGIONAL CYBERSPACE

MICHAEL SEXTON AND ELIZA CAMPBELL

INTRODUCTION

Much of the literature on foreign policy with respect to cyberspace — indeed, much of this book — has been focused on "admiring the problem," an all-too-common endeavor in this area of research. The rapid invention and spread of the internet has been such an all-encompassing societal transformation that there is no limit to the amount of ink that can be spilled to document all the associated challenges. It is glaringly obvious today that, for all its benefits, the internet age has introduced wide new avenues for government surveillance and interstate conflict. Edward Snowden's revelations of U.S. government surveillance and front-page American cyber spats with Iran, Russia, China, and North Korea make it clear that more can and must be done to rein in the dangers and excesses of this new technology.

This is even clearer when studying the downsides of the digital transformation in the Middle East. The early 2010s' "techno-optimism" that social media would overthrow the region's sclerotic autocrats and usher in a utopian, democratic, and peaceful age has quickly faded. Civilians are at great risk of being hacked and surveilled by their governments for exercising their human rights of free assembly and speech, and the amassing of offensive capabilities by rival militaries has introduced another, murkier domain for interstate conflict. The roots of these problems — the anarchy of the international system, autocratic paranoia toward dissent, and a domain that by construction prioritizes connectivity and profit over security — present a thorny set of challenges.

But we should not allow pessimism to fester into cynicism and apathy. Every age has its challenges. The exorbitant callousness of Enlightenment Age European monarchies brought about the spread of democracy on two continents (however imperfect and messy). The revolting inequities of the early Industrial Age spurred international taboos on child labor, normalized 40-hour workweeks, and inspired global labor movements that persist today. We do not propose any sweeping, conclusive solutions here — indeed, those aforementioned reforms leave a great deal of room for progress to this day — but we do propose some incremental policies and approaches that can help constrain the dangers and take advantage of the opportunities of the cyber domain in the Middle East.

We have identified two families of cyber policy challenges that are especially prominent in the Middle East: the questions presented by the growing private hacking tool industry, and the wide gradient of interstate cyber conflict. The supply and demand of hacking tools developed specifically for legal intercept and lawful search purposes is especially pronounced in the Middle East. Interstate cyber conflict (much like traditional political conflict) between American allies and adversaries alike is also particularly stubborn in the region. Both of these problems are challenging if not impossible to solve, but well within America's ability to influence.

INTERSTATE CYBER CONFLICT

As the previous chapters make clear, cyberspace is an especially unstable domain of conflict in the Middle East. Israel and Iran have engaged in a series of tit-for-tat cyberattacks in recent years; ISIS and the Syrian Electronic Army have carried out many loud, if not highly sophisticated, cyber operations since the onset of the Syrian civil war; the Gulf Cooperation Council (GCC) rift with Qatar has spilled into cyber disputes both grave and petty.

Insecurity and instability in Middle East cyberspace is, of course, in some ways a proxy for, or outgrowth of, underlying political and economic insecurity in the region writ large. Most, if not all, of the current conflicts or tensions in MENA cyberspace are intertwined with existing interstate tensions, and are unlikely to be resolved without close attention to this larger context. A truly lasting and persistent cyber peace is probably contingent on the resolution of these conflicts — a policy goal vastly exceeding the ambitions of this book.

That said, we maintain that some progress can be made in this domain. To a foreign policy realist or pessimist, the Joint Comprehensive Plan of Action (JCPOA) — a multilateral deal in which Iran agreed to forfeit its prerogative to build nuclear weapons — would be a baffling historical anomaly, and yet indeed it was negotiated and signed (until it collapsed). We maintain that a similar diplomatic initiative, even if incremental and fragile, may be possible and worth pursuing in this domain as well.

First, we ought to acknowledge some fault on the part of the United States in creating this problem. By launching Operation Olympic Games — better known by the virus name Stuxnet — against Iran's nuclear reactor in Natanz in coordination with Israel, the U.S. quite literally fired the first shot in this domain. It is not at all surprising that Iran would retaliate for this aggression, however justifiable, by developing and deploying its own offensive cyber capabilities. Any American initiative toward stabilizing this space regionally should begin with a recognition that the U.S. has itself contributed to its destabilization.

That said, with America's firm diplomatic and security ties to a multitude of regional rivals — Turkey, Israel, Qatar, Saudi Arabia, Egypt, and the United Arab Emirates (UAE) — there is no other country we see as better positioned politically to negotiate a stabilization to interstate cyber conflict.

This leads us to our broad approach for this problem: outside-in negotiations of cyber non-aggression, beginning with American allies and partners, and culminating in a coalition negotiation of cyber non-aggression with Iran.

CYBER PEACE — BETWEEN U.S. ALLIES

The first step to negotiating any form of "cyber peace" is to define what sorts of activities we hope to proscribe and which we are willing to tolerate. This is no easy task, given many governments perceive any information contrary to their regime's interests as tantamount to a cyberattack. Authorities in Bahrain, for example, have accused Qatar of "cyber terrorism" for "implementing a 'systematic plan' to harm the image of Bahrain and its people"[1] — a charge that we would characterize as a disinformation or influence campaign, rather than the grave label of cyber terrorism.

In other cases, cyber conflict is so bound up in broader political and information space tensions that domain-specific deescalation may be unfeasible. Consider the intersection of cyberattack (against the Qatar News Agency), allegations of media bias and incitement (against Al-Jazeera), and social media disinformation campaigns in the blockade against Qatar. Any negotiated settlement restricting the use of cyberattacks is unlikely without settling all these tangentially associated issues. Indeed, any "cyber peace" negotiation involving Qatar and the blockading quartet — Saudi Arabia, the UAE, Bahrain, and Egypt — may simply be unfeasible without a larger effort on the part of U.S. and other diplomats and stakeholders to work toward de-escalation of regional tensions.

The Tallinn Manual[2] is the best, most comprehensive legal work to guide the negotiation of a cyber non-aggression pact between America's allies and partners in the region. The original Tallinn Manual was published in 2013, authored by legal experts within the NATO Cooperative Cyber Defense Centre of Excellence (CCDCOE) in Tallinn, Estonia. Its development in Estonia is no historical accident: In 2007, Estonia — a NATO member — suffered a devastating wave of denial of service (DOS) attacks that crippled its government, lasting weeks.[3] The attacks presented grave questions for NATO in the digital age: How does NATO's collective defense pact work in cyberspace? What even constitutes a cyberattack on a NATO member? Can — or should — a newfangled mode of attack trigger the full retaliatory response of this sprawling Cold War alliance?

The Tallinn Manual aims to take traditional international legal concepts around warfare and define what they mean in the cyber domain. A few definitions and principles within the Manual are worth affirming in the Middle East context in particular:

- "A cyber operation by a State directed against cyber infrastructure located in another State may violate the latter's sovereignty. It certainly does so if it causes damage." (pg. 16)

- "A State bears international legal responsibility for a cyber operation attributable to it and which constitutes a breach of an international obligation." (pg. 29)

- "The fact that a cyber operation does not rise to the level of a use of force does not necessarily render it lawful under international law." (pg. 44)

- "... [Cyber] espionage and cyber exploitation operations lacking a coercive element do not per se violate the non-intervention principle." (pg. 44)

- "A cyber operation constitutes a use of force when its scale and effects are comparable to non-cyber operations rising to the level of a use of force." (pg. 55)

- "Cyber operations executed in the context of an armed conflict are subject to the law of armed conflict." (pg. 75)

- "The civilian population as such, as well as individual civilians, shall not be the object of cyber attack." (pg. 113)

The Tallinn Manual imposes reasonable guardrails on state conduct in cyberspace that would be suitable to the Middle East. A cessation of cyber espionage in the region does not, at the time of this writing, seem realistic, and it is critical to establish that cyber activity like the use of social media bots[4] falls far below the threshold of a cyberattack. These acknowledgements do not imply that such activity is not an issue, but they simply are not as important as prohibiting the most lethal and destructive potential abuses of cyberspace. This underscores the importance of working carefully to simultaneously draw from previously existing frameworks for managing and analyzing conflict, while also acknowledging the unique and unprecedented risks and potential areas for tension escalation in the Middle East cyber domain. It is for this reason that such responses must be, on some level, regionally calibrated, and involve input and analysis from stakeholders living and working within the region itself.

To establish a more stable and safe Middle East cyberspace, the United States should first convene its regional allies and partners to agree on certain behavioral restrictions and principles of international cyber law. These should include:

- An affirmation that states bear legal responsibility for cyber operations attributed to themselves

- An affirmation that a cyber operation with scale and effects comparable to a non-cyber use of force can itself constitute a use of force

- A prohibition against destructive cyber operations against one another

- An affirmation that a cyber operation against civilians individually or as a group constitutes a violation of international law

The parties to this agreement would ideally include all of the U.S.'s allies and partners in the region, but this may not necessarily be feasible in a reasonable period of time. The U.S. should capitalize on supranational organizations like the Arab League or, more likely, the GCC to negotiate this agreement. This agreement should strive to include:

- All parties to the Qatar blockade, given its instigation by the cyberattack on the Qatar News Agency

    - As stated above, the thorny and multifaceted nature of the blockade may mean this agreement would have to follow after a broader resolution to the conflict.

- Every state reported to possess offensive cyber capabilities, namely:

- Morocco[5]
- Algeria[6]
- Egypt[7]
- Israel[8]
- Saudi Arabia[9]
- The UAE[10]

This, we should emphasize, is the easy part. Iran is by far the most destabilizing actor in Middle East cyberspace, but it would be misguided for the U.S. to strive to decrease tensions with Iran while those among its own regional partners remain high. With a unified (or at least stable) front, the U.S. will likely have better luck negotiating stabler cyber relations with its regional adversaries — most notably Iran.

CYBER PEACE — WITH U.S. ADVERSARIES

The U.S. has many adversaries in the Middle East, from Iran and Syria to non-state actors like Hezbollah and al-Qaeda in the Arabian Peninsula. First, we should disregard the prospect of any negotiation with U.S.-designated terrorist organizations, including al-Qaeda and its affiliates, ISIS, and Hezbollah. Of the "cyber-capable" adversaries that remain, we are mainly left with Syria and Iran — and Syria is functionally a client state of Iran. Thus, this chapter will focus primarily on negotiating cyber stability with Iran, but it should be noted that this will have implications for governments and militias with ties to Iran, such as Syria, Hezbollah, the Houthis, and Shi'a militias in Iraq.

To avoid unduly caricaturing Iran as a regional bête noire, we should note again that the U.S. and Israel carried out the Operation Olympic Games cyberattack[11] against Iran before the country could reasonably be characterized as a major cyber aggressor. This operation was in service of American, Israeli, and regional security, as well as the principle of nuclear nonproliferation, but it undoubtedly contravened the same principles of cyber non-aggression that this chapter argues should be established. We say this because Iran is reflexively dishonest about its cyber operations,[12] and neglecting to state this obvious fact that the U.S. and Israel (understandably) avoid admitting gives Iran cover to deflect and deny its own malicious activity.

Any sort of non-aggression pact with Iran would certainly be an ambitious and challenging undertaking. Iran's destabilizing actions and violations of international norms are many: violent suppression of dissent, offensive cyber operations, support for terrorism and militias, online influence operations, and a nuclear weapons program. An agreement with Iran to curb any one of these behaviors runs the risk of signaling that the others are acceptable or not a priority. This is a difficult, emotionally charged political issue: These are literally matters of life and death.

It may well be that, among the various forms of problematic Iranian activity, its cyber capabilities and operations are simply not the highest ranking issue. Certainly today, as Iran enriches uranium at levels above the limits stipulated in the JCPOA,[13] an agreement to limit offensive cyber operations should not be the top priority for American foreign policy toward Iran. Nevertheless, the threat of cyberattacks is severe — especially in the Middle East, where scorching climates and increasingly scarce water supplies make electric and water infrastructure particularly critical.

Assuming an existing agreement between the U.S. and its partners in the region, as outlined in the previous section, Iran would have a significant incentive to sign on to the same set of cyber non-aggression principles. America's partners and allies in the Middle East tend to be adversaries of Iran, giving Tehran a great deal to gain from acceding to the agreement.

The viability of Iranian assent would depend heavily on the regional partners to the agreement. With the increasing strategic alignment of Iran's adversaries — in particular Israel with the UAE, Egypt, and Saudi Arabia — any agreement without all these states would have limited utility for Iran. And while these Iranian adversaries may have apprehensions about a diplomatic agreement with Iran, as they did with the JCPOA,[14][15][16] they will have been involved and party to previous agreements, which should alleviate some anxiety. This could be a meaningful opportunity for the U.S. to recuperate some of the trust it lost by negotiating the JCPOA without the involvement of its regional allies and partners. Even if the deal with Iran ultimately fails, the prior version of the deal without Iran would still be a substantial boon to regional security and stability.

Some experts have noted that, because Iran's malicious activity takes so many forms, countering its behavior in one arena (e.g., nuclear, terrorism, cyber) simply pushes Iran to take destabilizing actions elsewhere. Again, we do not recommend prioritizing an arrangement to limit cyber operations over a renegotiated nuclear deal. Nuclear escalation notwithstanding, the risk of conflict spillover into Iranian support for militants or terrorists would be a difficult tradeoff, but worthwhile considering the particular danger of conflict in the cyber domain. The *medium* through which cyberattacks take place is constantly and rapidly changing, especially with the onset of 5G technology, making the challenge of securing it dramatically more challenging than defending against kinetic terrorism. And the nature of software attacks means they can wreak far more damage and havoc than intended, as seen in the 2017 NotPetya cyberattack.[17] The physical and intelligence challenge of defending against terrorism has certainly changed in the past two decades, but nowhere near as much as the challenge of defending against cyberattacks has changed.

THE ATTRIBUTION PROBLEM

This conversation would be incomplete without some discussion of the attribution problem.[18] Without a doubt, the challenge of accurately and credibly attributing a cyberattack would make enforcement of any "cyber peace" arrangement difficult. Even the United States government, with its staggering investigative and espionage capabilities, sometimes prompts good faith skepticism when it attributes responsibility for cyber activity.[19]

This skepticism is warranted and worth considering, but we should not allow it to derail the concept of a multilateral cyber peace agreement altogether. There have been cases of attribution where thorough sourcing and a high level of transparency have been convincing for good faith experts. Consider the assiduously detailed 2013 Mandiant report on China's APT 1 cyber espionage unit, which prompted little skepticism beyond the Chinese Foreign Ministry;[20] or the revelation that the U.S. attributed the 2015 Sony hack to North Korea because the National Security Agency (NSA) had in fact already penetrated the North Korean attack network,[21] quieting experts' prior skepticism.[22] This will be a challenge in the Middle East — it is already known that Russia is hijacking Iranian attack infrastructure to disguise its activity[23]— but it is not insurmountable.

The challenge of attribution as a U.S. foreign policy issue is touched on in the recent Cyberspace Solarium Commission's report.[24] We affirm the Commission's recommendations for greater transparency and information sharing between law enforcement, intelligence, the private sector, and international partners. These recommendations are neither groundbreaking nor conclusive, but they can and will enhance the credibility of attribution, which underpins all enforcement of behavioral norms in international cyberspace.

PRIVATE HACKING TOOL COMPANIES

Another critical issue in cyberspace in the Middle East is the prevalence of private companies manufacturing hacking tools. These tools, intended to combat terrorism and other serious crime, are frequently deployed against political dissidents and journalists.[25] The most notorious firm producing these tools is the Israeli NSO Group, the developer of the commercial spyware program Pegasus.

This article takes as given that the elimination of this sector altogether is not feasible. It is simply not realistic that governments will give up on efforts to crack encryption on electronic devices belonging to terrorists or other serious criminals. And as long as governments are willing to pay for software to crack those devices, companies will be driven by the profit motive to develop that technology.

Inarguably, however, the sector as it exists today is plagued by excesses. NSO Group's Pegasus spyware has been uncovered on the phones of Jamal Khasoggi's associates,[26] a *New York Times* journalist,[27] Pakistani government officials,[28] and even allegedly Amazon CEO Jeff Bezos.[29] The notion that each of these hacks occurred under real suspicions of terrorism or serious crime like human trafficking strains credulity. Something can and ought to be done to rein this in, or at least to lay the groundwork for regulation and limits around such powerful new tools.

As a disclaimer, the policies suggested herein will not realistically thwart *all* abuses of these tools. Inevitably, hacking tools will be used in excess even in the best of circumstances. Surveillance, by its nature, targets suspects *before* a preponderance of evidence has been accumulated against them. As such, some unwarranted victimization by these tools is — very unfortunately — inevitable. However, we should not allow these edge cases to deter us from pursuing regulation to rein in the bulk of these cases.

Again here we should acknowledge the U.S.'s complicity in the same issue we seek to solve. Cyberpoint International — a firm heavily staffed with former NSA officials — played a crucial role in transferring offensive cyber capabilities from the United States to the UAE.[30] This took place shortly after 9/11, when the reality of an unprecedented threat of attack by terrorists deeply changed priorities for and limits around the U.S. intelligence and law enforcement communities. Regardless, however, this technology broadly speaking has been used in excess of its original intentions. Some acknowledgement of the U.S.'s role in this problem is appropriate as the U.S., again, is best positioned to address it.

EXISTING REGULATIONS

The Wassenaar Arrangement — an agreement limiting the export of weapons — is presently the best framework for regulating the sale of these tools at an international level. Originally negotiated in 1995,[31] the Arrangement was amended in 2013 to restrict the sale of hacking tools and then again in 2017 to carve out exceptions for vulnerability disclosure and other defensive cyber activity.[32] The agreement has no Middle Eastern parties apart from Turkey, although Israel claims to abide by its limitations.[33]

Other legal mechanisms with influence over the private hacking tool market include international human rights law, torts, and national-level export regulations. While all of them can, to a degree, rein in the abuse of these hacking tools against non-criminal civil society actors, it is unrealistic to suppose litigation and atomized national regulations can structurally and sustainably bring the industry under control. A strategic, international, legal policymaking effort is necessary to meaningfully regulate the sale of these tools.

THE HACKING TOOL KILL CHAIN

To limit the excesses of the hacking tool industry, we need to consider the kill chain connecting their development and abuse. At any point in the kill chain, regulation can step in to avoid the tools' abuse.

The Hacking Tool Kill Chain

Toolmaker	Medium	Gov't	Use	Abuse

At an international level, there should be an agreement building upon the basis of the Wassenaar Arrangement that first requires these hacking tool firms to register with their respective governments in order to sell or export their tools (*de facto* this is already the case, but it should be codified internationally). This should be part of an expansion of the parties to the Arrangement to include countries in the Middle East, in particular Israel[34] and the UAE. Selling these tools without registration should be criminalized in the respective jurisdictions — on par with doing so on the online black market. This licensing system will allow greater oversight and transparency.

Each party to the new arrangement should develop an oversight board to track the sale and use of these tools. The board does not need to be a novel entity — it can be incorporated into the responsibilities of existing bodies, such as the Bureau of Industry and Security of the U.S. Department of Commerce. These respective boards should track 1) who the clients are (states as well as agencies — law enforcement, intelligence, etc.), 2) the frequency with which the tools are used, and 3) what percentage of the tools' uses have resulted in law enforcement action. Of the tool uses that have not resulted in law enforcement action, there should be a randomized audit to determine the evidentiary basis for their use.

At an international level, monitoring parties should convene to review the statistics and audits on these tools. In addition, the U.S. and other allies should endeavor under existing democracy-building and development work to organize trainings for civil society and human rights organizations to help disseminate information about potential threats to and incursions on civil liberties that could be facilitated by the use of hacking tools. Like any newly deployed tool, the use of hacking tools in security and governance is in an early enough stage that such information, along with greater efforts to set up frameworks and norms for their use, is still in active development, and a range of partners can and should be party to these discussions. The limited and careful use of such technologies by governments to prevent serious crime and prosecute criminals — including crimes that flourish in unregulated online spaces, like radical extremist violence, trafficking in persons, and child sexual exploitation — can be effective and efficient, as long as it is carefully regulated.

Hacking tool companies that are found to have developed tools that were abused repeatedly — above a certain threshold that we lack the visibility to determine — should face consequences, proportionate to the frequency and severity of the abuse. This may be a limitation on the permitted sales of their tools, up to a termination of their export permit altogether for a lack of compliance. International consequences may include a cessation of contracts. While ultimately responsibility is with the end user of these tools, the companies developing them have a profit incentive to sell them as widely as possible with minimal oversight, which regulators have a responsibility to control.

There is little to be done by governments to reduce the risk of abuse at the level of the medium — i.e., the technology platforms the hacking tools are delivered through. At the very least, victims of egregiously wrongful hacking — cases with no evidentiary basis whatsoever — should be permitted to sue the governments or toolmakers involved. This sort of transparency would alert software platforms to vulnerabilities and permit them to patch their systems, allowing some remediation of the vulnerability hoarding and disclosure imbalance that law enforcement and intelligence agencies inevitably contribute to.[35]

Governments that are found to have abused the tools should also face consequences for their abuse. This bar for excessive use should be lower than that for hacking tool companies themselves, as developers should not ultimately bear all responsibility for the abuse of a plug-and-play system after it is sold. Again we lack the visibility to declare precisely what that bar should be, but possible consequences should include private complaints and, without remedial action, a cessation of permits to sell to the agencies involved.

GOVERNMENTAL COMPLIANCE

The exemplar of this problem as it exists today is the rampant sale of hacking tools like Pegasus by NSO Group in Israel, which brings us to the final requirement for this updated Wassenaar Arrangement to work: Government parties must hold each other accountable to enforce these export regulations. NSO Group is a company with a high profit incentive and little appetite for non-cosmetic self-regulation, aligned with a government that is willing to look the other way when those tools are sold widely and notoriously abused. NSO bears some responsibility for failing to self-regulate, but as long as the market for these tools exists, excesses are almost inevitable, and this is where the government must step in. Israel's government, unfortunately, has not shown the wherewithal to do so; the authors speculate the government is happy to sell their nation's tech talent to make bedfellows as strange as the government of Uzbekistan.[36] It is an unfortunate blemish for a country whose technology sector, by and large, has a track record of encouraging and incubating creative and innovative products, with the potential to do much more.

Government incentives to comply in good faith with such an agreement — or indeed to sign on to it at all — will be difficult to create. Law enforcement and national security agencies have a natural desire to retain some hacking capabilities to track and prevent serious criminal activity like terrorism and human trafficking, and countries with the talent to develop these capabilities at scale have an incentive to export them — especially Israel, which has few natural allies (but many adversaries) in the Middle East and Central Asia.

However, in a region with few democratic governments — where political dissent by groups like the Muslim Brotherhood is conflated with terrorism[37][38][39] — there is ample risk that these tools will be used to target journalists and activists who pose no credible violent threat. This is why the U.S. will need to apply diplomatic pressure in service of the digital privacy and freedom of expression that this market threatens. It may also be the case that U.S. government engagement with civil society organizations working in and around the Middle East will be an important part of elevating ongoing dialogue about and knowledge of the kinds of new tools available to governments attempting to stifle free speech and political accountability in the region.

It is not unprecedented for governments to perform this oversight even when it is geopolitically nonoptimal to do so. A bipartisan group of members of the U.S. Congress in 2019 wrote a letter to the secretary of state and director of national intelligence expressing concern about this market,[40] including the sale of these tools to the UAE, despite the fact that U.S.-Emirati cooperation is so close the CIA does not collect human intelligence there.[41] Of course this is only a small first step.

It is also not unheard of for a company selling these tools to operate somewhat responsibly. Cyberpoint International — which has been scrutinized for its role in transferring offensive cyber capabilities from the U.S. to the UAE — is not reported to have engaged in similar activities since the termination of its contract in 2015.[42] Cellebrite is an Israeli firm that develops similar tools for bypassing the security of a smartphone in police custody,[43] and while it has been the subject of some critical press,[44] it is nowhere near as notorious as NSO Group. Other mobile forensic companies like Micro Systemation AB, Paraben Corporation, and Magnet Forensics receive almost no media coverage at all. This is not to say that any of these companies is beyond reproach, but that there is a real possibility for this industry to exist without incessant, flagrant excesses — or at least ones that we are able to identify in our research.

One concrete, actionable policy that could quickly rein in the excesses of this industry would be an indefinite moratorium on the licensing of hacking tools that are deployed "in the wild," i.e., remotely on devices that have not been physically seized. By no means would this be a panacea, but it would deter the sheer volume of spurious lawful interceptions using tech like Pegasus, which can remotely infect a device with no more effort than it takes to send a text message. Governments would still have the capability to digitally search impounded devices and thereby identify and disrupt suspected terror or human trafficking networks — typical doomsday scenarios imagined by the "going dark" debate[45] — but they would not be able to hack dissidents abroad without cooperation from local law enforcement.[46]

This, we should emphasize, is a pathway toward harm reduction rather than elimination. It will remain an enduring prerogative for governments to maintain a capacity to conduct lawful intercept operations for the purposes of law enforcement and intelligence, just as it ought to remain the prerogative for technology companies like Apple and Facebook to deploy the strongest possible encryption to protect customers' privacy. The alternative solution — an encryption backdoor — is utterly unworkable[47] and rightfully has been almost universally opposed by technologists for decades. The acceptance and regulation of the hacking tool industry is, right now, the most realistic strategy to mollify these entrenched and diametrically opposed interests. This framework should only constitute part of a broader foreign policy that advances liberal values and penalizes human rights abuses, whether digital or not.

CONCLUSION

The Middle East is and will likely remain a deeply unstable region in cyberspace for years to come, even in the best of circumstances. Macro trends like climate change and the automation of work bode ill for the prospect of a peaceful and prosperous Middle East in our lifetime. Water is becoming more scarce, the demand for petroleum products is becoming more erratic and precarious, and economic disenfranchisement remains prevalent. Nondemocratic governments are modernizing their tools of political suppression, making the social contract between citizens and their governments more fragile.

These trends underscore the need for a proactive and forceful American foreign policy in the Middle East. Preserving human and national security in the region cannot be accomplished through the military alone, but requires a rich diplomatic corps continuously advancing norms of responsible behavior in and out of cyberspace. This work is arduous and unglamorous, and at times it will miss the mark, but the region and the United States are better off for it.

Preventing interstate cyber conflict and implementing sensible regulations around hacking tools are two salient contemporary foreign policy prerogatives for the United States in Middle East cyberspace. As of this writing, these two issues are, at best, on track to remain constant into the medium-term future. We do not presume that the policy recommendations herein will arrest these trends entirely — we reject the false dichotomy that the U.S. must either "solve" or abandon problems this thorny — but something can and, indeed, must be done about them.

Endnotes

1. Al Sherbin, Ramadani. "Bahrain uncovers Iran and Qatar cyber terrorism network." *Gulf News*. May 20, 2019. https://gulfnews.com/world/gulf/bahrain/bahrain-uncovers-iran-and-qatar-cyber-terrorism-network-1.64065789.

2. NATO Cooperative Cyber Defense Centre of Excellence, "Tallinn Manual 2.0 on the International Law Applicable to Cyber Operation," *Cambridge University Press*, February 2017.

3. McGuinness, Damien. "How a Cyber Attack Transformed Estonia." *BBC News*. BBC, April 27, 2017. https://www.bbc.com/news/39655415.

4. Bots are operated on social media networks, and used to automatically generate messages, advocate ideas, act as a follower of users, and as fake accounts to gain followers themselves. It is estimated that 9-15 percent of Twitter accounts are social bots.

   "What Are Bots: Bot Types & Mitigation Techniques." Learning Center. Imperva, July 7, 2020. https://www.imperva.com/learn/application-security/what-are-bots/.

5. Vavra, Shannon. "Moroccan Journalist Targeted by NSO Group Spyware, Amnesty International Says." *CyberScoop*. CyberScoop, June 22, 2020. https://www.cyberscoop.com/nso-group-spyware-amnesty-international-omar-radi-morocco/?category_news=technology.

6. Parkinson, Joe, Nicholas Bariyo, and Josh Chin. "Huawei Technicians Helped African Governments Spy on Political Opponents." *The Wall Street Journal*. Dow Jones & Company, August 15, 2019. https://www.wsj.com/articles/huawei-technicians-helped-african-governments-spy-on-political-opponents-11565793017.

7. Bergman, Ronen, and Declan Walsh. "Egypt Is Using Apps to Track and Target Its Citizens, Report Says." *The New York Times*. The New York Times, October 3, 2019. https://www.nytimes.com/2019/10/03/world/middleeast/egypt-cyber-attack-phones.html.

8. Reed, John. "Unit 8200: Israel's Cyber Spy Agency." *The Financial Times*, July 10, 2015. https://www.ft.com/content/69f150da-25b8-11e5-bd83-71cb60e8f08c.

9. Kirkpatrick, David D. "Israeli Software Helped Saudis Spy on Khashoggi, Lawsuit Says." *The New York Times*. The New York Times, December 2, 2018. https://www.nytimes.com/2018/12/02/world/middleeast/saudi-khashoggi-spyware-israel.html.

10. Bing, Christopher. "Special Report: Inside the UAE's Secret Hacking Team of U.S. Mercenaries." *Reuters*. Thomson Reuters, January 30, 2019. https://www.reuters.com/article/us-usa-spying-raven-specialreport/special-report-inside-the-uaes-secret-hacking-team-of-u-s-mercenaries-idUSKCN1PO19O.

11. "How a Secret Cyberwar Program Worked." *The New York Times*. The New York Times, June 1, 2012. https://archive.nytimes.com/www.nytimes.com/interactive/2012/06/01/world/middleeast/how-a-secret-cyberwar-program-worked.html?ref=middleeast.

12. Alireza Miryousefi, spokesman for Iran's Mission to the United Nations, has said "The Iranian government does not engage in cyberwarfare" Nakashima, Ellen, and Joby Warrick. "Foreign Intelligence Officials Say Attempted Cyberattack on Israeli Water Utilities Linked to Iran." *The Washington Post*. WP Company, May 10, 2020. https://www.washingtonpost.com/national-security/intelligence-officials-say-attempted-cyberattack-on-israeli-water-utilities-linked-to-iran/2020/05/08/f9ab0d78-9157-11ea-9e23-6914ee410a5f_story.html.

13. "Iran Triples Stockpile of Enriched Uranium in Breach of Nuclear Deal." *The Guardian*. Guardian News and Media, March 3, 2020. https://www.theguardian.com/world/2020/mar/03/iran-triples-stockpile-of-enriched-uranium-in-breach-of-nuclear-deal.

14. Al Otaiba, Yousef. "One Year After the Iran Nuclear Deal – Op-Ed by Ambassador Yousef Al Otaiba." UAE Embassy in Washington, DC, April 3, 2016. https://www.uae-embassy.org/news-media/one-year-after-iran-nuclear-deal---op-ed-ambassador-yousef-al-otaiba.

15. Sharon, Itamar, Jonathan Beck, and Avi Lewis. "Netanyahu: World Powers Took a Gamble on Our Shared Future." *The Times of Israel*, July 14, 2015. https://www.timesofisrael.com/world-powers-nuclear-deal-with-iran-july-14-2015/.

16. Salisbury, Peter. "Risk Perception and Appetite in UAE Foreign and National Security Policy." Chatham House, July 2020. https://www.chathamhouse.org/sites/default/files/2020-07-01-risk-in-uae-salisbury.pdf. pg. 14.

17. Greenberg, Andy. "The Untold Story of NotPetya, the Most Devastating Cyberattack

in History." *Wired*. Conde Nast, August 22, 2018. https://www.wired.com/story/notpetya-cyberattack-ukraine-russia-code-crashed-the-world/.

18. Newman, Lily Hay. "Why Is It So Hard to Prove Russia Hacked the DNC?" *Wired*. Conde Nast, June 3, 2017. https://www.wired.com/2016/12/hacker-lexicon-attribution-problem/.

19. Laughland, Oliver. "FBI Director Stands by Claim That North Korea Was Source of Sony Cyber-Attack." *The Guardian*. Guardian News and Media, January 7, 2015. https://www.theguardian.com/world/2015/jan/07/fbi-director-north-korea-source-sony-cyber-attack-james-comey.

20. Wan, William, and Ellen Nakashima. "Report Ties Cyberattacks on U.S. Computers to Chinese Military." *The Washington Post*. WP Company, February 19, 2013. https://www.washingtonpost.com/report-ties-100-plus-cyber-attacks-on-us-computers-to-chinese-military/2013/02/19/2700228e-7a6a-11e2-9a75-dab0201670da_story.html.

21. Sanger, David E., and Martin Fackler. "N.S.A. Breached North Korean Networks Before Sony Attack, Officials Say." *The New York Times*. The New York Times, January 19, 2015. https://www.nytimes.com/2015/01/19/world/asia/nsa-tapped-into-north-korean-networks-before-sony-attack-officials-say.html.

22. Schneier, Bruce. "We Still Don't Know Who Hacked Sony." *The Atlantic*. Atlantic Media Company, December 8, 2016. https://www.theatlantic.com/international/archive/2015/01/we-still-dont-know-who-hacked-sony-north-korea/384198/.

23. Stubbs, Jack. "Hacking the Hackers: Russian Group Hijacked Iranian Spying Operation, Officials Say." *Reuters*. Thomson Reuters, October 21, 2019. https://www.reuters.com/article/us-russia-cyber/hacking-the-hackers-russian-group-hijacked-iranian-spying-operation-officials-say-idUSKBN1X00AK.

24. "Report." Cyberspace Solarium Commission, March 2020. https://www.solarium.gov/report. pgs. 46-47.

25. Mazzetti, Mark, Adam Goldman, Ronen Bergman, and Nicole Perlroth. "A New Age of Warfare: How Internet Mercenaries Do Battle for Authoritarian Governments." *The New York Times*. The New York Times, March 21, 2019. https://www.nytimes.com/2019/03/21/us/politics/government-hackers-nso-darkmatter.html.

26. Kirkpatrick, David D. "Israeli Software Helped Saudis Spy on Khashoggi, Lawsuit Says." *The New York Times*. The New York Times, December 2, 2018. https://www.nytimes.com/2018/12/02/world/middleeast/saudi-khashoggi-spyware-israel.html.

27. Hubbard, Ben. "Someone Tried to Hack My Phone. Technology Researchers Accused Saudi Arabia." *The New York Times*. The New York Times, January 28, 2020. https://www.nytimes.com/2020/01/28/reader-center/phone-hacking-saudi-arabia.html.

28. Kirchgaessner, Stephanie. "Israeli Spyware Allegedly Used to Target Pakistani Officials' Phones." *The Guardian*. Guardian News and Media, December 19, 2019. https://www.theguardian.com/world/2019/dec/19/israeli-spyware-allegedly-used-to-target-pakistani-officials-phones.

29. Lyons, Kim. "The FBI Is Investigating the Bezos Hack." *The Verge*. The Verge, January 31, 2020. https://www.theverge.com/2020/1/31/21117180/fbi-bezos-hack-amazon-saudi-arabia-nso.

30. Schectman, Joel, and Christopher Bing. "Made in America." *Reuters*. Thomson Reuters, November 6, 2019. https://www.reuters.com/investigates/special-report/usa-raven-whitehouse/.

31. "About Us." The Wassenaar Arrangement, July 15, 2020. https://www.wassenaar.org/about-us/.

32. Waterman, Shaun. "The Wassenaar Arrangement's Latest Language Is Making Security Researchers Very Happy." *CyberScoop*. CyberScoop, August 1, 2018. https://www.cyberscoop.com/wassenaar-arrangement-cybersecurity-katie-moussouris/.

33. "Israeli Statement at the Conclusion of the Wassenaar Arrangement Outreach Delegation Visit." Israel Ministry of Foreign Affairs, November 20, 2019. https://mfa.gov.il/MFA/PressRoom/2019/Pages/Israeli-statement-at-the-conclusion-of-the-Wassenaar-Arrangement-Outreach-Delegation-visit-20-November-2019.aspx.

34. While Israel claims to voluntarily abide by the Wassenaar Arrangement's export controls, it is not a signatory to the deal and its exports of hacking tools likely violate the Arrangement's later amendments.

35. Armerding, Taylor. "US Intelligence Can't Break Vulnerability Hoarding Habit." *Naked Security*,

36. Marczak, Bill, John Scott-Railton, Sarah McKune, Bahr Abdul Razzak, and Ron Deibert. "HIDE AND SEEK: Tracking NSO Group's Pegasus Spyware to Operations in 45 Countries." The Citizen Lab, May 8, 2020. https://citizenlab.ca/2018/09/hide-and-seek-tracking-nso-groups-pegasus-spyware-to-operations-in-45-countries/.

37. Cary, Glen, and Alaa Shahine. "U.A.E. Supports Saudi Arabia Against Qatar-Backed Brotherhood." *Bloomberg*, March 9, 2014. https://www.bloomberg.com/news/articles/2014-03-09/u-a-e-supports-saudi-arabia-against-qatar-backed-brotherhood.

38. "Egypt's Muslim Brotherhood Declared 'Terrorist Group'." *BBC News*. BBC, December 25, 2013. https://www.bbc.com/news/world-middle-east-25515932.

39. "Saudi Arabia Declares Muslim Brotherhood 'Terrorist Group'." *BBC News*. BBC, March 7, 2014. https://www.bbc.com/news/world-middle-east-26487092.

40. Malinowski, Tom, Eliot Engel, Adam Schiff, Mike Gallagher, Jason Crow, Will Hurd, Colin Allred, Abigail Spanberger, André Carson, and Eric Swalwell. "Surveillance Letter." Congressman Tom Malinowski, May 17, 2020. https://malinowski.house.gov/sites/malinowski.house.gov/files/Surveillance%20letter%20-%20signed%20final.pdf.

41. Roston, Aram. "Why the CIA Doesn't Spy on the UAE." *Reuters*. Thomson Reuters, August 26, 2019. https://www.reuters.com/article/us-usa-emirates-spying-insight/why-the-cia-doesnt-spy-on-the-uae-idUSKCN1VG0V3.

42. Schectman, Joel, and Christopher Bing. "Made in America." *Reuters*. Thomson Reuters, November 6, 2019. https://www.reuters.com/investigates/special-report/usa-raven-whitehouse/.

43. Zetter, Kim. "When the FBI Has a Phone It Can't Crack, It Calls These Israeli Hackers." *The Intercept*, October 31, 2016. https://theintercept.com/2016/10/31/fbis-go-hackers/.

44. Cox, Joseph. "Cellebrite Sold Phone Hacking Tech to Repressive Regimes, Data Suggests." *Vice*, January 12, 2017. https://www.vice.com/en_us/article/aekqjj/cellebrite-sold-phone-hacking-tech-to-repressive-regimes-data-suggests.

45. The "going dark" debate refers to a policy debate over encryption, typically between law enforcement and technologists. As increasingly sophisticated encryption schemes are implemented in customer technology, they render it intractable for law enforcement to act upon warrants and carry out lawful interception; however, any encryption "backdoor" would be exploitable by criminals or foreign spies, critically undermining the security of the devices and messaging services.

"Attorney General William P. Barr Delivers Keynote Address at the International Conference on Cyber Security." The United States Department of Justice, July 23, 2019. https://www.justice.gov/opa/speech/attorney-general-william-p-barr-delivers-keynote-address-international-conference-cyber.

46. Kirchgaessner, Stephanie. "Exclusive: Saudi Dissident Warned by Canadian Police He Is a Target." *The Guardian*. Guardian News and Media, June 21, 2020. https://www.theguardian.com/world/2020/jun/21/exclusive-saudi-dissident-warned-by-canadian-police-he-is-a-target.

47. Hayden, Michael. "Encryption Backdoors Won't Stop Crime But Will Hurt U.S. Tech." Bloomberg.com. *Bloomberg*, December 10, 2019. https://www.bloomberg.com/opinion/articles/2019-12-10/encryption-backdoors-won-t-stop-crime-but-will-hurt-u-s-tech.

About the Middle East Institute

The Middle East Institute is a center of knowledge dedicated to narrowing divides between the peoples of the Middle East and the United States. With over 70 years' experience, MEI has established itself as a credible, non-partisan source of insight and policy analysis on all matters concerning the Middle East. MEI is distinguished by its holistic approach to the region and its deep understanding of the Middle East's political, economic and cultural contexts. Through the collaborative work of its three centers — Policy & Research, Arts & Culture and Education — MEI provides current and future leaders with the resources necessary to build a future of mutual understanding.

Assertions and opinions in this publication are solely those of the authors and do not reflect the views of The Middle East Institute.

Made in the USA
Monee, IL
04 November 2020